ROUTLEDGE LIBRARY EDITIONS:
LABOUR ECONOMICS

Volume 3

INTERNATIONAL LABOUR STATISTICS

INTERNATIONAL LABOUR STATISTICS

A Handbook, Guide, and Recent Trends

Edited by
R. BEAN

Routledge
Taylor & Francis Group
LONDON AND NEW YORK

First published in 1989 by Routledge

This edition first published in 2019
by Routledge
2 Park Square, Milton Park, Abingdon, Oxon OX14 4RN

and by Routledge
52 Vanderbilt Avenue, New York, NY 10017

Routledge is an imprint of the Taylor & Francis Group, an informa business

British Library Cataloguing in Publication Data
A catalogue record for this book is available from the British Library

ISBN: 978-0-367-02458-1 (Set)
ISBN: 978-0-429-02526-6 (Set) (ebk)
ISBN: 978-0-367-07544-6 (Volume 3) (hbk)
ISBN: 978-0-429-02133-6 (Volume 3) (ebk)

Publisher's Note
The publisher has gone to great lengths to ensure the quality of this reprint but points out that some imperfections in the original copies may be apparent.

Disclaimer
The publisher has made every effort to trace copyright holders and would welcome correspondence from those they have been unable to trace.

International Labour Statistics

A Handbook, Guide, and Recent Trends

Edited by R. Bean

ROUTLEDGE
London & New York

First published 1989
by Routledge
11 New Fetter Lane, London EC4P 4EE
29 West 35th Street, New York, NY 10001

Wordprocessed by Vibes, Brighton.
Printed in Great Britain

British Library Cataloguing in Publication Data

International labour statistics: a handbook,
guide, and recent trends.
1. Labour market. Statistical analysis
I. Bean, R. (Ron), *1938–*
331.12′028

ISBN 0-415-02179-0

Library of Congress Cataloging in Publication Data

International labour statistics.

Includes index.
1. Labor and laboring classes — Statistics.
2. Labor supply — Statistics. 3. Economic history —
1971– — Statistics. I. Bean, R. (Ron), 1938–
HD4826.I636 1989 331.1′021 88-31678
ISBN 0-415-02179-0

CONTENTS

FIGURES AND TABLES

Figures

Tables

Tables

CONTRIBUTORS

R. Bean is Senior Lecturer, Department of Economics and Accounting, University of Liverpool.

Paul Blyton is Senior Lecturer at the Cardiff Business School, University of Wales, College of Cardiff.

S. Creigh is Economic Adviser with the Employment Market Research Unit, Department of Employment, London.

K. Holden is Senior Lecturer, Department of Economics and Accounting, University of Liverpool.

James J. Hughes is Pro-Vice Chancellor and Professor of Industrial Relations at the University of Kent, Canterbury.

Robert Price is Lecturer in the Industrial Relations Research Unit, University of Warwick.

George F. Ray is Senior Research Fellow at the National Institute of Economic and Social Research, London.

ABBREVIATIONS

Eurostat	Statistical Office of the European Communities
ILO	International Labour Office
IMF	International Monetary Fund
OECD	Organization for Economic Cooperation and Development

**	Not available
-	Not applicable

PREFACE AND ACKNOWLEDGEMENTS

The object of this book is not merely to provide a convenient and accessible source of labour-market data on an international basis, although it does centralize, and co-ordinate from a range of sources, basic statistical information appertaining to the labour force for a large number of countries. Rather, the emphasis is placed upon providing a tool for assisting and guiding users of international labour statistics. Following a general introduction, for eight key aspects relating to the labour markets of major developed, capitalist economies (OECD countries) there are individual chapters written by specialists in the particular subject areas. These discuss the nature of the data sources and statistical compilations, highlight cross-national trends over the past ten to fifteen years, and elucidate the inherent difficulties of cross-country comparability, as well as potential pitfalls of interpretation of which users are often insufficiently aware. The remainder of the book, compiled by the editor, provides a summary of key labour-market statistics, on an individual country basis, for 24 OECD and 20 other (including some Third-World) countries.

It is intended to be of use to two main groups of readers: first, students and researchers involved in labour-market analysis who require an awareness of the nature and quality of the relevant statistics (since, for instance, the testing of economic models of the workings of labour markets can only be as good as the available data will permit); and second, business managements who are concerned with labour conditions within particular countries as one possible, influencing factor in decisions on investment and trade, and who need to be informed of the labour-market aspects of the international economic environment.

Grateful acknowledgement is expressed to the embassies, high commissions, and statistical offices of the various countries which supplied data, as well as to trade unions and employers' organizations, and to the following for permission to reproduce copyright material: the International Labour Office, the Organization for Economic Co-operation and Development, US Bureau of Labor Statistics, and the World Bank (in World Development Reports, New York: Oxford University Press).

Part 1: A guide to the use of labour statistics

1 LABOUR STATISTICS IN INTERNATIONAL PERSPECTIVE

R. Bean

INTRODUCTION

Within developed market economies it is the labour market bringing together buyers and sellers of labour services, which allocates labour among different kinds of employment and, since it constitutes an important source of income for most of the population, also determines the distribution of labour earnings and conditions of employment. Furthermore, the workings of labour markets are central to economic-policy considerations since the unemployment rate and consumer price index, for instance, provide simple yardsticks - and are regarded as key indicators - for attempting to measure the overall performance of an economy, as well as for comparing economic performance among nations. It is frequently claimed that the higher and persistent levels of unemployment throughout most industrialized countries in recent years constitute the leading economic problem of our time, reflecting both unused labour resources and loss of potential output. The costs of unemployment for the economy, however, include not only lost production but reductions in tax receipts, together with increases in government transfer payments.

The labour market itself also provides an important interface between the economic and social systems since, although labour is a factor of production, 'the worker is a human being, and his work involves social as well as technical relations. Work is not merely the way to get a living but a way of life ... a field of conflicts and loyalties, anxieties and reassurances'[1] in which the occupational and social structures are interlocked. Thus, although wage and earnings levels are arrived at in a market as a price and a distributive share, they can depend not only on the impersonal balance of supply and demand but upon custom, notions of fairness and equity, together with the balance of power between groups and classes.[2] Similarly, unemployment has social as well as economic ramifications because - as Guy Routh has recently observed:

> work, with its regular routine and activities, forms an essential framework for the personality, giving the worker status and a sense of identity ... [whereas] alienation and anomie accompany loss of a job and the inability to find one [so that] the unemployed are bystanders, excluded from participation in this life process, unless they can enter sub rosa through the black economy.[3]

The unemployment rate may therefore be utilized not only as an indicator of the supply of unused labour in an economy but also as an index of economic and related social hardship, stemming from loss of income and consumption which, in turn, may influence government policy on the extent of job creation, special training programmes, income support schemes, and other welfare measures. The Bureau of Labor Statistics in the United States of America was, in fact, established originally in order to meet a growing demand for information on labour conditions so as to provide a basis for improved labour standards, and in its early days was viewed as part of a movement for social reform.[4] In the United Kingdom a similar, early concern of official labour statistics was with the conditions of the 'wage-receiving class', and post-1945 the 'figures of registered unemployment were commonly regarded as perhaps the most important ... indicators on which to base public policies of demand management, regional growth, the control of inflation and welfare provisions'.[5] Labour-force measures, however, are used not only for the analysis of the economic and social forces of employment and unemployment but also in estimating labour productivity and, within Third-World countries, as a basis of planning for economic development and to help decide on whether labour-intensive, or capital-intensive, techniques should be used in the production process.

In relation to the labour market statistical data are necessary for analysis upon which to anchor observations and base recommendations since statistics 'both mould and reflect our perceptions of reality of a given social and economic situation'[6] and they are valuable resources in producing and evaluating knowledge. Undoubtedly the measurement of any economic variable is vital where it acts as a guide to policy makers and, since the labour market itself is a complex phenomenon, measurement of its performance necessitates the careful development and use of a range of measures that will capture the many aspects and different dimensions of its operations.[7] For instance, when examining labour demand, attention needs to be directed not only to the number of persons employed and the rate of growth of numbers employed but also to the utilization of those already employed and the number of hours worked, since the aforesaid measures neglect changes in hours worked (and therefore possibly underemployment) by those already in work (see chapter 7). Similarly, in order to assess the extent of labour-market slack the unemployment measure needs supplementing because in many countries, including Australia,[8] it is argued that there is a significant number of 'hidden' unemployed persons or 'discouraged' job seekers, who, having dropped out of the labour force and therefore not appearing in the official unemployment statistics, would actively seek work if labour-market employment conditions were more favourable, given prevailing wages.

Additional measures such as labour-force participation or activity rates - showing the proportion of the population of a given age group offering their services in the labour market - are therefore important from a planning standpoint to help gauge the productive potential of an economy and to facilitate higher rates of participation for particular population groupings. Other useful, but less widely used, measures of labour-market conditions include the 'employment-population' ratio which relates the employment level to population size and answers the question 'what proportion of the population of working age is actually employed?' It indicates whether or not an economy is generating jobs at a fast enough pace to provide employment for a constant proportion of the population.[9]

CONCEPTUAL AND MEASUREMENT DIFFICULTIES

There has been a good deal of criticism in recent years concerning the adequacy and measurement methods of particular labour-force statistics.[10]

There is some ambiguity, for instance, in the concept of 'employment' across different societies which makes it hard to define optimal policies (see chapter 2). More difficult is the measurement of unemployment which is a complex and multi-dimensional phenomenon. This measurement can sometimes be controversial since,

> When rates are low, public interest also is low. When rates rise, controversy is likely to rise, particularly with respect to what the figures mean. Some argue that the figures are too low and do not reflect the true extent of labour underutilization in times of rising unemployment. Others contend the figures are too high and do not reflect the reality of the job market.[11]

Such problems hinge on how unemployment is defined, operationally specified, and compiled, and, in order to consider the merits and limitations of any labour-market measure like this, it is essential, as a preliminary, that the objective of that measure is clearly defined.[12] One use of unemployment data is to assess current economic conditions and short-term prospects, that is, as a cyclical indicator, whereas other users require the data as a measure of how well the economy relieves the economic and psychological hardships experienced by job seekers.[13] Since there are a variety of different purposes for which unemployment data may be required - as well as differences in the methods of measurement - there is, as chapter 3 makes clear, no one, correct measure.[14]

In those countries such as the UK where unemployment insurance (rather than household surveys and censuses) has been used as the main source of unemployment statistics since 1920, there are further problems in using an administrative system as a proxy for an economic and social concept like unemployment. In fact, two very different concepts of unemployment are implied in questioning people about their employment status, availability and job-seeking activities, and in bureaucratic regulations relating to who can and cannot claim unemployment benefit. In the UK the official monthly unemployment figures have become an issue of major political controversy. They are a good illustration of the way in which the definition of a social problem can alter both its size and shape since it was contended in the mid-1980s that 'by excluding or ignoring certain groups the government has managed to stabilize unemployment at about 3.3 million over the past two years (and on at least two occasions actually to reduce it).'[15] More generally, some observers would maintain that political positions are inevitably embedded in supposedly factual and technical statistical data since the data themselves are social products which are not simply collected but produced. Thus 'statistical data cannot be interpreted without reference to their underlying theoretical assumptions [since] all data ... are structured by the conceptual framework that is applied as well as by the technical instruments used in their production'.[16]

In the case of Italy, unemployment figures - along with many other Italian statistics - are said to be subject to an unusually high margin of error which in part reflects the large role played by the 'black', or 'underground', economy in that country. This submerged and unreported economy concerns tax avoidance, the illegal employment of students, pensioners, and foreign workers, as well as double-job holding, together with the officially unemployed who have black jobs - estimated at some two million. The authorities claim to have discovered 6.6 million cases of black employment, (lavoro nero), equivalent to 1.5 million full-time jobs, which would push up the number of employed persons in Italy by 7.4 per cent to 22.5 million and would significantly reduce the unemployment statistics.[17]

Conceptual difficulties and measurement errors also affect other types of statistics relating to the labour force such as strikes (industrial disputes). Indeed, Shalev maintains that strike statistics are 'some of the most over-abused and least understood of man's many attempts to freeze and condense richly dynamic social events into static, artificial and misleadingly accurate arithmetic'.[18] Other things being equal, smaller, shorter, and more localized disputes are less likely to secure statistical inclusion in the official figures for a particular country. Also, in a recent study in New Zealand, it was found that over a three-month period in 1984 the official statistics underestimate the actual number of workers involved in stoppages in that country by 47 per cent, and the number of working days lost by 42 per cent.[19]

Furthermore, in most countries there will be inaccuracies of strike reporting because of either insufficient resources being devoted to the collection of the statistics, or a wish to use them for particular purposes. In this respect companies desirous of projecting an image of industrial harmony might overlook certain disputes when making their returns, or underestimate the number of workers taking part. Alternatively, they could inflate their figures with a view to securing unfavourable publicity, and perhaps adverse government attention, towards the strikers. In the case of the metalworking industry in Sweden, for example, even though unofficial strikes are clearly in breach of the peace obligation imposed by Swedish law, and therefore illegal, only about 3 per cent of them have ended up before the Labour Court. Employers were reluctant to report them, partly for fear of escalating the conflict and thereby damaging their future relations with the union. It was also felt that such action would reflect negatively upon the firm's management, adversely affecting its public-relations image and making personnel recruitment more difficult.[20] It has further been pointed out that the collection of strike statistics in individual countries tends to reflect the particular historical attitude adopted towards strikes themselves with, for example, some countries such as Italy still using a system of measurement which grew out of the view of strikes as a potential act of civil commotion;[21] hence the local police are still the focus for strike reporting by employers.

In relation to Third-World countries there are particular problems concerning the collection and interpretation of socio-economic data, even though this information can be of great value in social and economic development and in policy formulation. One study has noted the 'incomplete, fragmentary and defective nature of the data available in Africa',[22] where the economies are largely agrarian and where there are conceptual and measurement difficulties in applying western-type definitions to the African context. For instance, employment is more difficult to measure because of the sharing of the work among family members - and hence a less clear-cut distinction than in industrialized countries between breadwinners and others - as well as the great variations in intensity of work at different seasons of the year. Thus in Tanzania,

> the terms 'employed' and 'working' are often more applicable to an industrially advanced nation than to one with a large subsistence economy .... The wide divergence between the unemployment rates in rural and urban areas testifies to the difficulties in making the distinction between 'employed' and 'unemployed'. The term 'employed'

> could easily be associated with wage employment, which would apply to a large sector of the urban situation. Hence, the distinction between 'employed' and 'unemployed' is more appropriate in urban areas than in rural areas where wage employment is a very small portion of the total employment.[23]

As regards unemployment, the International Labour Office (ILO) often receives requests for unemployment statistics for countries which do not possess either employment agencies (so that there is no unemployment count), or labour-force surveys.[24] Certainly, in many countries - particularly on the African continent - any attempt to collect data via sample surveys and census methods is fraught with difficulties, including not only the lack of skilled manpower or funds to carry them out but also 'the illiteracy of the majority of the population and vagueness about time periods, particularly ages, the difficulty (both physical and mental) of communications, and cultural factors such as the belief that misfortune will follow the disclosure of certain facts. There is also resistance to questioning and falsification of results for economic and political reasons'.[25] These problems are further exacerbated in relation to obtaining accurate data on employment and unemployment in that, so long as unskilled manpower is relatively abundant, both governments and individual enterprises may lack interest in securing a good statistical picture of the unemployment situation.

Even when unemployment statistics are available in developing countries, they may give an unreliable and possibly misleading guide to what is happening there. One ILO study, using available unemployment statistics from 1975-80, was said to be 'worthless' to the extent that even comparing census or labour-survey data on employment to labour supply gave unemployment rates of as much as 60 per cent in some countries such as Costa Rica, Egypt, Jamaica, Republic of Korea, Peru, and Tunisia.[26]

Consequently, in view of all these considerations, the statistics (especially) of little-developed countries need to be treated with some caution.

INTERNATIONAL COMPARISONS

Given the differences between the definitions, scope, and coverage of the data, the methods used for compiling them and the ways in which the data are presented, further problems are encountered when utilizing national statistics in an attempt to assess international comparative performance, in order to examine the position of one country relative to that of another. In fact, international comparisons of labour statistics can be extremely hazardous. There are some differences, for instance, in such an apparently straightforward concept as the working-age population, since this has been defined as those persons aged 15 and over in Australia, Canada, Japan, and West Germany. Yet it is defined as those aged 16 and over in the USA and those aged 16 to 74 in Sweden. Furthermore, the working-age population refers to the civilian non-institutionalized population in Canada and the USA, whereas in Australia and West Germany it relates to the civilian population, and in Japan and Sweden to the total resident population.[27]

However, as regards international labour-force comparisons it would appear that employment is a firmer and more objective concept than unemployment, which involves uncertainties about whether jobless persons are actually seeking and are available for work, in order to be classified as unemployed, and consequently employment is somewhat easier to define and measure. By contrast, one comprehensive ILO study, in presenting a table of unemployment rates over the course of time in nine industrialized countries, clearly states that, although a useful guide to relative trends, 'because of differences in the sources and methods of data collection, in the scope and coverage of each national series and in the concepts and criteria used to identify the unemployed, they are not intended for inter-country comparisons'[28] (see chapter 3). By no means all such studies, however, are so explicit in their caveats about those statistics which are not directly comparable.

We may also note that in the case of Spain unemployment reached 20 per cent of the civilian labour force in 1984, as against only 1 per cent in 1970, and there was a very rapid increase in unemployment of 17 percentage points, in comparison with an average increase in European Economic Community countries of 8.6 points, over the period 1970-83. But it has to be recognized that these figures may overstate the extent of the unemployment problem in Spain because of the incidence of the underground economy there, as well as of fraudulent practices in unemployment registration, which may be higher than in most EEC countries.[29] Conversely, one reason for the relatively low unemployment rate in West Germany for many years is that in times of labour shortage the economy has relied upon guest workers who then returned to their home countries as employment conditions worsened. As a result the West German employed labour force has been reduced without any concomitant increase in unemployment.[30]

The measurement of unemployment in Japan is also particularly instructive in this respect. It has been argued that the (internationally) relatively low Japanese unemployment rate (2.5 per cent on average, 1977-80, whilst the rates in other industrialized countries rose markedly) is partly a consequence of distinctive and inadequate measurement techniques in comparison with those in other countries, since some of the jobless who would be included among the unemployed elsewhere are kept out of the statistical labour force in Japan. For instance, the 'temporarily ill' are considered as being out of the labour force (and therefore not unemployed) because they are not looking for work, whereas in US labour-force concepts they are counted among the ranks of the unemployed. The reason appears to be that 'the Japanese cannot stand the thought that a person should suffer double misfortunes: unemployment and illness. By classifying the temporarily ill as not in the labour force, the Japanese spare them the shame of having to be designated as unemployed'.[31] As well as differences in statistical methods and definitions arising from distinctive social and cultural attitudes the unemployment rate in Japan is also kept down in other, related ways as well. Labour slack tends to be pushed into underemployment (on reduced hours, or temporary lay-offs) and hidden unemployment - which does not show up in the official statistics - as a result of the 'lifetime employment' system in Japan in which permanent employees are still retained and paid even when there is no work for them.

Again, in the case of strikes, because they also are highly complex social phenomena, the problems already alluded to of measuring their magnitude become even greater in cross-national comparisons, since there are significant methodological differences between countries in the collection and processing of strike data and in terms of minimum, threshold levels of recording, which can also vary over the course of time (see chapter 9).

The major source of international data on industrial disputes, the ILO Year Book of Labour Statistics clearly states that:

> Various methods are used for calculating the number of working days lost, and these data, as well as the statistics of workers involved, are often approximations only. Because of this variation between countries in definitions, sources, scope and statistical treatment of data at country level, any comparison of the magnitude and relative importance of industrial disputes should be made with extreme care. (1986, 919)

However, the problems can be mitigated, to some extent, if only trends are being examined.

As a result of this kind of difficulty, any approach towards international comparisons utilizing various labour market data must be appraised with an understanding of the definitional variations which present problems in making such comparisons meaningful and valid. It is necessary to warn against the careless or reckless use of statistics when making comparisons between countries without taking account of differences and varying definitions, although, as Mitchell has wryly observed, 'one can find little comfort ... in the fact that failure to observe such warnings is one of the main reasons why statistics have sometimes been held to be worse than "damned lies".'[32]

INTERNATIONAL STATISTICAL SOURCES

The major work of statistical reference on labour-force matters from an international standpoint is the ILO Year Book of Labour Statistics which brings together in systematic form a mass of data from some 183 countries and territories, with the information presented usually spanning the last ten years. Nine major topics are included which comprise: the total and economically active population, employment, unemployment, hours of work, wage rates and earnings, labour costs, consumer price indices, occupational injuries, and industrial disputes - although there are gaps on at least some of these topics for many of the countries. The objective of the ILO data is the collation and international dissemination of the official statistics supplied by the individual countries themselves. The ILO's Bureau of Statistics does not adjust the data with a view to achieving cross-national comparability (apart from its 'Estimates and projections of the economically active population' - where adjustments are made to provide comparable data), 'although the typographic uniformity of the tables may unwittingly suggest more comparability than in fact exists'.[33] However, the ILO does intend to publish comparable estimates of annual average employment and unemployment for a number of countries in future.

Also, for more than sixty years the ILO has endeavoured to enhance the international comparability and standardization of national labour statistics, as well as providing guidance on data collection, analysis, and classification (especially to countries with less developed statistics), mainly through organizing international conferences of labour statisticians. These conferences pass resolutions (often called 'guidelines') for the promulgation of statistical standards in order to help achieve international standardization in concepts, terminology, and measures, although they are not mandatory on member countries. As regards unemployment statistics, for instance,

> Practice in individual countries varies considerably, reflecting in part the constraints imposed by the system for obtaining the statistics and

> in part the uses, circumstances and traditions of the country concerned. When the figures are compiled from administrative sources (as in the United Kingdom and many other countries) and not from specially designed surveys of the labour force, there are commonly difficulties in meeting the ILO recommendations.[34]

The ILO recommendations on standards are reviewed at intervals when changes may be made in the terminology and methods of presentation of particular labour statistics. To illustrate, at the 13th International Conference of Labour Statisticians (1982) the definitional boundary of the 'economically active population' was extended to include unpaid household work, not only if it is being produced for the market, as was previously the case, but also if it is primary production for own consumption (e.g. vegetables, eggs, and milk).[35]

As a further step in the standard-setting activities of the ILO, at the 71st International Labour Conference a Convention on labour statistics was adopted reflecting the need for more comprehensive and precise information in order to assist in planning and monitoring economic and social progress. Improving upon an earlier instrument, the Convention obliges ratifying states to produce statistics that will be progressively expanded with data so as to provide a detailed picture of the country as a whole, including wage structure and distribution, labour costs, consumer-price indices, household expenditure, occupational injuries, and industrial disputes. However, in the case of developing countries - many of which are weak in the compilation of accurate statistics - a flexibility clause enables them to apply the provisions of the Convention selectively and progressively, although at the same time taking into account ILO standards and guidelines as regards concepts, definitions, and methodology.[36]

In addition to the Year Book the ILO also publishes a quarterly Bulletin of Labour Statistics, with supplements in the intervening months, to complement and update the annual data given in the Year Book for employment and unemployment, hours worked, wages and consumer price indices. The Bulletin also includes regular articles of professional interest to labour statisticians. Detailed ILO estimates and projections of the economically active population are published in six volumes for the various continents (Economically Active Population, Estimates and Projections: 1950-2025 3rd edition 1986). A number of detailed guides to the sources and methods for the series published in the Year Book and Bulletin are also available.[37]

A further important source of international labour statistics is the Organization for Economic Co-operation and Development (OECD). For twenty-four OECD member countries Labour Force Statistics, published annually and (since 1975) quarterly, gives detailed statistics on population, labour force, employment, and unemployment as well as participation rates for a more limited number of member countries. Recent changes in labour force, wages, and prices are presented in its quarterly publication Main Economic Indicators. Like the ILO, the OECD also emphasizes with regard to its labour force data that:

> The standardized presentation of the tables does not imply that the corresponding series for the various countries are comparable. Differences exist between countries in the matter of general concepts, classification and the methods used for obtaining the data. International comparisons must therefore be approached with caution; the rates of change can be considered as more comparable than the

absolute figures and for some series the transformed data (indices, percentages etc.) should be used.[38]

An important feature, however, of the OECD data is that, in order to facilitate cross-country comparisons, the unemployment rates (expressed as a percentage of the total labour force) for sixteen major industrialized countries have since 1971 been adjusted as necessary and to the extent that the available data will permit, so as to conform to the ILO criteria and definitions. Consequently, these standardized rates are more comparable than the unemployment rates based on national definitions, which are also shown. The standardized unemployment rates are also published twice a year in the OECD Economic Outlook.

Since the early 1960s the United States Bureau of Labor Statistics (BLS) has published unemployment rates, adjusted for all known, major differences of coverage and definition to a statistically comparable base approximating to US definitions and concepts, for seven other major industrial countries, recently extended to ten - USA, Canada, Australia, Japan, and six European countries. These figures, together also with similarly adjusted, comparative labour-force and employment statistics, participation rates, and employment - population ratios are published in the Monthly Labor Review. The Bureau notes that although precise comparability may not be attained, the adjusted figures provide a better basis for international comparisons than the figures regularly produced by each country. Also, because the OECD and BLS use similar methods of adjustment, for most countries there is little difference between the unemployment rates emanating from these two sources.

A useful source of data on wages, hourly labour costs, and the structure of earnings for EEC member countries is EUROSTAT (Statistical Office of the European Communities) which has also published a handbook entitled A Guide to Current Sources of Wage Statistics in the European Community (1984). There are similar publications on Industrial Disputes: Methods and Measurement in the European Community (1982), Working Time Statistics (1984), and Trade Union Membership (1985). Regular series on EEC member countries' employment and unemployment (in which member countries compile data on a comparable basis directly, rather than adjusting national data), working population (including activity rates), as well as industrial stoppages are also available.

FORMAT OF THE BOOK

Once the nature, sources, methods of compilation, and some pitfalls of interpretation of international statistical information relating to the labour force have been examined in general terms, the remaining chapters in the first part of the book are concerned specifically with statistics of eight key aspects of the labour market, for a more limited group of (some 20-24) major developed, capitalist economies for which comprehensive statistical data is available. For each subject area a commentary is presented by a specialist contributor on the compilation, limitations, and interpretation of the available data, together with a review of the major comparative, cross-national trends which can be discerned over the past ten to fifteen years. It will be apparent that over the past decade substantial changes have taken place in both the structure and performance of labour markets, emanating from changes in various economic factors such as the oil-price crises in 1974 and 1978, together with the subsequent slowdown in economic growth and the increase in international competitive pressures, although the labour-force response to these changes has varied markedly in different countries.

In chapter 2 labour-force and employment measures are discussed and recent trends delineated. There are undoubtedly wide international differences in the proportion of the population of working age actually offering their labour-force services. In 1981, for instance, when the overall labour-force participation rate in the USA was 64 per cent, it was 67 per cent in Sweden, but only 52 per cent in Germany and 48 per cent in Italy. Data on the relative movement of participation rates can help to explain the marked long-term differences in labour-force trends among industrialized countries since, although the USA and Japan have both had similar rates of population growth over the past twenty years, the labour force in the USA has grown much more rapidly than that in Japan because participation rates for women and youths have risen in the USA, whereas they have been falling in Japan.[39]

Since the 1930s the industrialized countries of the western world have relied upon unemployment statistics in order to evaluate both the economic state of the labour market and the social conditions of the labour force itself. In chapter 3 it is shown that, although in countries such as the UK and USA the level and rate of unemployment are probably the most widely quoted of all statistics, comparisons are frequently made with little qualification or reference to variations in the definition of unemployment, or in the administrative arrangements for collecting the relevant statistics. Furthermore, the unemployment rate itself may not always be a good measure of the degree of tightness in the labour market since it reflects only embodied labour i.e. it is a 'persons' measure. It is also largely a supply-side measure and may, therefore, be a very poor indicator of any imbalance between the demand for and the supply of labour services.[40]

Wage-rate and earnings data for the labour force are discussed in chapter 4. Wage (and labour-cost) data on comparative levels of remuneration are important in relation to international trade and competitiveness, as well as providing crucial insight into the well-being of the working population, and furthermore it has been noted that the lack of reliable wage statistics can sometimes also prove a serious handicap in efforts to settle labour disputes.[41] There is a basic distinction to be drawn between the narrower concept of wage rates and the broader magnitude of earnings and it is important that the user of such statistics should be aware of the implications of the one which is being employed in any particular statistical series. Moreover, because the purchasing power of nominal wages differs as between countries, consumer-price indices are required in order to throw light on the amount of goods and services which can actually be purchased with wages (see chapter 5). Historically, in the case of the UK at the turn of the century, these indices were intended to show the effect of changing food prices upon the living standards of manual workers, to complement the wages statistics. Nowadays, however, the general index of retail prices in the UK is much more broadly based:

> It is extensively used within government as a key economic indicator of the level of inflation, and now occupies a crucial role in the index-linking of many government payments, including social security benefits, public sector occupational pensions ... and personal tax allowances. It is also widely used outside government in the context of pay negotiations, private sector pension schemes and private contractual arrangements for which a widely accepted measure of general inflation is required.[42]

International surveys of consumer prices are undertaken in order to make estimates of what are termed 'purchasing-power parities' (PPPs). These may be regarded as retail-price indices which measure differences in purchasing power between countries, as against changes over time in a single country.[43] The problem is that international economic comparisons are conventionally carried out by using exchange rates for converting individual currencies, thereby providing data in a common currency but valued at different sets of prices. PPPs provide data in a common currency valued at a common set of prices and may be used, for instance, by companies who wish to compare earnings levels in different countries.

As well as the money payments which employees receive from their employers in return for their labour services a further important concept is that of labour costs, which represent the total costs incurred by the employers in the employment of labour. These include not only direct wage costs but also, inter alia, additional items of fringe benefits, employers' social security payments, and the cost of vocational training. The Research department of the Swedish Employers' Confederation (SAF) in Stockholm produces an international survey, on an annual and comparable basis, for some fifteen countries relating to wages and total labour costs. These statistics form the basis of chapter 6 in which the concept and recent cross-national trends of labour costs are fully explored. The ILO also publishes a series on labour costs in manufacturing, on the basis of individual countries' currencies, in its Year Book but warns that care should be taken in using the figures since national definitions of labour costs differ from the recommended standard definition. Since labour costs are a major component of the cost of manufactured goods, labour costs per unit of output, in conjunction with the exchange rates among currrencies, play a major role in determining the relative price of goods sold on the world market.

A further source of international statistical information on unit labour costs on both a national-currency and a US-dollar basis is the series for the USA, Canada, Japan, and nine European countries, in the form of indices, produced by the BLS and published in the Monthly Labor Review. The series also includes manufacturing output per hour (a labour productivity measure), total hours, and compensation per hour - where compensation is defined as wages and salaries plus employers' contributions for social insurance and other employee-benefit programmes. However, because of data limitation and the technical problems in comparing the levels of manufacturing output among countries, the BLS statistics are to be used to facilitate analysis of country-by-country time-series trends (i.e. the movements over a number of years), rather than for cross-national (level) comparisons at a particular point in time.[44]

Statistics of hours of work, as well as wages, are an important economic indicator and are used for helping to forecast economic and business conditions. In particular, 'changes in average hours of work per week or in the amount of overtime worked ... usually point to a shift in the level of business activity earlier than other economic indicators such as productivity'.[45] One major instrument which has been canvassed as a way of adjusting labour supply to demand and thereby reducing existing high levels of unemployment in many countries is the reduction of contractual working hours, generally referred to as 'work sharing'. This policy option has received a good deal of attention in recent years in countries such as West Germany, France, and the Netherlands. Indeed, it has been said that 'in the late 1970s the European trade union movement exhibited an uncritical faith in the shorter working week as a virtually autonomous method of creating jobs'.[46] Another related possibility for reducing working time is the greater control of overtime working and the extension of annual holidays. In the case of the former it has been suggested that in West Germany, for instance, the reduction of overtime to the standard working hours would create more than one million new jobs.[47] Variations in hours of work among countries and the statistical backdrop to these policy considerations are dealt with in chapter 7.

Another comparative labour-market indicator - although somewhat less used due to limited data availability - is the extent of trade-union membership, and changes in the number of union members, among employees within different countries. Although data on levels of membership and union growth do not provide any precise quantitative index of the industrial and political power of unions, nevertheless the two are broadly related since 'at the very least union growth is a necessary condition, a prerequisite for the exercise of union power'.[48] The collation and an assessment of the data, together with a discussion of recent trends in union membership growth across a number of countries, are presented in some detail in chapter 8.

In the final chapter, 9, there is a comprehensive discussion of the validity of various measures of industrial disputes examined from an international viewpoint, as well as data concerning recent cross-national trends in work stoppages. Interest in comparative strike statistics has increased with the expansion of multinational enterprises since the strike record, as one indicator of the industrial relations 'climate', may influence the decision to invest in a new plant within a new location. Furthermore, strike statistics may be used to evaluate the effectiveness of government policies in the area of industrial relations or, on a comparative basis, as one index of the efficacy of particular countries' industrial-relations systems. Conceptual and practical problems arise, however, when making such international comparisons. Although, since the 1920s, the ILO has laid down guidelines in order to establish a consistent approach to the enumeration and classification of industrial disputes, in the case of France, West Germany, Italy, and the UK, at least, it would seem that 'only scant reference is given to the recommendations, as evidenced in the still wide differences of measurement between the countries'.[49]

In the second part of the book there is provided a summary of key labour-market, factual data - the most recent information available - country by country for a total of 44 countries, centralizing the available statistical data from a number of different sources. The countries for which data are provided have been selected on the basis of their importance for international trade and investment, subject to the constraints provided by the actual availability of statistical information about the labour force for these countries. In general, the data are comprehensive and updated for the OECD countries, but less so for other countries.

Finally, there is a table of statistics relating to the membership of the 16 International Trade Secretariats affiliated to the International Confederation of Free Trade Unions. These bodies are organizations which group together under one international umbrella national trade unions within particular sectors of the economy throughout various countries. They have attained increased importance as a result of the growth of multinational corporations and their activities include the dissemination of information on terms and conditions of employment of their affiliates around the world, and international assistance during industrial disputes.[50]

NOTES

1 E.H. Phelps Brown (1962) The Economics of Labor, New Haven: Yale University Press: 5.

2 ibid., 6.

3 G. Routh (1986) Unemployment: Economic Perspectives, London: Macmillan; 1.

4 Janet L. Norwood (1985) 'One hundred years of the Bureau of Labor Statistics', Monthly Labor Review, vol. 108, January: 4. For the UK see P. Dworkin (1986) 'The Department of Employment - labour market statistics 100 years on', Statistical News: Developments in British Official Statistics, London: HMSO, no. 73, May: 8.

5 W.R. Garside (1980) The Measurement of Unemployment: Methods and Sources in Great Britain 1850-1979, Oxford: Blackwell: 4.

6 G.M.K. Kpedekpo and P.L. Arya (1981) Social and Economic Statistics for Africa, London: Allen and Unwin: 8.

7 H.V.J. Moir and C. Robinson, 'Labour market measurement: a review of some popular labour market measures', in R. Blandy and O. Covick (eds.) (1984) Understanding Labour Markets in Australia, Sydney: Allen and Unwin: 77.

8 P. Striker and P. Sheehan (1981) Hidden Unemployment: The Australian Experience, Institute of Applied Economic and Social Research, University of Melbourne.

9 See Carol B. Leon (1981) 'The employment-population ratio: its value in labor force analysis', Monthly Labor Review, vol. 104, February.

10 See for instance Economic Council of Canada (1976) People and Jobs: A Study of the Canadian Labour Market, Ottawa; Supply and Services; National Commission on Employment and Unemployment Statistics (1979) Counting the Labor Force, Washington: US Government Printing Office; and J. Mouly (1977) 'Employment: a concept in need of renovation', International Labour Review, vol. 16.

11 J. Shiskin and R.L. Stein (1975) 'Problems in measuring unemployment', Monthly Labor Review, vol. 98, August: 3.

12 R. Blandy and O. Covick, op. cit., 62.

13 J. Shiskin (1976) 'Employment and unemployment: the doughnut or the hole?', Monthly Labor Review, vol. 99, February: 3-4.

14 The US Bureau of Labor Statistics, for instance, publishes seven different unemployment rates, with different durations of unemployment, and some with adjustments to put part-time work on to a full-time-equivalent basis.

15 M. Slattery (1986) Official Statistics, London: Tavistock Publications: 83.

16 J Irvine, I. Miles, and J. Evans (eds.) (1979) Demystifying Social Statistics, London: Pluto Press: 5.

17 The Times, 5 August 1987, and F. Modigliani, F. Padoa Schioppa, and N. Rossi (1986), 'Aggregate unemployment in Italy, 1960-1983', Economica, vol. 53: 245.

18 M. Shalev, 'Lies, damned lies and strike statistics: the measurement of trends in industrial conflict' in C. Crouch and A. Pizzorno (1978) The Resurgence of Class Conflict in Western Europe since 1968, London: Macmillan; vol. 1: 1.

19 R. Harbridge (1987) 'The (in) accuracy of official work stoppage statistics in New Zealand', New Zealand Journal of Industrial Relations, vol. 12, no. 1: 33.

20 W. Korpi (1978) 'Workplace bargaining, the law and unofficial

strikes: the case of Sweden', British Journal of Industrial Relations, vol. XVI: 362.

21 K. Walsh (1983) Strikes in Europe and the United Sates: Measurement and Incidence, London: Frances Pinter: 4.

22 Kpedekpo and Arya, op. cit., 15. On the availability of statistical data elsewhere see E. Blauvelt and J. Durlacher (1981) Sources of Asian/Pacific Economic Information, London: Gower.

23 A.K. Dey and N. Mogil, 'Economic Characteristics' in B. Egero and R.A. Henin (eds.) (1973) The Population of Tanzania: An Analysis of the 1967 Census, Dar es Salaam: Bureau of Statistics: 132.

24 R. Turvey (1986) 'The International Labour Office (ILO) Bureau of Statistics', Statistical News: Developments in British Official Statistics, London: HMSO, no. 73, May: 11.

25 Kpedekpo and Arya, op. cit., 7.

26 M. Hopkins (1983) 'Employment trends in developing countries, 1960-80 and beyond', International Labour Review, vol 22: 477.

27 Monthly Labor Review (1986) vol. 109, May: 11.

28 D.H. Freedman (ed.) (1979) Employment: outlook and insights, Geneva: ILO: 43.

29 J.J. Dolado, J.L. Malo de Molina, and A. Zabalza (1986) 'Spanish industrial unemployment: some explanatory factors', Economica, vol. 53: 313.

30 Employment Gazette (1980) 'International unemployment statistics', LXXXVIII: 833.

31 K. Taira (1983) 'Japan's low unemployment: economic miracle or statistical artifact?' Monthly Labor Review, vol. 106, July. See also C. Sorrentino (1984) 'Japan's low unemployment: an in-depth analysis', ibid., vol. 107, March.

32 B.R. Mitchell (1982) International Historical Statistics: Africa and Asia, London: Macmillan: vii.

33 R. Turvey, op. cit., 11.

34 Employment Gazette (1980) 'International unemployment statistics': 834.

35 See M.V.S. Rao and F. Mehran (1984, 4) 'Salient features of the new international standards on statistics of the economically active population', Bulletin of Labour Statistics, ILO: ix.

36 See International Labour Review (1985) 'The 71st session of the International Labour Conference, June 1985', vol. 124, no. 5.

37 See for instance ILO, Statistical Sources and Methods, volume 3. Economically Active Population, Employment, Unemployment and Hours of Work (Household Surveys), 1986 which provides methodological descriptions of the statistics for 46 countries.

38 OECD (1987) Labour Force Statistics 1965-85, Paris.

39 E. Sorrentino (1983) 'International comparisons of labor force participation, 1960-81', Monthly Labor Review, vol. 106, February: 23. See also P.J. McMahon (1986) 'An international comparison of labour force participation, 1977-84', ibid., vol. 109, May.

40 Moir and Robinson, op. cit., 73.

41 K.M. Bashir (1979) 'An integrated system of wages statistics', International Labour Review, vol. 118: 371.

42 P. Dworkin, op. cit., 9.

43 ibid. Eurostat publishes PPPs for the twelve EEC member states.

44 See A. Neef (1986) 'International trends in productivity and unit labor costs in manufacturing', Monthly Labor Review, vol. 109, December. The data relate to the period 1960-85.

45 K.M. Bashir, op. cit.

46 M. White 'Working time and employment: a negotiable issue?' in P.E. Hart (ed.) (1986) Unemployment and Labour Market Policies, Aldershot: Gower: 12.

47 W. Franz and H. König (1986) 'The nature and causes of unemployment in the Federal Republic of Germany since the 1970s: an empirical investigation', Economica, vol. 53: 219.

48 G.S. Bain and R. Price, 'Union growth: dimensions, determinants and density' in G.S. Bain (ed.) (1983) Industrial Relations in Britain, Oxford: Blackwell: 3.

49 K. Walsh (1982) 'Industrial disputes in France, West Germany, Italy and the United Kingdom: measurement and incidence', Industrial Relations Journal, vol. 13, no. 4: 66.

50 See R. Bean (1985) Comparative Industrial Relations: An Introduction to Cross-National Perspectives, London: Croom Helm: 8.

2 WORKING POPULATION AND EMPLOYMENT

Paul Blyton

INTRODUCTION

The International Labour Office (ILO) and the Organization for Economic Co-operation and Development (OECD) collect information on a variety of aspects relating to the population and employment profiles of their member countries. In this chapter the OECD has been used as the primary source of information; where ILO data have been drawn upon, any differences in definitional criteria employed by the two organizations has been indicated. OECD information on working populations and employment appears in a number of different forms and types of publication, some of them containing historical time series as well as current data (such as Labour Force Statistics 1966-1986 published by the OECD in 1988), and others brought up to date either annually (e.g. Employment Outlook, published annually in September since 1983), or quarterly (Quarterly Labour Force Statistics which reports data on fourteen of the twenty-four OECD countries).

Having detailed statistics on various aspects of the working population and labour force is particularly useful at the present time, since, as we discuss in detail below, significant changes have been occurring in recent years which will continue to be important in the future. Prominent among these is the marked ageing of the populations in most industrialized countries, which wil substantially alter the ratio of those in paid employment and those retired from full-time work; the implications of this extend not only to public-policy areas such as the provision of welfare services to the elderly, but also to questions relating to the funding of pension schemes and even the markets for goods and services targeted at the elderly population.

Other important developments include the forthcoming decline in the number of young people leaving school, changes in the participation rates of men and women in the labour market and, in particular, the increase in the number of married women with children who are seeking paid employment. Added to this is the changing nature of employment, most notably the growth of the service sector, occurring at a time of widespread shrinkage in the numbers working in industry and in agriculture. In some countries almost seven out of ten employees are now located in the service sector - a situation which some analysts have taken to represent the transition from an industrial to a post-industrial society. Further, given the continued high levels of unemployment in many industrialized countries, the extent to which services can create additional jobs has become an important national issue. As we discuss further below, the indications are that service employment within the OECD will continue to grow but probably at a slower rate than was evident in the 1970s.

Linked to the growth in services and in female participation has been a substantial growth in part-time working within the OECD; in a number of countries one in five jobs is now part-time. Comparisons between countries are complicated by variations in the definitions of part-time work; however, the widespread growth is clear and the role of part-time work in the employment profiles of corporations and entire nations has become more apparent since the beginning of the 1970s.

In part, this growth in part-time employment is one aspect of a broader move by managements to develop a greater degree of flexibility in their workforces. Part-time work increases flexibility by allowing labour to be used at periods when demand is heaviest (for example, during lunchtime in high-street department stores). Other means to increase manpower flexibility have included a greater use of temporary workers in a number of countries; an increased reliance on self-employed workers to undertake specific tasks on a fee-paying basis; and the growing trend away from single-skilled toward more company-specific multi-skilled employees. In some instances this search for greater flexibility has been technology driven, with developments in computer-based equipment allowing a greater degree of flexibility, which managers have sought to match through greater flexibility in the workforce. Objectives of increasing labour productivity and reducing unit labour costs have also been important stimuli to efforts to increase workforce flexibility.

Given the strength of international competition, and the arrival of newly industrializing countries on world markets, coupled with the relatively slack labour markets (and resulting weakened trade unions) in many industrial countries, we may anticipate that this drive for greater flexibility will continue in coming years and become more prominent in the service sector which, up to now, has concentrated mainly on part-timers as a means to introduce flexibility. Overall, it would appear that the pattern of employment will continue to display many of the changes already evident in most industrial countries, with both manufacturing and service sectors undergoing major transformations in the number and composition of workers employed.

WORKING POPULATION

Population of working age

A variety of measures have been used by different international bodies to encapsulate the notion of 'population of working age', or that proportion of the total population considered potentially eligible for employment. Some consensus does exist, however, that the boundaries of this group should be 15 and 64 years inclusive. This span is generally used by the OECD in its published statistics for most countries, and will be used here. The general increase in school-leaving ages (i.e. the age after completion of the compulsory years of schooling) which has occurred over the past twenty years, together with a widespread reduction in actual ages of retirement resulting from participation in early retirement schemes (see chapter 7), has tended to undermine the validity of the 15- and 64-year boundary posts; increasingly 16 to around 62 years represents a truer indication of the population of working age. However, for the time being, and to ensure comparability with previous statistical compilations, the 15 - 64-years span remains widely employed.

Table 2.1 indicates that in the OECD as a whole there has been a fairly stable annual growth rate of just over 1 per cent in the population of

Table 2.1 Growth in the population of working age (15-64): average annual growth rates

	1973-5	1975-9	1980-2	1983	1984	1985[a]
	%	%	%	%	%	%
Australia	1.9	1.8	1.9	1.6	1.5	1.7
Austria	0.2	0.6	1.4	0.9	1.0	0.3
Belgium	0.8	0.7	0.6	0.8	-0.1	-0.2
Canada	2.6	2.0	1.5	1.2	1.1	1.0
Denmark	0.2	0.4	0.7	0.4	0.4	0.4
Finland	0.7	0.4	0.7	0.7	0.6	0.3
France	0.7	0.7	1.4	1.2	1.1	0.7
Germany	0.1	0.4	1.4	1.0	0.6	0.3
Greece	0.7	1.3	1.3	1.1	0.8	0.8
Iceland	2.1	1.5	1.7	1.6	1.3	1.2
Ireland	1.9	1.7	1.4	1.2	1.4	1.3
Italy	0.6	0.7	1.0	1.3	1.6	0.8
Japan	0.9	0.8	0.7	1.0	1.1	1.1
Luxemburg	1.8	0.3	0.7	0.9	0.4	0.4
Netherlands	1.4	1.4	1.2	1.1	1.2	1.1
New Zealand	2.6	0.9	1.2	2.2	1.7	1.7
Norway	0.6	0.6	0.7	0.7	0.8	0.6
Portugal	3.3	1.0	1.2	1.4	1.3	1.2
Spain	1.0	1.3	1.0	1.1	1.1	1.0
Sweden	-0.1	0.2	0.4	0.2	0.3	0.1
Switzerland	-0.4	0.2	1.4	0.7	0.8	0.5
Turkey	3.0	2.7	3.3	3.1	3.0	2.8
United Kingdom	0.1	0.5	0.6	0.7	0.9	0.4
United States	1.7	1.7	1.1	0.9	1.0	0.9
North America	1.8	1.7	1.1	0.9	1.0	0.9
OECD Europe	0.7	0.9	1.3	1.2	1.2	0.8
Total OECD	1.1	1.2	1.2	1.1	1.1	0.9

Sources: OECD (1986) Employment Outlook
OECD (1960-84) Historical Statistics

a Secretariat estimates.

1984 population of working age	1984 total population	Proportion of total population in 15-64 age category
000s	000s	000s
10,250	15,544	65.9
5,071	7,552	67.1
6,581	9,855	66.8
17,111	25,128	68.1
3,388	5,112	66.3
3,326	4,882	68.1
36,082	54,947	65.7
42,655	61,175	69.7
6,460	9,900	65.3
152	240	63.3
2,113	3,535	59.8
39,000	56,344	69.2
81,550	120,020	67.9
254	366	69.4
9,816	14,424	68.1
2,110	3,258	64.8
2,652	4,140	64.1
6,212	9,613	64.6
24,673	38,387	64.3
5,397	8,337	64.7
4,448	6,505	68.4
28,701	48,825	58.8
37,104	56,488	65.7
156,907	236,682	66.3
174,018	261,810	66.5
264,085	400,627	65.9
532,013	801,259	66.4

working age in the period 1973-85. This is slightly faster than the growth in the total OECD population (rising annually at about 0.8 per cent during this period). In part, this reflects the working through of the 1950s and 1960s 'baby boom' into the working population a generation later. The peaking of births in the USA and Canada occurred in the late 1950s, in most European countries in the mid-1960s, and in Australia and Japan not until the 1970s. In addition, the population of working age in certain countries and regions (Australia, Canada, New Zealand, the USA, and Northern Europe) has been significantly influenced by the net inflow of migrant workers, though more so in the early 1970s than in the last decade; the post-1980 recession reduced the flows of migrants considerably.[1]

The average OECD growth rate in the population of working age subsumes considerable variation between individual member countries, with some demonstrating a slow growth rate for part or all of this period ('slow' being defined here as less than 0.5 per cent increase per annum) - for example, Austria, Denmark, Finland, the Federal Republic of Germany, Luxemburg, and the United Kingdom; others exhibiting a growth pattern similar to the OECD average, e.g. Netherlands, Spain; and a third group exhibiting a much higher growth rate (in excess of 1.5 per cent annually), for example, Australia, New Zealand and, most notably, Turkey. However, despite these variations in the actual rate of change, there is virtually no variation in the direction of that change. All countries show net growth in their working-age populations; only three countries (Belgium, Sweden, and Switzerland) have epxerienced individual years where the population of working age has declined slightly.

In the OECD as a whole, the population of working age comprised just under two-thirds (66.4 per cent) of the total population in 1984. In most OECD countries this proportion lies between 64 and 68 per cent. Exceptions to this include, on the high side, the Federal Republic of Germany (70 per cent), Italy and Luxemburg (69 per cent), and, on the low side, Ireland (60 per cent) and Turkey (59 per cent).

In passing, table 2.1 also indicates the huge population differences between the countries making up the OECD. In 1984 the majority of members (thirteen out of the twenty-four) had populations of less than 10 million and two - Iceland and Luxemburg - were populated by considerably less than half a million. At the other extreme, the USA, with its population of more than two hundred million, is almost double the size of any other member. Two countries, the USA and Japan, together account for more than 44 per cent of the total OECD population; seven of the twenty-four countries (France, Germany, Italy, Japan, Turkey, the UK, and the USA) contain over four-fifths of the OECD population.

The labour force and participation rates

The 'labour force' comprises that part of the population of working age who are active in the labour market (i.e. who are employed, including the self-employed, or are currently unemployed). Some differences exist, however, in the definition of the labour force adopted by individual countries e.g. in Italy the minimum age is 14, in Finland the range is 15-74 and in Norway and Sweden (up to 1986) it is from 16 to a maximum age of 74. Such differences in the minimum age of the working population may be important for considerations of youth-labour markets, and the maximum age in the Scandinavian countries will have some effect on labour-force-participation-rate comparisons as between these countries and others (since these rates are derivative measures). Changes in the size of the labour force can be caused either by changes in the population of working age, and/or by changes in the labour-force-participation rate, i.e. the proportion of the population of working age who are active in the labour market (see below). For most countries the source of these data is a labour-force survey of households. From table 2.2, it is evident that, in the OECD as a whole, the labour force grew throughout the 1973-85 period. Again, however, this overall average masks significant variation between member countries and, in particular, fails to reflect a reverse trend in several countries for parts of that period (e.g. in Germany and Switzerland during the 1970s, the UK in the early 1980s, and Belgium and Portugal during the mid 1980s). Further, in recent years North America and Australia have demonstrated a much more rapid growth in their labour force than Europe or Japan.

Of the two possible contributors to changes in the size of the OECD labour force over the past two decades, it has been the continued growth in the working-age population that has been the major determinant of the increase.[2] Overall, the participation rate in the OECD has changed much less in the period (see table 2.3). The participation rate was very stable between 1970 and 1975 and then increased slowly from 68.3 per cent in 1975 to 69.3 per cent in 1979, primarily as a result of increases in North America and, to a lesser extent, Japan. Since 1979 the overall participation rate has changed very little; a small decrease in OECD European countries has been offset by a continued rise in the participation rate in North America.

Certain countries, however, do show a much greater rate of change over the 1975-85 period; for example, the increased participation rates in Canada, Denmark, Finland, Iceland, Japan, Norway, and the USA, together with the decreased participation rates in countries such as France, Germany, Spain, and Turkey. Table 2.3 also indicates wide cross-national diversity in the proportions of the populations of working age active in the labour market, and the tendency for this diversity to persist over time. On the one hand, in the Nordic countries the participation rate in recent years approaches four out of five, whereas in half the OECD member countries the proportion was below two-thirds, and in at least one case (Spain) the participation rate was only a little above one in two of the population of working age.

More insight can be gained into these participation rates by examining the specific changes in male and female participation rates (table 2.4). In general the picture is one of a decrease in the rate of male participation in the labour force (by over 3 per cent in the OECD as a whole between 1975 and 1984) and an increase in female participation rates (by over 6 per cent over the same period). In the majority of countries both trends are evident, though the decline in male participation rates is dominant in Luxemburg and Switzerland, while the increase in female participation is relatively more marked in Canada, Denmark, Japan, Netherlands, Sweden, and the United States. Of the twenty-four OECD countries, only seven do not fit this general pattern of declining male and increasing female participation rates. In four of these (Austria, Finland, Greece, and Norway) there is no evidence of a declining male participation rate, while in the remaining three (Germany, Spain, and Turkey) there is little or no indication of a growth in female participation since 1975. Indeed, in the case of Turkey, the female participation rate (and the combined male and female participation rates) appears to have fallen considerably over the 1975-84 period.

These are exceptions, however, to the broader trend which is evident

Table 2.2 Labour force: average annual growth rates

	1973-5	1975-9	1980-2	1983	1984	1985[a]	1984 labour force
	%	%	%	%	%	%	000s
Australia	1.9	1.3	1.2	1.3	2.0	2.3	7,138
Austria	-0.8	1.0	2.7	-0.2	2.1	-0.2	3,363
Belgium	1.0	0.9	0.5	0.4	0.0	-0.7[b]	4,214
Canada	3.7	3.0	1.6	1.9	1.8	1.9	12,474
Denmark	0.8	1.4	0.3	1.2	-0.4	1.1[b]	2,720
Finland	1.3	1.4	1.6	0.7	1.0	1.2	2,600
France	0.8	1.0	0.8	-0.3	0.6	0.1	23,830
Germany	-0.6	0.0	0.6	0.2	0.1	0.8	27,618
Greece	0.3	0.8	3.6	2.7	0.1	0.9[b]	3,811
Iceland	2.6	1.7	3.9	1.2	1.1	1.0[b]	116
Ireland	1.1	1.6	1.9	1.0	0.4	0.8[b]	1,314
Italy	0.8	1.2	0.8	1.1	1.0	0.8	23,407
Japan	0.0	1.3	1.1	2.0	0.7	0.6	59,270
Luxemburg	2.1	0.0	0.3	0.1	0.4	1.9[b]	161
Netherlands	1.2	1.0	3.2	1.3	1.0	-0.4[b]	5,896
New Zealand	3.1	1.4	1.4	1.1	1.2	1.2[b]	1,371
Norway	2.0	2.2	1.3	1.3	0.3	1.6	2,031
Portugal	1.5[a]	1.5	-0.4	6.1	-1.1	-0.9[b]	4,544
Spain	0.4	-0.7	0.9	0.8	-0.2	0.6	13,675
Sweden	1.9	0.8	0.5	0.4	0.4	0.8	4,391
Switzerland	-2.3	-0.2	0.4	-0.8	0.0	0.8	3,177
Turkey	2.0	1.4	1.3	1.3	1.3	1.3[b]	18,516
United Kingdom	0.5	0.7	-0.3	-4.1	5.6	1.8	27,014
United States	2.3	2.8	1.5	1.2	1.8	1.7	115,763
North America	2.4	2.8	1.5	1.3	1.8	1.7	128,237
OECD Europe	0.7	0.7	0.8	0.0	1.3	0.8[b]	172,398
Total OECD	1.2	1.5	1.1	0.8	1.4	1.1[b]	368,414

Source: OECD (1986) Employment Outlook

a data refer to 1974-75
b Secretariat estimates

Table 2.3 Participation rates[a]

	1975	1979	1982	1983	1984	1985
	%	%	%	%	%	%
Australia	70.5	69.2	69.6	69.3	69.6	70.1
Austria	63.8	64.9	66.3	65.6	66.3	65.9
Belgium	63.8	64.1	64.2	64.0	64.0	63.7[b]
Canada	68.1	70.8	71.9	72.4	72.9	73.6
Denmark	76.8	79.8	80.4	80.9	80.3	80.9[b]
Finland	72.5	75.5	77.9	77.9	78.2	78.8
France	67.9	68.5	67.3	66.4	66.0	65.7
Germany	67.9	66.8	65.6	65.1	64.7	65.1
Greece	56.6	55.4	58.5	59.4	59.0	59.1[b]
Iceland	71.6	72.0	76.5	76.2	76.1	76.0[b]
Ireland	62.6	62.4	62.9	62.8	62.2	61.9[b]
Italy	59.0	60.2	60.5	60.4	60.0	60.0
Japan	70.4	71.8	72.3	73.0	72.7	72.3
Luxemburg	65.2	64.4	63.8	63.3	63.4	64.3[b]
Netherlands	57.3	56.5	60.1	60.2	60.1	59.2[b]
New Zealand	65.0	66.3	66.0	65.3	65.0	64.6[b]
Norway	69.7	74.5	76.4	76.9	76.6	77.4
Portugal	72.2	73.6	71.6	74.9	73.1	71.7[b]
Spain	62.0	57.3	56.3	56.1	55.4	55.2
Sweden	78.5	80.5	81.2	81.3	81.4	81.9
Switzerland	74.8	73.8	73.2	72.0	71.4	71.6
Turkey	74.3	70.6	66.8	65.6	64.5	63.6[b]
United Kingdom	73.5	74.2	73.1	69.6	72.8	73.8
United States	69.1	72.1	73.0	73.2	73.8	74.3
North America	69.0	72.0	72.9	73.1	73.7	74.2
OECD Europe	67.2	66.7	66.0	65.2	65.3	65.2[b]
Total OECD	68.3	69.3	69.3	69.1	69.2	69.4[b]

Source: OECD (1986) Employment Outlook

a Defined as the total labour force divided by the population of working age (15-64) at mid-year
b Secretariat estimates

Table 2.4 Male and female participation rates

	Male					
	1975	1979	1982	1983	1984	1985
	%	%	%	%	%	%
Australia	90.2	87.7	86.7	86.0	85.9	85.4
Austria	81.3	81.6	83.2	82.3	81.7	81.3
Belgium	83.5	80.8	79.0	78.1	77.6	**
Canada	86.2	86.2	84.9	84.7	84.6	84.8
Denmark	89.8	89.6	88.0	87.6	86.7	-
Finland	79.7	82.2	82.9	82.4	82.5	82.6
France	84.3	82.8	80.0	78.4	77.4	76.3
Germany	87.0	84.5	81.4	80.6	79.9	79.8
Greece	-	79.0	81.4	79.3	78.0	**
Ireland	89.9	88.7	87.5	87.1	86.6	**
Italy	84.5	82.6	81.7	81.0	79.6	79.2
Japan	89.7	89.2	89.1	89.1	88.4	87.6
Luxemburg	91.1	88.8	86.6	85.1	84.3	**
Netherlands	83.2	79.0	80.7	80.0	78.8	**
New Zealand	88.6	87.3	86.2	84.7	83.7	**
Norway	85.9	87.0	87.2	86.6	86.2	86.0
Portugal[a]	95.5	90.9	87.6	90.6	89.0	**
Spain	92.5	82.6	80.0	79.5	78.4	77.4
Sweden	89.2	87.9	86.3	85.9	85.4	85.7
Switzerland	97.7	94.6	92.1	90.6	89.5	89.6
Turkey	92.1	-	87.5	86.9	86.5	**
United Kingdom	92.1	90.5	89.1	87.5	87.1	87.7
United States	85.4	85.7	84.8	84.8	85.0	84.9
North America	85.5	85.7	84.8	84.8	85.0	84.9
OECD Europe[b]	87.3	84.6	82.6	81.6	80.7	**
Total OECD[b]	87.2	85.9	84.7	84.2	83.8	**

Source: OECD (1986) Employment Outlook

[a] Labour-force data include a significant number of persons less than 15 years and 65 years and over
[b] Excluding Greece and the Netherlands

Female					
1975	1979	1982	1983	1984	1985
%	%	%	%	%	%
50.1	50.3	52.0	52.1	52.9	54.3
47.6	49.1	50.3	49.7	51.5	51.1
44.0	47.4	49.4	49.8	50.4	**
50.0	55.5	58.9	60.1	61.2	62.4
63.5	69.9	72.6	74.2	73.8	**
65.6	68.9	72.8	73.4	73.8	75.0
51.2	54.1	54.6	54.3	54.7	55.0
49.6	49.6	50.0	49.7	49.7	50.4
-	32.8	36.3	40.0	40.4	**
34.5	35.2	37.6	37.8	37.0	**
34.6	38.7	40.2	40.7	41.0	41.3
51.7	54.7	55.9	57.2	57.2	57.1
38.3	39.8	41.2	42.0	42.5	**
31.0	33.4	39.0	39.8	40.8	**
41.1	45.0	45.5	45.7	46.0	**
53.3	61.7	65.3	66.8	66.7	68.3
51.5	57.3	56.6	60.1	58.2	**
32.4	32.4	33.0	33.1	32.7	33.3
67.6	72.8	76.0	76.6	77.2	78.0
51.9	53.0	54.0	53.3	53.1	53.3
55.4	-	44.3	42.5	40.7	**
55.1	57.9	57.0	57.0	58.5	59.8
53.2	58.9	61.4	61.9	62.8	64.0
52.9	58.6	61.2	61.7	62.7	63.8
46.4	48.6	49.2	49.2	49.6	**
49.8	53.4	54.9	55.3	55.9	**

both in countries where the female participation rate is high and low. Participation rates are particularly high in Scandinavia (ranging from, in 1985, 68 per cent in Norway to 78 per cent in Sweden); in contrast, in the Mediterranean countries of Greece, Italy, Spain, and Turkey, together with certain west European countries such as Ireland and the Netherlands, the female participation rate is much lower at around 40 per cent or below - and as low as 33 per cent in Spain.

Disaggregating the male and female trends further, certain age-related patterns are discernible; for example, a general decline in the youth participation rate in most European countries over the last decade, a general decline also (particularly in the 1970s) in the participation of older workers (55 years and above) and even a small decline in the participation of prime-age males (generally taken to be the 25-54-years age group), who have traditionally demonstrated the highest and most stable participation rate.[3] Among females the most notable trend is the rise in the participation of married women, particularly those with children.

What factors account for these changes in male and female participation rates? Both general and specific influences can be identified. First, participation rates are related to the level of economic activity - when the labour market is slack (as was the case in many OECD countries in the late 1970s and early 1980s) the 'discouraged worker' effect increases whereby some unemployed withdraw from the labour market and some who would normally enter that market do not do so due to a low expectation of gaining employment. This discouraged-worker effect seems to explain much of the decline in youth and male participation after the mid-1970s. In addition, the decline in older-worker participation was further stimulated by the spread of occupational pension schemes and the growth of early retirement provision both in state schemes and by companies using early retirement as a method of reducing the volume of manpower.[4]

The discouraged-worker argument is of more limited value in explaining trends in female participation, however. It is relevant in explaining the slow-down in the increase in female participation after 1979 (and particularly in the period 1981-3). In the OECD as a whole female participation rose by 3.6 percentage points between 1975 and 1979, and by 2.5 percentage points between 1979 and 1984; in a number of individual countries such as Denmark, New Zealand, and Norway this deceleration was much more marked than the OECD average suggests. However, in the female group the discouraged-worker effect was insufficient to nullify a persistent 'added worker' effect whereby individuals not previously active in the labour market begin to seek employment.[5] Among the female population it has been married women with children who have been the most prominent 'added workers'.

What accounts for this increased activity of women in the labour market? There appear to be a number of supply and demand factors at work. On the one hand, the widespread decline in manufacturing employment has reduced the number of jobs traditionally undertaken by men; correspondingly the substantial growth in the service sector over the past two decades has increased the available employment opportunities for women. Further, many service-sector jobs lend themselves easily to being offered as part-time jobs - a working arrangement which many women with family responsibilities have found particularly suitable (part-time working and the growth of service sector employment are discussed in more detail below). Another factor stimulating the demand for female workers is that on average, and for various reasons (of which direct discrimination is only one), they are cheaper to employ than their male counterparts. In Britain, for example the average female wage is only about two-thirds that of the average male wage.[6] Moreover the average hourly rate for part-time workers is significantly lower than that of their full-time counterparts. Again using the British example, average hourly pay of women part-time workers is only about four-fifths that of full-time females and for men the average hourly part-time wage is only two-thirds that of the full-time average.[7] An OECD summary of nine industrial countries similarly found that in only one (Australia) were part-time hourly wages not lower than full-time equivalents.

An increased interest in employment, particularly among married women with children, has matched employers' desire for more female labour (especially part-time workers). Various people have pointed to a wide range of objective and subjective factors stimulating greater female participation, including the greater availability of part-time jobs, rising inflation, lower birth rates, increasing material aspirations, better education, the greater social isolation of women (due to greater geographical mobility), growing male unemployment, and changing attitudes towards female domestic roles.[8]

Economic cycles will continue to affect the participation rates of both men and women, through the influence of the 'discouraged worker' and 'added worker' effects. However it appears that overall, female participation rates will continue to rise, albeit at a slower rate, and that the participation of older males will continue to fall. Because of ceiling effects, the increase in female participation is likely to be most evident in those countries where the female participation rate is currently below the OECD average.

Future changes in size of labour force

The International Labour Office has calculated projected changes in the size of 'economically active populations' up to the year 2025. This notion of economically active population is similar to the OECD's use of the term 'labour force'. The ILO defines 'economically active populations' as comprising all persons who furnish the supply of labour for the production of economic goods and services, i.e. 'all employed and unemployed persons (including those seeking work for the first time). It covers employees, wage earners, employers, own-account workers, unpaid family workers, members of producers' cooperatives and members of the armed forces'[9] (although national practices vary in terms of the treatment of the latter group).

For measuring the economically active population, and thus for the correct application of the definition of employment (and unemployment), a clear understanding of both the concept and boundary of 'economic activity' is an essential requirement. As the ILO has stated:

> Economic activity covers production for sale (market production) and certain types of production for own-consumption (non-market production). It excludes unpaid domestic activities .... The rationale for the inclusion of certain types of non-market production and the exclusion of others ... lies in the importance of the activities in many countries and the frequent existence of 'close' market parallels i.e. the existence of identical or very similar goods and services which are usually also available on the market. There are also practical considerations involved. When the same persons are engaged in both market and non-market production, it is, in practice, often impossible to measure the two components separately.[10]

From 1950 to the present, almost all the OECD countries have shown a continuing increase in the size of their economically active populations, partly as a result of a continued natural growth in population (and the reaching of working age by the post-war baby boom), partly through changes in participation rates (see above), and partly due to net migration inflows. This growth has been particularly marked in North America, Australia, and New Zealand, where a high degree of immigration has acted to swell the size of the labour force. The European average growth rate from 1950 to 1985 has been much less than half the North American average (see table 2.5 below).

Table 2.5 Annual rates of growth of economically active population 1950-2025: European and North American averages

	Europe	North America
	%	%
1950-1960	0.55	1.24
1960-1970	0.63	1.85
1970-1980	0.67	2.41
1980-1985	0.76	1.25
1985-1990	0.47	0.89
1990-2000	0.28	0.79
2000-2010	0.04	0.60
2010-2020	-0.23	0.13
2020-2025	-0.35	0.06

Source: ILO (1986) Economically Active Population, Estimates and Projections: 1950-2025, vol. 4, 3rd edition. Copyright 1986, International Labour Organisation, Geneva

Following a widespread and relatively vigorous period of growth, the general picture more recently for many individual countries has been of a slowing down in the growth of this economically active section of the population to below 1 per cent increase per annum (see table 2.6). Indeed, in many cases a reversal of this upward trend is anticipated by the first decades of the next century. Only in Ireland and Turkey is a 1 per cent annual growth rate anticipated after the year 2000. By 2025 the size of the economically active population of nineteen of the twenty-four OECD countries is projected to be declining, and in certain cases (West Germany, Switzerland) by more than 1 per cent per annum.

This slowing down and subsequent reversal of the growth of economically active populations will be accompanied by a significant ageing in the population as average life expectancy increases. As more people continue to survive to an older age (and fewer enter the job market due to the 'baby-bust' phenomenon which has followed the baby boom in many countries), the section of the population over retirement age will increase significantly relative to those of working age. In general the proportion of industrial populations over 65 years was approximately one in ten in 1950 and had increased to one in eight by 1980. In many countries projections indicate that this proportion will have reached one in five by 2025, with some countries (e.g. Sweden and Switzerland) approaching a proportion of one in four (see ILO[11] for projections of population change in different age categories). This shift in the balance between working-age and post-working-age populations raises many questions about the provision of welfare services and more generally about the financing of an ageing population. Indeed, this question could become even more salient, should a fundamental medical or social breakthrough occur in coming years (such as a major decline in cigarette smoking or the more effective treatment of cancer or heart disease) which would further improve life expectancy rates.

EMPLOYMENT

Overall growth

In 1984 total employment in the OECD as a whole was about 337 million, 9 million more than it had been in 1982. Between 1975 and 1979 total employment increased at an annual rate of $1\frac{1}{2}$ per cent, a rate of growth faster than that recorded in the 1960s and early 1970s.[12] This accelerated growth in the later 1970s was predominantly due to a very high growth rate in employment in North America (see table 2.7). However, with the sharp economic downturn after 1979 employment growth fell rapidly, with 1982 representing the year of greatest fall (when total employment in the OECD declined by more than half a percentage point). After 1982 employment recovered slowly in 1983 and more vigorously in 1984. This post-1982 growth in employment has not, however, been uniform across the different OECD countries, reflecting variations in economic recovery and growth. The growth in civilian employment in Australia and North America has been considerably stronger than that in Europe; almost 11 million jobs were created in North America between the end of 1982 and the end of 1985, and in both 1984 and 1985 the employment growth in North America was more than four times the average achieved by the OECD Europe countries. Indeed, employment in certain European countries (France, Ireland, Portugal) continued to decline in 1985. Turning to the projected developments in employment, the OECD forecast that employment growth in Australia and North America would continue to outstrip the growth within Europe. In the light of the continued growth in the population of working age (see above), this slower growth in employment in Europe suggests that unemployment in many European countries is likely to remain at or near its present levels for some years (see chapter 3).

Employment distribution by sector

Most of the jobs created in the post-1982 recovery have come in services, and the shift from agricultural and industrial employment to service-sector employment is the primary employment change in the last two decades, a shift which accelerated during the 1970s. The OECD defines services as 'activities other than those which produce goods';[13] these activities include retail and distribution, transport and communications, financial and business services, and social and personal services. The service sector can also be differentiated in terms of public and private services, market and non-market services, and services to producers or households. In the OECD as a whole, approximately six employed people in every ten work in service

Table 2.6 Economically active population and annual rates of growth, 1950-2025

	Australia[1]		Austria		Belgium		Canada		Denmark		Finland	
	A	B	A	B	A	B	A	B	A	B	A	B
	000s	%	000s	%	000s	%	000s	%	000s	%	000s	%
1950	3,417	**	3,467	**	3,503	**	5,438	**	2,077	**	2,009	**
1960	4,169	2.01	3,384	-0.24	3,513	0.03	6,675	2.07	2,092	0.07	2,024	0.07
1970	5,353	2.53	3,112	-0.83	3,609	0.27	8,706	2.69	2,380	1.30	2,200	0.84
1980	6,744	2.34	3,364	0.78	3,948	0.90	11,849	3.13	2,704	1.29	2,381	0.79
1985	7,364	1.78	3,504	0.82	4,092	0.72	12,723	1.43	2,784	0.58	2,488	0.88
1990	7,963	1.58	3,570	0.37	4,151	0.29	13,360	0.98	2,852	0.48	2,552	0.51
2000	8,964	1.19	3,563	-0.02	4,152	0.00	14,461	0.80	2,877	0.09	2,605	0.20
2010	9,775	0.87	3,485	-0.22	4,073	-0.19	15,174	0.48	2,734	-0.51	2,525	-0.31
2020	10,245	0.47	3,273	-0.63	3,841	-0.59	15,101	-0.05	2,526	-0.79	2,364	-0.66
2025	10,399	0.30	3,120	-0.95	3,729	-0.59	15,024	-0.10	4,402	-1.00	2,292	-0.62

	France		Germany		Greece		Iceland		Ireland		Italy	
	A	B	A	B	A	B	A	B	A	B	A	B
	000s	%	000s	%	000s	%	000s	%	000s	%	000s	%
1950	19,248	**	23,293	**	3,089	**	63	**	1,284	**	20,417	**
1960	19,741	0.25	26,178	1.17	3,385	0.92	69	1.03	1,118	-1.37	20,723	0.15
1970	21,579	0.89	26,907	0.28	3,412	0.08	88	2.45	1,124	0.05	20,955	0.11
1980	23,559	0.88	28,336	0.52	3,668	0.73	117	2.88	1,259	1.14	21,936	0.46
1985	24,639	0.90	29,403	0.74	3,780	0.60	127	1.63	1,367	1.65	22,763	0.74
1990	25,404	0.61	29,311	-0.06	3,852	0.38	136	1.35	1,481	1.63	23,339	0.50
2000	26,486	0.42	27,432	-0.66	3,947	0.24	153	1.21	1,723	1.52	23,310	-0.01
2010	26,638	0.06	25,650	-0.67	4,061	0.29	166	0.77	1,986	1.43	22,549	-0.33
2020	25,648	-0.38	23,304	-0.95	4,089	0.07	166	0.02	2,179	0.93	21,786	-0.34
2025	25,071	-0.45	21,718	-1.40	4,068	-0.11	164	-0.24	2,236	0.52	21,078	-0.66

1 Including Christmas Island, the Cocos (Keeling) Islands, and Norfolk Island

	Japan		Luxemburg		Netherlands		New Zealand		Norway		Portugal	
	A	B	A	B	A	B	A	B	A	B	A	B
	000s	%	000s	%	000s	%	000s	%	000s	%	000s	%
1950	36,650	**	137	**	4,013	**	730	**	1,396	**	3,458	**
1960	44,721	2.01	132	-0.31	4,076	0.16	887	1.96	1,406	0.07	3,399	-0.17
1970	53,259	1.76	131	-0.15	4,718	1.47	1,099	2.17	1,606	1.34	3,387	-0.04
1980	57,097	0.70	152	1.55	5,461	1.47	1,334	1.96	1,962	2.02	4,346	2.53
1985	59,772	0.92	155	0.43	5,861	1.42	1,458	1.80	2,039	0.77	4,563	0.98
1990	62,202	0.80	155	-0.04	6,153	0.98	1,570	1.49	2,128	0.86	4,740	0.76
2000	64,352	0.34	149	-0.38	6,313	0.26	1,736	1.01	2,254	0.57	5,129	0.79
2010	62,414	-0.31	141	-0.59	6,114	-0.32	1,849	0.64	2,252	-0.01	5,452	0.61
2020	60,974	-0.23	129	-0.86	5,606	-0.86	1,877	0.15	2,153	-0.45	5,568	0.21
2025	60,856	-0.04	124	-0.87	5,300	-1.12	1,853	-0.26	2,085	-0.64	5,558	-0.04

	Spain		Sweden		Switzerland		Turkey		UK		USA	
	A	B	A	B	A	B	A	B	A	B	A	B
	000s	%	000s	%	000s	%	000s	%	000s	%	000s	%
1950	10,686	**	3,074	**	2,135	**	11,954	**	23,403	**	65,178	**
1960	11,564	0.79	3,272	0.62	2,505	1.61	13,963	1.57	24,320	0.39	73,171	1.16
1970	11,956	0.33	3,728	1.31	2,981	1.75	16,071	1.42	25,512	0.48	87,222	1.77
1980	12,895	0.76	4,163	1.11	3,062	0.27	19,090	1.74	26,765	0.48	109,872	2.34
1985	13,725	1.25	4,237	0.35	3,173	0.72	21,385	2.30	27,432	0.49	116,800	1.23
1990	14,456	1.04	4,319	0.38	3,212	0.25	23,696	2.07	27,766	0.24	122,005	0.88
2000	15,539	0.73	4,409	0.21	3,147	-0.21	28,752	1.95	28,068	0.11	132,017	0.79
2010	16,181	0.41	4,212	-0.46	2,971	-0.57	34,949	1.97	28,032	-0.01	140,406	0.62
2020	16,711	0.32	3,931	-0.69	2,710	-0.92	40,406	1.46	27,044	-0.36	142,579	0.15
2025	16,728	0.02	3,793	-0.71	2,567	-1.08	42,673	1.10	26,299	-0.56	143,116	0.08

Source: ILO (1986) Economically Active Population, Estimates and Projections: 1950-2025, vol. 1 Asia; vol. 4 N. America, Europe, Oceania and USSR, 3rd edition. Copyright 1986, International Labour Organisation, Geneva

Notes: A Total economically active population
B Average annual rates of growth over previous decade (half decade for 1980-5, 1985-90 and 2020-5 periods)

Table 2.7 Overall growth in employment: average annual growth rates

	1973-5	1975-9	1980-2	1983	1984	1985
	%	%	%	%	%	%
Australia	0.5	1.0	0.8	-2.2	3.5	3.1
Austria	-1.1	0.9	1.9	-0.8	2.4	0.0
Belgium	-0.1	0.1	-1.7	-1.1	0.0	0.3[b]
Canada	2.9	2.8	-0.3	0.8	2.5	2.8
Denmark	-1.3	1.1	-2.0	0.7	2.9	2.2[b]
Finland	1.3	0.4	1.0	0.5	1.0	1.0
France	0.1	0.5	-0.2	-0.5	-1.0	-0.3
Germany	-2.1	0.2	-1.2	-1.5	0.1	0.7
Greece	0.1	0.9	2.0	0.5	-0.2	0.6[b]
Iceland	2.5	1.7	3.7	0.9	0.9	0.6[b]
Ireland	0.3	1.6	-0.3	-2.0	-1.3	-0.7[b]
Italy	1.1	0.7	0.0	0.2	0.4	0.5
Japan	-0.3	1.2	0.9	1.7	0.6	0.7
Luxemburg	2.0	-0.1	0.0	-0.2	0.3	1.7[b]
Netherlands	-0.4	1.0	0.3	-1.4	0.8	0.7[b]
New Zealand	3.0	1.0	0.7	-1.1	1.1	0.5[b]
Norway	1.6	2.3	0.9	0.6	0.7	2.2
Portugal	-1.4[a]	0.5	-0.2	5.1	-1.8	-0.6[b]
Spain	-0.5	-1.9	-1.6	-0.8	-4.1	0.2
Sweden	2.3	0.7	-0.1	0.1	0.7	1.0
Switzerland	-2.5	-0.1	0.3	-1.3	-0.2	0.9
Turkey	1.6	1.3	0.9	0.7	1.3	0.3[b]
United Kingdom	0.0	0.3	-2.8	-5.4	6.2	1.4
United States	0.4	3.5	0.1	1.3	4.1	2.0
North America	0.6	3.4	0.1	1.3	3.9	2.1
OECD Europe	0.0	0.4	-0.7	-1.1	0.8	0.5[b]
Total OECD	0.2	1.5	-0.1	0.2	1.9	1.2[b]

Source: OECD (1986) Employment Outlook

a Data refer to 1974-5
b Secretariat estimates

Projections		
1986	1987	1984 Employment
%	%	000s
3.5	2.0	6,533
0.3	0.3	3,235
0.3	0.3	3,668
2.8	1.5	11,075
1.5	0.8	2,489
0.0	0.0	2,442
0.0	0.0	21,518
1.0	1.3	25,352
-0.3	-0.3	3,501
1.0	0.8	114
0.3	1.3	1,110
0.3	0.3	21,015
0.5	0.5	57,660
1.3	1.3	158
0.8	0.3	5,074
0.0	0.0	1,293
2.0	0.8	1,970
0.3	1.0	4,141
0.8	1.0	10,774
0.3	0.0	4,255
0.8	0.5	3,142
1.0	1.0	15,611
0.5	1.0	23,984
2.0	2.0	107,224
**	**	118,299
0.5	0.8	153,554
1.3	1.3	337,339

Figure 2.1 Proportions employed in agriculture, industry, and services in fourteen OECD countries, 1986

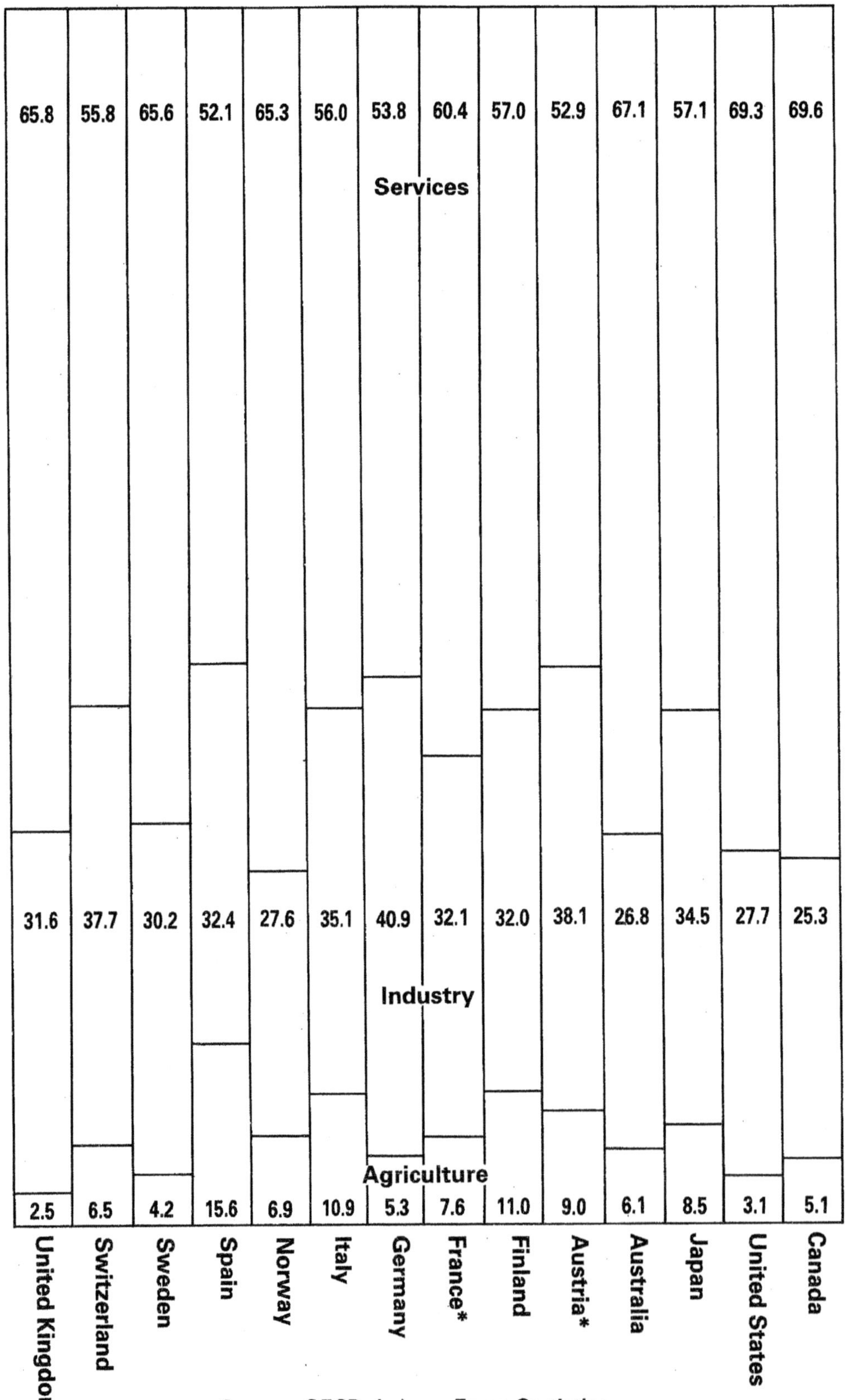

Source: OECD, *Labour Force Statistics*
*1985 figures

activities. In 1971 the corresponding figure was five out of ten and in 1961, just over four out of ten. As figure 2.1 indicates, in 1986 the proportion of people working in services in some countries was much higher than the OECD average - in North America, the proportion of employed people in the service sector is almost seven-tenths of total employment. In contrast, the proportion working in services is substantially lower in more recently industrialized countries, where the level of agricultural employment is still significant. For example, by 1982 the proportion of employed people working in the service sector in Turkey was still below one-quarter, and in Portugal and Greece, in the same year, services accounted for 37 per cent and 42 per cent respectively of total employment. While the distinction between mature and newly industrialized countries is easily identifiable in the proportion of employees engaged in services, what is more surprising perhaps is the variations evident between those countries that have long been industrialized. From figure 2.1 it is evident for example, that West Germany and Austria maintain a relatively far higher proportion of their total employment in industry than in services, compared to North America and Australia; further, given Switzerland's reputation as a banking, financial, and tourist centre, it is less dependent on service-sector employment than might have been supposed.

Service-sector employment has grown markedly since the mid-1960s. In the period 1975-82 employment in services in the OECD grew by 23.5 million - an average of 2 per cent - with growth being stronger in North America and Japan than in Europe. Even before the 1960s the service sector had been the main source of job creation; however, since the 1970s it has been the only sector to be a net creator of jobs in most OECD countries (Japan and the United States being notable exceptions to this). However, although less sensitive to cyclical variation in economic activity than industrial employment, the growth in service employment has tended to slow down in the last decade, particularly during recessionary periods when producers demand fewer services (e.g. business services and transportation), households reduce consumption (partly due to higher unemployment), and governments tend to reduce employment growth in the public sector. Table 2.8 indicates that in the OECD as a whole the growth rate in service-sector employment fell from an annual average of 2.6 per cent in the late 1970s to 1.5 per cent in the early 1980s, though recovering the former growth rate in 1984 (the last year for which full data is published, though the figures for 1985 that are available suggest a growth rate at least as strong as 1984). In North America this deceleration was even more marked: in Canada service-employment growth fell from an annual average of 3.2 per cent in the late 1970s to 1.4 per cent in the early 1980s; the corresponding figures for the United States were 3.5 per cent and 1.7 per cent. Yet sufficient has been the underlying growth of services that even in the major recession of the early 1980s, few countries experienced an actual decline in service-sector employment. In the industrial sector, in contrast, an annual increase in the OECD of just under 1 per cent in the later 1970s was transformed into a 2.5 per cent decline in the early 1980s (a rate of decline which reached almost 7 per cent in the UK). However, in 1984 employment in industry in the OECD grew at a rate of just under 1 per cent. Though full data for 1985 were not available at the time of writing, it is suggestive that of the fourteen countries on which statistics were available, the majority were reporting a positive growth in industrial employment - the first time those increasing had been in the majority since the mid-1970s.

The numbers employed in agriculture have been steadily declining

Table 2.8 Distribution of civilian employment by sector: average annual growth rates

	Agriculture						Industry	
	1973-5	1975-9	1980-2	1983	1984	1985	1973-5	1975-9
	%	%	%	%	%	%	%	%
Australia	-2.0	-0.5	0.5	1.0	-3.1	2.2	-1.6	-1.1
Austria	-3.0	-3.8	-2.1	-1.8	-2.5	-4.4	-2.1	-0.1
Belgium	-2.8	-3.5	-2.3	-0.9	0.0	**	-1.8	-2.7
Canada	-0.7	1.1	-2.2	5.2	-0.2	0.7	0.6	2.5
Denmark	0.2	-6.3	0.6	0.0	-6.8	**	-4.6	2.0
Finland	-5.6	-1.6	-0.3	-3.2	-2.6	-4.8	1.9	-0.6
France	-4.1	-3.0	-3.2	-2.3	-2.2	-2.8	-1.1	-1.1
Germany	-4.0	-4.4	-1.5	-0.3	-0.1	0.0	-4.4	-0.4
Greece	-2.0	-2.5	-0.4	4.3	-2.2	**	0.7	2.7
Iceland	0.0	-3.8	-3.9	0.0	0.0	**	2.9	1.4
Ireland	-3.4	-1.8	-3.9	-2.1	-3.7	**	0.3	2.0
Italy	-3.2	-2.2	-6.7	0.2	-4.0	-5.3	1.2	-0.2
Japan	-3.2	-1.9	-2.5	-3.1	-3.6	-0.6	-2.2	0.5
Luxemburg	-4.3	-4.9	0.0	-12.5	0.0	**	0.7	-3.1
Netherlands	-1.7	-0.6	-1.0	3.3	-0.4	**	-2.6	-0.8
New Zealand	0.8	1.9	2.9	-2.7	0.7	**	2.8	-0.6
Norway	-8.3	0.3	-1.9	-6.4	-4.8	3.6	2.3	-1.0
Portugal	-1.9[a]	-1.8	-3.9	-1.1	1.8	**	1.0[a]	1.8
Spain	-5.4	-4.6	-3.2	-2.2	-4.1	-5.5	1.5	-2.8
Sweden	-2.8	-1.9	-0.2	-3.0	-4.8	-4.6	1.9	-2.1
Switzerland	-2.0	-1.6	-1.4	-0.9	-0.5	-1.4	-5.4	-1.7
Turkey	-0.1	0.5	0.0	-0.3	-0.4	**	3.8	2.0
United Kingdom	-3.3	-0.7	-0.9	-1.1	-0.8	-0.3	-2.3	-0.7
United States	-0.9	0.0	0.6	-0.8	-2.0	-3.8	-3.5	4.1
North America	-0.9	0.2	0.2	0.0	-1.8	-3.1	-3.1	4.0
OECD Europe	-1.6	-1.6	-1.9	-0.6	-1.5	**	-1.3	-0.6
Total OECD	-1.8	-1.4	-1.7	-0.9	-1.9	**	-1.9	0.9

Source: OECD (1986) Employment Outlook

a Data refer to 1974-5

				Services					
1980-2	1983	1984	1985	1973-5	1975-9	1980-2	1983	1984	1985
%	%	%	%	%	%	%	·%	%	%
-0.8	-6.2	1.5	1.6	2.7	2.0	2.4	0.0	4.1	3.9
-2.8	-3.4	-0.5	0.0	3.2	1.9	1.4	0.6	0.9	0.9
-5.3	-3.4	-2.1	**	1.5	2.0	0.2	0.1	1.1	**
-3.9	-2.9	3.8	1.3	4.4	3.2	1.4	2.0	2.2	3.6
-5.2	0.7	-2.8	**	0.7	1.8	-0.4	0.7	6.5	**
-0.1	-1.5	-0.8	-1.0	3.3	1.7	2.2	2.8	2.9	3.5
-2.1	-2.6	-3.3	-2.8	1.9	2.3	1.4	1.1	0.5	1.4
-2.9	-3.4	-0.9	-0.1	0.4	1.4	0.3	-0.1	1.0	1.4
0.2	-1.5	-3.0	**	1.8	2.4	5.1	-0.8	3.2	**
2.5	0.0	0.0	**	3.5	3.2	5.6	1.7	1.7	**
-2.2	-6.8	-3.3	**	2.0	2.8	2.1	1.0	0.5	**
-1.1	-2.3	-4.2	-2.1	3.2	2.5	2.7	2.2	4.5	3.4
0.2	1.4	0.8	0.8	1.8	2.4	2.0	2.7	1.2	0.8
-3.4	-3.6	-1.9	**	4.1	2.8	2.8	2.1	2.1	**
-3.8	-5.0	-2.6	**	1.2	2.1	2.3	-0.3	2.3	**
-0.8	-2.6	0.7	**	3.7	1.9	1.2	-0.1	1.5	**
0.4	-3.8	1.5	0.4	3.1	4.5	1.4	3.5	1.2	2.7
1.0	-1.4	-2.5	**	3.7 a	2.5	1.5	17.0	-3.4	**
-4.7	-1.8	-6.3	-1.4	0.2	1.2	1.2	0.7	-2.2	3.7
-3.2	-1.1	0.4	1.3	3.3	2.7	1.4	0.9	1.4	1.3
-1.0	-3.3	-0.7	0.8	0.1	1.3	1.4	0.2	0.2	1.1
1.8	2.4	3.7	**	5.5	3.2	2.8	2.3	3.8	**
-6.8	-4.3	-0.7	-0.6	1.9	1.2	-0.5	0.4	3.0	2.1
-3.5	0.0	5.8	0.5	2.6	3.5	1.7	2.0	3.8	3.0
-3.5	-0.3	5.6	0.6	2.8	3.5	1.7	2.0	3.6	3.0
-2.9	-2.7	-2.0	**	1.8	1.9	1.1	1.1	1.8	**
-2.5	-1.3	0.9	**	2.2	2.6	1.5	1.7	2.5	**

throughout the 1973-85 period. It is worth noting that in several countries, the small totals now employed in agriculture give rise to apparently large fluctuations year by year; in practice these fluctuations are often the result of relatively small numbers moving into and out of agriculture (in table 2.8 Luxemburg and Norway are examples of apparently vigorous movements in and out of agriculture).

Disaggregating the service sector points to some interesting variation in scale of activity and patterns of growth. In the OECD overall, nearly one person in two employed in services works in personal and social services; one in three is employed in distribution, one in ten in transport and communications and one in eight in financial or business services.[14] During the 1976-82 period there was strong growth (2.5-5 per cent per year) in banking and insurance, business services, and social services, and in some countries, distribution; in contrast, much lower growth rates were demonstrated in transport and communications. From a summary of the whole service sector, it would appear that social services represented the main source of new service-sector jobs in the later 1970s and early 1980s; in the manner in which it is generally used (for example, by the OECD) this category of social services contains not only traditional central and local government services, but also public and private educational services, and public and private health care.

It is not yet clear whether the slow-down in the growth of service-sector employment reflects the general economic situation prevailing in OECD countries or whether the various services are beginning to use up their capacity to create jobs. The extent to which micro-electronics can be applied to many services as well as industrial situations may suggest that in future at least parts of the service sector (those capable of standardizing their 'production') will experience a higher level of 'jobless growth' and gradually reduce their labour intensity; signs of this are already occurring in banking and retailing where increased automation has been accompanied by an increased tendency to hire part-time rather than full-time workers (see next section). At the same time, technological developments may well generate a new demand for services, for example, in the education and leisure fields. Overall, given favourable economic conditions and rising household incomes, the level of employment in services looks set to continue to rise at least into the next decade, though is likely to grow at a smaller rate than that demonstrated in the 1970s.

Part-time working

The level of part-time working has increased rapidly over the past twenty years, with growth being particularly strong during the 1970s, and part-time employment has now established itself as a major component of total employment; indeed, in some areas (e.g. Scandinavia) one in four of the work force is now employed part-time.

Precise inter-country comparisons of part-time working are hindered by different national definitions of what constitutes part-time working. Some attempts have been made to construct more general criteria for classifying part-time work. The ILO, for example, defines part-time employment as 'work on a regular and voluntary basis for a daily or weekly period of substantially shorter duration than current normal or statutory hours of work.[15] Yet such broad definitions clearly raise as many problems as they solve. What for example should constitute 'substantially shorter duration'? How is the 'voluntary' nature of part-time working to be measured? Should seasonal and casual part-time workers be included or excluded? How are special groups to be treated - for example, school teachers who formally work less than average hours but who nevertheless view their job as full-time? Not all these problems are satisfactorily solved by the national and international bodies who compile data on part-time working. In general, one or both of two criteria are used by individual countries in assessing the level of part-time working: first, the hours worked by an individual; second, self-assessment by survey respondents as a full-time or part-time worker. The latter criterion is particularly evident in data from household surveys in EEC countries. The former, on the other hand, is simpler and more clear-cut; however one problem in using the hours measure over a long period of time is that gradual reductions in the normal 'full-time' week have implications for what constitutes part-time working. In comparing part-time working across several countries an added difficulty is that different countries use different cut off points - e.g. 30 or 35 hours - to denote part-time working. Table 2.9 gives some indication of the national variations in how part-time working is defined. (These definitions are used by the OECD in compiling its own statistics, such as those reported in tables 2.10 and 2.11). Clearly this variation in definitions of part-time work militates against very fine distinctions being drawn between countries (particularly when we take multiple job holding into account, which seems to be more prevalent in some countries, such as Italy, than in others).[16]

Yet, despite these definitional problems, it is still possible to compile a general picture of trends in part-time working and the extent to which these are being replicated in different industrial countries. First, table 2.10 which reports changes in part-time working in nineteen OECD countries indicates that in almost all cases (Ireland and Italy being exceptions) the extent of part-time working as a proportion of total employment rose significantly in the decade after the first oil crisis in 1973. In some countries this rise has been particularly marked: in Belgium, for example, up by 143 per cent (albeit from a relatively low base in 1973); Australia (51 per cent); Canada (45 per cent); and Sweden (41 per cent). Most countries report a rise in the proportion of part-time working in both male and female employment; however, the number of males involved in part-time working remains relatively small - in general, four out of five part-timers are women and in some cases (e.g. Germany, Luxemburg, and the UK) this proportion of females in the total part-time group reaches nine out of ten; only in Greece and Italy (both countries with relatively low levels of registered part-time work) does the proportion of males in the total part-time group reach one third. Second, despite a broad similarity in the trend of part-time working, the importance of part-time working varies greatly between countries with, at the extremes, countries such as Italy in 1983 maintaining less than one-sixth the proportion of part-timers that Norway reported. In four countries (Denmark, Netherlands, Norway, and Sweden) part-time work comprised more than one fifth the total employment in 1983; in contrast, in eight countries (Austria, Belgium, Finland, France, Greece, Ireland, Italy, and Luxemburg) the part-time share in total employment was less than one-tenth. Third, as we have noted, women make up the great majority of part-time workers and this aspect of employment constitutes an important element in overall female employment. In Britain for example, more than two-fifths of women in employment work part-time.[17] Among the female-employment group, it is married women with children who are predominant in part-time jobs. This is also true elsewhere, though in addition North America (and to a lesser extent Australia) has a sizeable student part-time workforce;[18] the USA in particular has also

Table 2.9 Definitions of part-time employment

EEC	Part-time workers are in principle those who declared themselves to be part-time at the time of the Labour Force Sample Survey. In some countries responses are checked against other criteria, e.g. in France, a part-time job is judged to be one where the number of hours worked is less than 30 hours.
Australia	Those who usually work less than 35 hours and did so during the survey week.
Austria	Employees whose normal weekly hours are less than 36 hours. Self-employed excluded.
Canada	Workers who usually work less than 30 hours. Those who usually work less than 30 hours but consider themselves to be employed full-time are classified as full-time workers.
Finland	Those whose normal hours are less than 30 hours in their main job.
Japan	Non-agricultural employees who actually worked less than 35 hours during the reference week.
New Zealand	Those who regularly worked less than 30 hours per week.
Norway	Those who actually worked less than 35 hours during the survey week.
Sweden	Those who usually work less than 35 hours per week.
USA	Those who usually work less than 35 hours per week and who were at work and actually worked less than 35 hours during the reference week because of non-economic reasons (i.e. voluntarily) in non-agricultural industries. Those who worked less than 35 hours because of economic reasons are excluded.

Source: OECD (1985) Employment Outlook

witnessed a significant growth in older workers engaged in part-time work.

In many countries the growth in part-time working represented a major source of employment growth in the 1970s; in some, it was even the dominant source. For example, in Britain between 1971 and 1981 the net increase of 360,000 employees comprised an 800,000 decrease in the number of full-time workers and the creation of over 1 million part-time jobs.[19] More generally, in seven other European countries (Belgium, Denmark, France, Germany, Luxemburg, Norway and Sweden) part-time growth exceeded full-time growth in the 1973-81 period.[20] In contrast, in North America during this period less than one in five of the fourteen million jobs created during this period were part-time.

As a whole, part-time jobs were affected by the post-1980 recession less than full-time jobs. Since the low point of the recession in 1982, the level of full-time jobs in certain industrial countries has recovered at a faster rate than the growth in part-time employment (table 2.10). In particular, in the United States the growth in part-time working accounted for just under 7 per cent of the net employment growth over the period 1982-85; full-time employment also grew slightly faster than part-time in Norway and Sweden during this period. However, in the remaining six countries in table 2.11 the growth in part-time employment was more rapid, leading to a higher share of part-time employment in total employment in 1985.

What factors lie behind the accelerated growth in part-time employment since the 1960s? Many of the reasons are similar to those explaining greater female participation discussed earlier (not surprisingly, given that much of the increase in female participation has been into part-time jobs). Thus on the demand side, the growth in the service sector, the desire for greater flexibility, and the search for lower labour costs (part-timers not only typically earn less per hour than their full-time counterparts but also have poorer fringe benefits) have stimulated employer interest in part-time work. This has been matched by favourable supply-side conditions, in particular a growing desire among prime-age women for employment.

Looking to the future, it seems likely that in the short and medium terms at least, part-time employment will continue to grow, possibly towards an average in many OECD countries of one in four of the total workforce (a proportion already reached in parts of Scandinavia). The continued emphasis on flexibility and improving competitiveness through lower labour costs, together with the likely continued growth in service-sector employment, all point to a further rise in part-time employment in coming years.

Other changes in employment

The growth in part-time working is not the only instance of a move away from the norm of workforces being comprised of full-time, permanent workers. In other ways too workforces are becoming more heterogeneous as employers search for greater productivity, lower labour costs, and a more effective basis on which to adjust to market and technological changes. Particularly reflective of these management objectives (and of the slack labour markets in many industrial countries in recent years) is the growth of temporary forms of work. Temporary employment is not a new phenomenon. Those activities which are highly seasonal (e.g. agriculture, tourism) have long used temporary employees; in the early moves out of a recession a degree of temporary working has traditionally been used until signs of recovery are more certain. However, with an increasing emphasis on flexibility to meet market and technological changes, there is some indication that temporary working is becoming more widespread. Unfortunately information on temporary work is sparse and anecdotal, in part because of the lack of an agreed definition. The difficulties of comparison are compounded by the various forms that temporary work can take. As a result, definitions tend to be broad; in Britain, for example, temporary workers are defined by the Manpower Services Commission as 'those who describe their jobs as (i) seasonal, temporary or casual, or (ii) under contract or for a fixed period of time'.

Where studies have been conducted (e.g. UK, France, and the United States) there is some indication that the number of temporary workers is increasing, though they remain a small (and in the United States a very small) proportion of the total workforce.[21] The proportion of temporary workers in the total workforce may grow somewhat in coming years, particularly in countries where labour markets remain relatively slack;

Table 2.10 Size and composition of part-time employment, 1973-83

	Part-time employment as a percentage of:									Women's share in part-time employment		
	Total employment			Male employment			Female employment					
	1973	1979	1983[a]	1973	1979	1983[a]	1973	1979	1983[a]	1973	1979	1983[a]
	%	%	%	%	%	%	%	%	%	%	%	%
Australia	11.4	15.5	17.2	3.4	5.1	6.1	27.3	34.5	35.9	79.6	78.8	77.8
Austria	6.4	7.6	8.3	1.4	1.5	1.5	15.6	18.0	19.8	85.8	87.8	88.4
Belgium	3.8	6.0	8.1	1.0	1.0	2.0	10.2	16.5	19.7	82.3	89.3	84.0
Canada	10.6[b]	12.5	15.4	5.1[b]	5.7	7.6	20.3[b]	23.3	26.2	69.5[b]	72.1	71.3
Denmark	21.2[b]	22.7	23.7	4.7[b]	5.2	6.6	45.1[b]	46.3	44.7	86.8[b]	86.9	84.7
Finland	6.7[c]	6.7	8.3	3.3[c]	3.2	4.5	10.5[c]	10.6	12.5	72.8[c]	74.7	72.1
France	7.2	8.2	9.7	2.6	2.5	2.6	14.7	17.0	20.1	77.9	82.0	84.6
Germany	10.1	11.4	12.6	1.8	1.5	1.7	24.4	27.6	30.0	89.0	91.6	91.9
Greece	**	**	6.5	**	**	3.7	**	**	12.1	**	**	61.2
Ireland	6.7[b]	5.1	6.7	2.7[b]	2.1	2.7	16.8[b]	13.1	15.7	71.4[b]	71.2	72.0
Italy	6.4	5.3	4.6	3.7	3.0	2.4	14.0	10.6	9.4	58.3	61.4	64.8
Japan	7.9	9.6	10.5	4.6	5.2	4.8	14.7	18.4	21.1	60.9	64.5	70.7
Luxemburg	6.7	5.8	6.9	1.0	1.0	1.0	18.4	17.1	18.8	77.8	87.5	90.0
Netherlands[d]	8.7	11.1	21.2	2.4	2.8	6.9	26.2	31.7	50.3	80.2	82.5	78.4
New Zealand	10.8	13.3	14.6	4.7	5.0	5.2	22.0	26.2	28.3	71.3	76.8	79.0
Norway	23.5[b]	27.3	30.0	8.7[b]	10.6	11.7	47.6[b]	51.6	54.8	77.0[b]	76.8	77.3
Sweden	18.0	24.2	25.4	3.7	6.5	7.3	38.8	46.2	46.2	88.0	85.2	84.6

Table 2.10 cont.

United Kingdom	16.0	16.4	19.1	2.3	1.9	3.3	39.1	39.0	42.4	90.9	92.8	89.6
United States[e]	14.0	14.4	14.4	7.2	7.4	7.6	23.8	24.1	23.3	68.4	69.8	70.3
	(16.6)	(17.6)	(20.0)	(9.4)	(10.1)	(12.5)	(27.9)	(27.9)	(29.4)	(65.5)	(66.9)	(65.0)

Source: OECD (1984) Employment Outlook

a The number of non-declared persons in the 1983 data for the EEC countries is distributed between full-time and part-time employment
b 1975
c 1976
d Data for 1983 are not comparable with earlier years because of a change in the definition of part-time workers
e Part-time workers for economic reasons are excluded from both part-time and total employment. Data in parenthesis show the results of including this group in the calculations

Table 2.11 Contributions of full- and part-time employment to employment changes: selected countries, 1982-5

	Both sexes		Male		Female		Part-time employment as a percentage of total employment	
	Full-time	Part-time	Full-time	Part-time	Full-time	Part-time	1982	1985
	000s	000s	000s	000s	000s	000s	%	%
Australia	+142	+144	+31	+25	+111	+119	16.5	18.0
Canada	+445	+223	+191	+62	+254	+160	14.4	15.5
Finland	+26	+20	0	+7	+26	+12	7.6	8.2
France[a]	-450	+372	-373	+83	-77	+289	9.1	10.9
Japan[b]	+1,680	+550	+860	+60	+830	+490	10.4	11.0
Norway[c]	+41	+10	+11	0	+31	+9	28.8	28.6
Sweden	+104	-25	+69	-9	+135	-16	25.6	24.6
Great Britain[d]	+131	+563	+86	+126	+44	+437	19.2	21.2
United States	+7,116	+509	+3,529	+91	+3,586	+417	18.2	17.4

Source: OECD (1986) Employment Outlook, 18

a Data for 1982 refer to April-May and data for 1985 to March
b Data refer to employees in non-agricultural industries
c Persons for whom hours of work were unspecified are excluded from both full-time and part-time employment. These numbered 30,000 (1.5 per cent of total employment) in 1985
d Data refer to period from spring 1983-spring 1985. Persons for whom hours of work were unspecified are distributed proportionately between full-time and part-time employment

where labour becomes scarce, however, employees' desire for job security will militate against employer moves to increase the proportion of temporary workers.

The growth in self-employment represents another way in which the working population is becoming more heterogeneous. The ILO includes among the self-employed 'employers, own-account workers, members of producers' cooperatives and unpaid family workers'. However, many countries do not collect information specifically on producer co-operatives; moreover, unpaid family workers are in practice often omitted from figures on the self-employed. In a recent analysis of self-employment, for example, the OECD focused solely on 'employers and own-account workers, that is persons who operate their own economic enterprise or who follow a profession or trade on their own account'.[22]

Definitional problems still remain but, despite these, the general picture is one of the numbers of self-employed growing at about the same pace as increases in total employment (hence the proportion of self-employed remains fairly stable). Overall, in the twenty-three countries in table 2.12, one in ten workers is self-employed, though this varies from more than one in four in Greece to less than one in twenty in the Netherlands and Sweden. Certain countries show a significant growth in self-employment: Australia, Italy, and the UK, for example, have all experienced a proportional increase in self-employment; in contrast, self-employment in Austria declined significantly during the 1970s and early 80s. However, because the proportional growths and declines have been relatively small, the average proportion in self-employment in the OECD has changed relatively little since the early 1970s.

CONCLUSION

By way of conclusion, let us recap on the main patterns to emerge in the working populations and employment groups within the OECD over the past decade and a half. At the same time it is worth reiterating that the OECD member countries are highly diverse in their size and character, so any summary statements and averages will necessarily often disguise a marked variation between countries. This having been said, a number of broad trends can nevertheless be identified. First, the OECD countries display a general growth in the population of working age which on average comprises about two-thirds of the total population of individual countries. Among those of working age, the proportion of women who are active in the labour market has risen considerably in many countries in recent years and looks set to rise further in the coming period. Among males, on the other hand, the level of participation has tended to fall slightly in the period under discussion.

As for employment, the recent period after the 1980 recession has seen employment growing much more vigorously in North America than in Europe. In both areas service employment has been the major (or the only) job-creating sector. Now, more than six out of every ten workers in the OECD are employed in the service sector; continued growth in services is anticipated, but at a lower rate than previously experienced. Closely associated with the growth of services and the increase in women's working has been the rise of part-time employment. In some countries, other forms of employment, such as temporary working and self-employment, have also become somewhat more prominent in recent years.

Several of these trends are likely to continue at least well into the next decade. Longer-range projections, however, show certain reversals

Table 2.12 Proportion of total employment which is self-employed* (armed forces and agricultural sector excluded)

	1969	1973	1979	1981	1984
	%	%	%	%	%
Australia	9.3	9.5	12.4	12.1	12.4
Austria[a]	13.1	11.7	8.9	8.6	7.9
Belgium	11.9[b]	11.0	11.2	11.5	12.3
Canada	**	5.8[c]	6.7	6.4	7.4
Denmark	**	9.7[c]	9.2	8.3	8.4[d]
Finland	**	**	**	**	6.9
France	**	9.7	8.7	8.7	9.1[d]
Germany	8.3	7.6	7.7	7.6	8.2
Greece	**	**	**	27.8	27.3
Iceland[a]	10.2	8.3	7.0	7.0	7.3[d]
Ireland	9.6[e]	10.1	10.4	9.6	11.4
Italy	**	17.8	18.7	19.6	20.6[d]
Japan	14.6	14.1	14.0	13.6	13.0
Netherlands	**	3.7[c]	4.1	5.6	4.9[d]
New Zealand	7.5[e]	9.1[f]	**	8.4	**
Norway	7.6[g]	7.6	6.4	6.6	6.3
Portugal	**	11.5[h]	12.1	11.6	**
Spain	16.1[b]	16.3	15.9	16.3	17.9
Sweden	5.6[b]	4.8	4.5	4.6	4.6
Switzerland	7.6[b]	**	7.5	**	**
Turkey	25.0[b]	25.0[c]	20.8[i]	**	**
United Kingdom[j]	6.5	7.3	6.6	7.9	9.6
United States	7.0	6.7	7.1	7.3	7.6
Unweighted average[k]	**	9.5	9.4	9.5	9.9

Source: OECD (1986) Employment Outlook, 44

* Luxemburg excluded
a Data include unpaid family workers
b 1970
c 1975
d 1983
e 1971
f 1976
g 1972
h 1974
i 1980
j Data may include some family workers
k Average calculated excluding Finland, Greece, New Zealand, Portugal, Switzerland, and Turkey

eventually occurring, notably in the size of the populations active in the labour market. However, this is still many years into the future and before that the growth in working populations raises major implications, not only for employment but also for the subject of the next chapter - unemployment.

NOTES

1 OECD (1985) 'The labour market implications of international migration in selected OECD countries', Employment Outlook: 47-63.

2 OECD (1986) Employment Outlook: 22.

3 OECD (1983) Employment Outlook: 18.

4 P. Blyton (1982) 'Early retirement: an EEC perspective', Three Banks Review, no. 136: 32-44.

5 OECD (1983) op. cit.

6 B. Chiplin and P.J. Sloan (1982) Tackling Discrimination at the Workplace, Cambridge: Cambridge University Press.

7 P. Glucklich and M. Snell (1980) Women, Work and Wages, London: Low Pay Unit.

8 A.T. Mallier and M.J. Rosser (1979) 'The changing role of women in the British economy', National Westminster Bank Quarterly Review: 54-65; G. Clark (1982) 'Recent developments in working patterns', Employment Gazette, vol. 90, no. 7: 284-8; OECD 'Part-time employment in OECD countries' in OECD (1983) Employment Outlook; P. Blyton (1985) Changes in Working time: An International Review, London: Croom Helm; Liba Paukert (1984) The Employment and Unemployment of Women in OECD Countries, Paris: OECD.

9 M.T. Dupré, R. Hussmanns, and F. Mehran (1987, 3) 'The concept and boundary of economic activity for the measurement of the economically active population', ILO, Bulletin of Labour Statistics.

10 ILO (1986) Economically Active Population, Estimates and Projections: 1950-2025, vol. 1, copyright 1986, International Labour Organisation, Geneva: ix. See also M.T. Dupré, R. Hussmanns, and F. Mehran; op. cit.

11 ILO (1986) ibid., table 2, pp. 17-157.

12 OECD (1983) Employment Outlook.

13 'The contribution of services to employment' in OECD (1984) Employment Outlook: 39.

14 ibid., 41.

15 ILO (1973) Part-time Employment: An International Survey: 3.

16 'Concealed employment' in OECD (1986) Employment Outlook: 66-79.

17 Clark, op. cit.

18 W.V. Deuterman and S.C. Brown (1978) 'Voluntary part-time workers: a growing part of the labor force', Monthly Labor Review, vol. 101, no. 6: 3-10.

19 Clark, op. cit.

20 OECD 'Part-time employment...', op. cit., 45.

21 OECD (1986) Employment Outlook: 20.

22 'Self-employment in OECD countries' in OECD (1986) Employment Outlook: 43.

3 UNEMPLOYMENT

James J. Hughes

INTRODUCTION

There is no simple, correct, method of measuring unemployment, or its rate. Indeed, as one commentator[1] has observed, 'no single way of measuring unemployment can satisfy all analytical or ideological interests'. As a consequence, several different measures of unemployment often exist for any one country, each calculated on a different basis, each serving a different purpose. Although one of these measures is usually regarded as the 'official' measure, one needs to be extremely cautious in making cross-country comparisons of unemployment because national definitions of official unemployment vary from country to country, as do methods of collecting the statistics.

Defining unemployment

Clearly the starting point for the measurement of unemployment is to define it. A text book[2] definition of unemployment might be as follows:

> Unemployment (U) is the total number of hours (H_d) that people want to work in a period, minus the number of hours (H_a) that they actually do work[3], i.e.
>
> $$U = H_d - H_a$$
>
> Expressing unemployment as a rate, u, gives
>
> $$u = \frac{U}{H_d}$$

Such a definition has the advantage that it takes account of the preferences of individual workers to work differing hours. However, it suffers from the practical disadvantage that it would be almost impossible to ascertain individual preferences for hours as well as individual patterns of hours actually worked. Concentrating on individuals rather than hours suggests the alternative definition:

> Unemployment is the number of people wishing to undertake paid employment (L) minus the number actually employed (E), i.e.
>
> $$U = L - E \quad \text{and} \quad u = \frac{U}{L}$$

While this definition suffers from the disadvantage that it does not take account of individual differences in hours, either in preferences or in actual hours, it has the practical advantage that it is much easier to count just people rather than people and hours. However, before the definition can be made operational, we need to take account of an important theoretical consideration, namely that we cannot talk of an individual supplying labour services except at a price. For example, one individual, A, who does not currently have a job but would like one, might be prepared to work but only if he were to receive a wage rate that is higher than that which is currently on offer. Individual B, with identical qualifications to A, is also without a job but would accept one at the current market rate. Should both be regarded as unemployed? The answer is 'no'; only those who are willing and able to accept a job offer at the current market wage should be included in the measure of unemployment. Thus individual B should be included but A excluded. Although A is excluded from current unemployment he is clearly part of a potential labour reserve.

The current market wage

Reference to the current market wage suggests that there is a unique wage rate for each occupation, or rather each job grade within each occupation. In practice this is not so. Empirical studies show that there is often a wide dispersion in rates and earnings for a particular grade of worker, even within local labour markets. It is this that provides the incentive for an unemployed worker to search the local labour market in the hope that he receives the best wage offer that is available, but from the point of view of measuring unemployment the absence of a unique rate makes it more difficult to distinguish between individuals A and B.

In practice the labour-market status of an individual who is not employed might have to be determined by the agency responsible for collecting unemployment statistics by reference to the individual's willingness to accept (or reject) job offers that are made to him. Thus, if the individual has refused a number of job offers at the prevailing local labour-market rate, the agency might deem that he is unavailable for work and should not therefore be counted as unemployed. Clearly such an 'availability' test can be applied by the agency only if it has information on job offers that have been made to those registered with it. Such a test cannot help identify those who have not been subjected to a vacancy recently but would not have accepted an offer anyway at the prevailing market rate. For such people the problem of determining whether they are in category A or B remains.

In addition to introducing an 'availability' test the agency might also insist upon a 'job search' test to determine what steps an individual has undertaken over some specified recent period in order to try to find a job. Those who fail the test will be deemed to have been not very active in job search and therefore excluded from the unemployment count.

ILO/OECD DEFINITION

In 1982 the International Labour Office (ILO) and the Organization for Economic Co-operation and Development (OECD) adopted a common definition of unemployment.[4] This is fairly lengthy and is reproduced in full below:

> (1) The 'unemployed' comprise all persons above a specified age who during the reference period were:

(a) 'without work', i.e. were not in paid employment or self-employment ....
(b) 'currently available for work', i.e. were available for paid employment or self-employment during the reference period; and
(c) 'seeking work', i.e. had taken specific steps in a specified recent period to seek paid employment or self-employment. The specific steps may include registration at a public or private employment exchange; application to employers; checking at worksite, farms, factory gates, market or other assembly places; placing or answering newspaper advertisements; seeking assitance of friends or relatives; looking for land, building, machinery or equipment to establish own enterprise; arranging for financial resources; applying for permits and licences, etc.

(2) In situations where the conventional means of seeking work are of limited relevance, where the labour market is largely unorganized or of limited scope, where labour absorption is, at the time, inadequate, or where the labour force is largely self-employed, the standard definition of unemployment is given in subparagraph (1) above may be applied by relaxing the criterion of seeking work.

(3) In the application of the criterion of current availability for work, especially in situations covered by subparagraph (2) above, appropriate tests should be developed to suit national circumstances. Such tests may be based on notions such as present desire for work and previous work experience, willingness to take up work for wage or salary on locally prevailing terms, or readiness to undertake self-employment activity given the necessary resources and facilities.

(4) Notwithstanding the criterion of seeking work embodied in the standard definition of unemployment, persons without work and currently available for work who had made arrangements to take up paid employment or undertake self-employment activity at a date subsequent to the reference period should be considered as unemployed.

(5) Persons temporarily absent from their jobs with no formal job attachment who were currently available for work and seeking work should be regarded as unemployed in accordance with the standard definition of unemployment. Countries may, however, depending on national circumstances and policies, prefer to relax the seeking work criterion in the case of persons temporarily laid off. In such cases, persons temporarily laid off who were not seeking work but classified as unemployed should be identified as a separate subcategory.

(6) Students, homemakers and others mainly engaged in non-economic activities during the reference period who satisfy the criteria laid down in subparagraphs (1) and (2) above should be regarded as unemployed on the same basis as other categories of unemployed persons and be identified separately, where possible.

THE UNEMPLOYMENT RATE

It is the rate of unemployment rather than the absolute number of people unemployed that indicates the severity of unemployment. In the introductory section the rate, u, was defined as U/L, where L = E + U. In principle, nothing could be simpler, the denominator is the total labour force size - sometimes referred to as the 'economically active population' - which can be decomposed into those employed (E) and those unemployed (U). In practice, not all countries - or rather, statistical agencies - agree on what should be included in the economically active population. As we shall see, concepts and methods of measuring U differ from one country to another. Likewise, there are differences in the measurement of E. Thus, even if all countries agreed on how to measure U, but disagreed on how to measure E, comparisons of unemployment rates would be distorted.

The first category of the active population that might be excluded from E is the armed forces (A). Where this occurs we are left with civilian employment E', and its counterpart the civilian labour force L', i.e.

$$L' = E' + U \quad \text{where} \quad E' = E - A$$

The 13th International Conference of Labour Statisticians[5] held in 1982 resolved that A should be included in labour force, that is that the denominator of u should be L rather than L'. Further, it resolved that civilian employment, E', should include the following groups:

(i) paid employment; i.e. all wage and salary earners;
(ii) self-employment; included here are employers, own-account workers and unpaid family workers.

Individuals in both groups who are not at work during the reference period, for reason of illness, injury, holiday, industrial dispute, etc., but still attached to a job, should be included. Likewise students, homemakers, and others who are mainly, but not exclusively engaged in non-economic activities during the reference week, should be included if they undertake some paid employment or self-employment.

Clearly, if the armed forces or any category of civilian employment is excluded from the labour force, or economically active population, the unemployment rate will be higher than it otherwise would be. In short, the magnitude of the unemployment rate will depend, to some degree, on the definition of labour force that is adopted.

SOURCE OF STATISTICS

There are basically three different sources from which unemployment statistics are derived. These are:

the record of claimants to unemployment benefit;
the register of job applicants at employment offices; and
labour-force sample surveys.

Unemployment benefit claimants

Here there are two sorts of scheme that give rise to unemployment statistics, compulsory state unemployment insurance schemes and those schemes administered by trade unions. The latter tend to have only partial coverage, given that trade union membership density is less than 100 per cent in most areas of activity. As a consequence, unemployment rates based on such data are likely to be untypical. On the other hand, compulsory schemes do not necessarily give rise to comprehensive coverage. Even when they cover all wage and salary earners, categories such as the self-employed, new entrants, and re-entrants into the labour force are often not covered by comprehensive schemes. However, a comprehensive system of state unemployment insurance involving registration at state-run employment offices can give rise to a fairly comprehensive system of unemployment statistics.

Employment office statistics

Data obtained from this source usually refer to the number of applicants for work on the registers of employment offices on some specified date each month (e.g. the last working day). Such data give rise to a snapshot view of what is usually a changing situation. Clearly, where registration at employment offices is not compulsory, data from this source will understate the true extent of unemployment. Such understatement might be particularly marked for less populated rural areas because for many workers the nearest local employment office is often some distance away, thus discouraging them from registering, even though they are available and searching for work. Also, where particular categories of workers are not accustomed to registering - perhaps because they believe they would receive little or no benefit from doing so - such categories will be underrepresented in the statistics obtained from this source.

As noted above, however, when there exists a compulsory and comprehensive scheme of unemployment insurance in which registration is a necessary condition for the receipt of benefit, employment-office registration will provide a more comprehensive measure of unemployment, with changes in the measure reflecting changes in the underlying conditions of the labour market, provided that there have been no legal or administrative changes in either the operation of the employment office or insurance scheme. Since there are differences in the organization and operation of employment offices from one county to another, as well as differences in insurance schemes, international rates derived from such sources are not strictly comparable.

Labour-force sample surveys

Labour-force surveys involve a sample of households, stratified at various stages to take account of such factors as the distribution of households between private and non-private dwellings, the distribution of the population between urban and rural areas, and other socio-economic considerations. The members of households in the sample are asked questions about their labour-market activity in order to determine whether they should be classified as employed or unemployed. The information is usually gathered either through personal or telephone interviews, but occasionally through a mailed questionnaire. The interviews (or questionnaries) are usually carried out (or sent out) during the same week each month, or sometimes at three-monthly intervals, with the information that is collected relating to the previous week (i.e. the survey or reference week).

Individuals who have not worked at all during the survey week but were available for work and engaged in search activity during some specified period prior to the survey week are designated as unemployed. Data from sample surveys includes individuals who might not be captured in the registration approach to measurement. This is particularly true for new entrants and re-entrants into the labour market, both of which groups might not have a strong incentive to register at employment offices if people in them are not entitled to unemployment benefit. For this reason, according to the ILO, surveys 'generally yield the best over-all statistics on unemployment'. Also, the continuity of any unemployment series based upon the survey method is less affected by legislative and administrative changes. Furthermore, the unemployment measures that result are more in line with the ILO/OECD definition and lend themselves more readily to international comparison.

SOURCES AND METHODS OF DATA COLLECTION IN OECD COUNTRIES

As Table 3.1 shows, of the twenty-four OECD countries, eleven have unemployment data derived from labour-market sample surveys, seven countries relying exclusively on this source. Sixteen countries derive data from employment-office registrations, and for twelve of them this is the only source. For most of the post-war period the UK has been a member of this latter group, but since October 1983 the count has been based on claimants to unemployment benefit, all others registering at employment offices being excluded. Four countries, Ireland, Norway, Spain, and Sweden regularly derive unemployment data from both sample surveys and employment offices and both sources are published in the ILO Year Book.

Table 3.1 Sources of unemployment data

1 Countries with survey data	2 Countries with employment-office data	3 Countries with claimant data
Australia	Austria	United Kingdom*
Canada	Belgium	
Finland	Denmark	
Ireland	France	
Italy	Germany	
Norway	Greece	
Japan	Iceland	
Portugal	Ireland	
Spain	Luxemburg	
Sweden	Netherlands	
United States	New Zealand	
	Norway	
	Spain	
	Sweden	
	Switzerland	
	Turkey	

Source ILO, Year Book of Labour Statistics (various issues, including 1986), Geneva

* Although the United Kingdom is now in column 3, from mid-1948 until October 1983 the count was based upon employment-office data.

Of those countries which use household surveys for obtaining information on unemployment, the US Current Population Survey is the longest established. It began life in 1940 and has been carried out monthly since then. In contrast, annual surveys were introduced in Ireland in 1983, although three biennial surveys had been carried out between 1975 and 1979. As table 3.2 shows, eight of the eleven countries that employ the survey method for generating unemployment data have done so for over 20 years.

Where the survey approach is employed, interviews are usually carried out in a specified week, with the information that is collected relating to the previous week (i.e. the survey or reference week). Both Australia and Sweden depart from this practice by interviewing over a two-week period, while in Portugal, where the survey is carried out twice-yearly, the survey period extends over the whole six months. Similarly, the quarterly survey in Spain extends over the whole quarter, while the annual survey in Ireland is carried out during April-May. What these different reference periods give rise to are, of course, different interpretations of the resulting measure of unemployment. Thus, while for the USA the monthly rate refers to a given week in the month (the week that includes the twelfth day), for Spain the rate is an average for the whole quarter and as such will take account of any tendency for unemployment to rise or fall during the quarter.

Even among countries adopting the survey approach the methods of data collection vary from one country to another. The personal interview of household members is the most popular method, although Japan, the USA and Sweden all adopt alternative methods. The former relies upon the mailed questionnaire, while in Sweden the telephone interview is the chosen method. In the USA two-thirds of households are interviewed by telephone, the remainder being covered by personal interviews.

Employment-office statistics on unemployment arise because people without jobs register themselves as applicants for work. In practice, the incentive to register will be strengthened if registration is a necessary condition for the receipt of unemployment benefit. However, those not covered by unemployment-insurance schemes, and therefore not eligible for unemployment benefit, will still have some incentive to register because through registration they are likely to learn of vacancies that they would not otherwise have heard about, and, through the free placement service, they might even be referred to some of these vacancies.

In eleven of the sixteen countries which derive unemployment data from employment-office statistics, and in the UK too where the count is now based upon claimants to unemployment benefit, registration is an essential condition for the receipt of unemployment benefit, and sometimes other social-security benefits also. In four 'employment-office' countries - Denmark, Ireland, Luxemburg and Spain - it is not possible to tell from the summary descriptions provided whether or not registration is an essential condition for the receipt of benefit. In all cases the unemployment count refers to a particular day of the month, although this was not always true for Denmark. Prior to 1979 the monthly count in Denmark was the average of four or five weekly counts carried out on a Wednesday. Since 1979 Denmark has conformed to standard practice in this group.

SEARCH AND AVAILABILITY TESTS IN OECD COUNTRIES

The survey approach to measurement, devoid as it is of registration data, usually includes some sort of search criterion in order to test an individual's motivation to try and find a job. Other things being equal,

Table 3.2 Countries with survey data: frequency and methods of data collection

Country	Starting year	Frequency of data collection	Method of data collection
Australia	1964	Monthly since 1978; quarterly prior to 1978 (survey carried out over two-week period)	Personal interviews
Canada	1945	Monthly since 1953; quarterly prior to 1953	Personal and telephone interviews
Finland	1959	Monthly since 1959	Since 1983, telephone interviews (92%), personal (7%); prior to 1983, mailed questionnaire
Ireland	1975	Annually since 1983; biennially to 1979; no survey 1981 (survey during April-May)	Personal interviews
Italy	1959	Quarterly since 1959	Personal interviews
Japan	1947	Monthly since 1947	Mailed questionnaire
Norway	1972	Quarterly since 1972	Personal interviews (60%); the remainder by telephone and mailed questionnaire
Portugal	1972	Twice yearly since 1972 (survey carried out over about a six-month period)	Personal interviews - preceded by letter of objectives
Spain	1964	Quarterly since 1975; twice yearly prior to 1975 (survey carried out throughout quarters)	Personal interviews
Sweden	1961	Monthly since 1970; quarterly prior to 1970 (survey carried out over two-week period)	Telephone interviews
United States	1940	Monthly since 1940	Telephone interviews (2/3); remainder by personal interviews

Source: ILO (1986) Economically Active Population, Employment, Unemployment and Hours of Work (Household Surveys), vol. 3 of Statistical Sources and Methods, copyright 1986, International Labour Organisation, Geneva.

whether or not a non-employed person will be counted as unemployed will depend upon whether or not he passes this search test. Clearly, like most tests, more people are likely to pass the search test the less severe the test is. For example, if it is stated that there must be evidence of search activity during the month immediately prior to the survey, this is a more stringent requirement than stating that there must be evidence of search activity sometime during the six months prior to the survey. Someone who satisfies the one-month rule also satisfies the six-month rule, but someone who satisfies the six-month rule does not necessarily satisfy the one-month rule. When comparing international measures of unemployment it therefore follows that, other things being equal, the country which has the more stringent search requirement will have a lower recorded rate of unemployment.

Table 3.3. summarizes the search requirement in each of the eleven countries employing the survey method. As can be seen, countries in groups 2 and 4, that is Finland, Italy, Portugal, Spain, Japan, and Sweden, tend to have the toughest search requirement, although in the case of Sweden this is weakened by exempting the unemployed from searching during the reference week if they are waiting for the results of search undertaken during the previous sixty days. In Ireland there is no general search requirement, only one that is applicable to re-entrants which requires them to have undertaken search during the reference week. Australia, Canada, and the USA adopt a four-week rule, while Norway alone has a two-month rule.

Table 3.3 Search requirements in countries adopting survey methods

Group		
1	Australia Canada United States	Had actively looked for work in the four weeks up to and including the reference week
2	Finland Italy Portugal Spain	Had actually looked for work during the reference week
3	Ireland	The only reference is to re-entrants who must have been actively looking for work during reference week
4	Japan Sweden	Had actively looked for work during reference period, or had been awaiting the results of earlier search (in case of Sweden, the previous sixty days)
5	Norway	Had actively looked for work during the last two months

Source: ILO (1986) Economically Active Population, Employment, Unemployment And Hours of Work (Household Surveys), vol. 3 of Statistical Sources And Methods, copyright 1986, International Labour Organisation, Geneva.

Many, although not all, national definitions of unemployment stress availability for work as being a necessary condition if those who are without a job are to be counted as unemployed. In practice this availability criterion is not often put to the test, no doubt because of the difficulty in devising an objective and reliable test. As was implied above, testing for availability really involves a two-stage process. First, it is necessary to test the willingness of individual job seekers to subject themselves (i.e. to apply) for reasonable job openings. Second, it is necessary to test their willingness to accept reasonable job offers. In practice, determining what is reasonable will rarely be clear cut and therefore designing an objective test of willingness is impossible. In order to determine whether the behaviour of someone who is unemployed is reasonable requires the exercise of judgement by another individual who knows something about the first individual's job searches, the job offers received and the individual's responses to these offers. Although the placement officers at an employment office will have some of this information, they are unlikely to be in possession of all of it. According to official definitions of unemployment reported to the ILO, only in Austria is the judgement of the placement officer crucial to the continued registration of inidividuals. This certainly used to be the case in the UK but the practice has lapsed, given that registration no longer takes place at the same office from which benefit payments are made.

In practice, given the difficulties of devising an objective test of availability, registration and reregistration might be regarded as a necessary first test of availability, although the fact that registration is often a necessary prerequisite for the receipt of benefit means that it is by no means a conclusive test.

Not all countries require workers to reregister periodically, and for those that do the frequency with which workers have to reregister varies. For example, in Norway individuals have to report every week, otherwise registration lapses. In New Zealand the requirement is to reregister once every two weeks, while in Greece, the Netherlands, and Sweden reregistration is required once a month.

DIFFERENCES IN OECD-COUNTRY DEFINITIONS

Notwithstanding the international definition of unemployment that has been adopted by both the ILO and OECD, and which is reproduced above, there are differences in the actual definition adopted from one country to another. As already noted, the different sources from which the statistics derive give rise to fundamentally different concepts of unemployment, namely registered as opposed to search unemployment. These different concepts of unemployment give rise to different measures of unemployment with different reference periods. Differences in the measures are compounded by differences in registration requirements and differences in the criteria of job search and availability for work that are adopted. All of these matters have been discussed, albeit briefly, above. In this section we discuss other differences in measured unemployment that arise from the differences in the coverage and scope of the statistics, particularly with regard to the age of those covered and the treatment of such groups as the mentally and physically handicapped, part-time job seekers, students, pensioners, new entrants and re-entrants into the labour force, the self-employed, and the temporarily stopped.

The different treatment of these groups in the different OECD countries is summarized in table 3.4. Before we discuss the main features

Table 3.4 The measurement of unemployment: international comparison of definitions

Country	*Age/coverage*	*Mental/ physical handicap*	*Part-time job seekers*	*Students*	*Pensioners*	*New entrants*	*Re-entrants*	*Self-employed*	*Temporarily stopped*
Australia (S)	15 and over		Included	Both full- and part-time students seeking full-time or part-time work included		Included	Included	Included	Included
Austria (EO)	Must have completed 9 years of schooling				From 1973 onwards pensioners registered only for purpose of receiving unemployment benefit excluded	Included except for those seeking apprenticeships			
Belgium (EO)	Wholly unemployed		Excluded			Excluded	Excluded	Excluded	Excluded (but separate data on temporarily stopped collected — these referred to as partially unemployed)

Canada (S)	15 and over; those living in Yukon, NW Territories and on Indian Reservations excluded	Included	Full-time students seeking part-time work included		Included	Included	Included	Included
Denmark (EO)	All wage and salary earners; also included are the partially unemployed, involuntarily working a reduced number of hours	Included since January 1977			Included	Included	Included since January 1977	Included
Finland (S)	15 to 74 years	Included	Part-time students included	Those with unemployment pensions included, although from 1986 onwards unemployed pensioners not seeking work excluded	Included	Included	Included	Included
France (EO)	All full-time job seekers, irrespective of age occupation or status	Excluded; only job seekers offering more than 30 hours per week included		Since 1972 those over 60 and in receipt of income maintenance benefits excluded				

Country	*Age/coverage*	*Mental/ physical handicap*	*Part-time job seekers*	*Students*	*Pensioners*	*New entrants*	*Re-entrants*	*Self-employed*	*Temporarily stopped*
Germany (EO) Federal Republic	14 and over; must be seeking employment of more than 3 months		Part-time housewives included; others must work at least 20 hours per week to be included			Included	Included	Included	
Greece (EO)	14 and over; younger if in possession of juvenile employment booklet.								
Iceland (EO)	16 and over					Included	Included		Included
Ireland (EO)	Partially unemployed included, beneficial occupiers of agricultural land excluded.					Excluded		Included; family workers also included.	Included
Ireland (S)	15 and over; includes all whose principal economic status is being unemployed.					Included	Included if interruption of working life is 12 months or more.		

Italy (S)	14 and over			Included since January 1977	Included since January 1977	Included	Included since January 1977	Included	Included
Japan (S)	15 and over; totally unemployed, Northern Territories excluded.		Included	Full- and part-time students seeking full- and part-time jobs included		Included	Included	Included	
Luxemburg (EO)	16 to 65; wholly unemployed wage and salary earners	Included provided that working incapacity rate does not exceed 66.7%				Included			
Netherlands (EO)	Males, 14 to 64, females, 15 to 64	Physical and mental condition must be no impediment to normal employment	Only job seekers offering 25 hours per week or more are included (prior to 1978, 30 hours per week)						Included
New Zealand (EO)	Wage earners and salaried employees					Included	Included		Included
Norway (EO)		Included if working capacity is 50% or more							
Norway (S)	16 to 74			Included	Included	Included	Included		Included

Country	*Age/coverage*	*Mental/ physical handicap*	*Part-time job seekers*	*Students*	*Pensioners*	*New entrants*	*Re-entrants*	*Self-employed*	*Temporarily stopped*
Portugal (S)	12 and over; (prior to 1983, 10 and over)					Included	Included		
Spain (S)	16 and over; whole country excluding Cueta and Melilla				Included	Included	Included	Included	Included
Spain (EO)	14 to 60; all workers prepared to work for minimum salary					Included	Included		
Sweden (S)	16 to 74			Part-time students seeking full- or part-time work included		Included	Included		Included
Sweden (EO)	Insured workers registering at local employment offices; in 1975 unemployment insurance covered only 65% of labour force								

Switzerland (EO)	15 and over; until 1983, wholly unemployed only; from 1984 onwards the partially unemployed included								Included
United Kingdom (BC)	Males, 16 to 65, females, 16 to 60	Excluded if unlikely to obtain work other than under special conditions	Excluded	Adult students excluded since March 1976	From April 1983 onwards certain categories of males aged 60 and over excluded	Non-claimant new entrants excluded		Excluded	Excluded since end of 1972
United States (S)	16 and over		Included	Full-time and part-time students seeking full-time or part-time work included	Included	Included	Included	Included	Included

Notes S Survey data
EO Employment Office data
BC Unemployment Benefit Claimants

of this table it is necessary to stress the need for caution in interpreting it. The two main sources for the information contained in it are the Technical Guide, volume 2 (1980), and Statistical Sources and Methods, volume 3 (1986) (see Sources). While the former contains limited information on all OECD countries, except Turkey, the latter contains only information on unemployment data deriving from household surveys. Thus for all those countries for which the data is derived from registration at employment offices (i.e. EO countries) the information is dated, lagging some five to six years behind that of countries undertaking surveys (i.e. S countries).

One further point needs to be borne in mind when interpreting table 3.4, namely that, where nothing is recorded in a particular column for any country, this means that the ILO sources do not make any specific reference to that group, or that reasonable inferences cannot be drawn from the concepts and definitions that are reported.

Age coverage

In any one country one would expect the minimum age for inclusion in the labour force to reflect the minimum school-leaving age, i.e. the age after completion of the compulsory years of schooling. As the Age/coverage column shows, the minimum age for inclusion in the unemployment count varies from 12 to 16 years, but for most countries lies within the range 14 to 16 years. In both Germany and Greece the minimum age for inclusion is 14, while in Scandinavian countries, the UK, and USA it is 16 years. The one country that lies outside this range is Portugal where the minimum age for inclusion is 12 years - and prior to 1983 was only 10.

At the other end of the life cycle many countries do not specify an upper age limit for excluding individuals from the unemployment count; this is found particularly in survey data. Other countries such as Finland, Norway, and Sweden have an upper age limit of 74, which is in marked contrast to other West European countries such as the UK, Netherlands, and Luxemburg where the upper age limit is 64-65 years, and for women in the UK only 60 years. The UK is the only country which reports different upper age limits for men and women, although in the Netherlands females do not count as unemployed until they are a year older than the males.

Generally, only those who are wholly unemployed are included in the count. However, EO counts in Denmark, Switzerland, and Ireland make some allowance for those who are not wholly but partially unemployed, that is for individuals who involuntarily are forced to work a reduced number of hours. At the other extreme Portugal ignores partial employment, at least where it amounts to less than fifteen hours per week and is accompanied by a desire on the part of the individual to work longer than fifteen hours. Those who worked less than fifteen hours per week but tried to find a full-time job during the survey week are counted as unemployed.

The only country which explicitly attempts to link the unemployment count to the current market wage (see above) is Spain where a condition for inclusion in the EO count is a willingness to work for the minimum salary.

Mental and physical handicap

Only four countries (none of them S countries) specifically mention mental and physical handicap in relation to unemployment. However, even among these four countries the treatment of this group varies. In Norway a handicapped individual is only included in the count provided that his working incapacity does not exceed 50 per cent. In Luxemburg the critical level of incapacity is 66.7 per cent. In both the Netherlands and the UK there is no explicit reference to the degree of incapacity, the individual being included only if his physical and mental condition are no impediment to normal employment.

Part-time job seekers

Table 3.4 contains information on part-time job seekers for eleven countries, five of which are S countries. All these S countries include part-time job seekers in unemployment. Of the other six countries only Belgium and the UK exclude part-time job seekers outright. In Germany part-time job seekers (other than housewives) must work a minimum of twenty hours per week to be included, while in the Netherlands and France the corresponding number of hours is twenty-five and thirty respectively.

Students

All S countries for which information is reported in table 3.4 count students as unemployed if they are without a job and seeking employment. However, even among these countries there are differences in treatment: for example, in Australia, Japan, and the USA all students, both full-time and part-time, are included irrespective of whether they are seeking full-time or part-time work; in contrast, only part-time students are included in Finland, while in Canada full-time students seeking part-time work only are included.

Pensioners

There is information on pensioners for only six countries. They are included in the survey data generated in Italy, Norway, Spain, the USA, and Finland, although the search criterion for pensioners in Finland has been tightened recently. In Austria they are also included if they are actively seeking work. In both France and the UK in recent years there has been a tendency to exclude certain categories of unemployed workers over 60 years of age.

New entrants and re-entrants

In survey-generated data, new entrants and re-entrants are always included in the unemployment count, provided they meet the usual criteria. In EO-generated data the treatment of these categories varies; for example, both are excluded in Belgium and the UK but included in several other countries such as Denmark, Germany, Iceland, New Zealand, and Spain.

Self-employed

Generally those who had previously been self-employed but have ceased to be so are included as unemployed in survey-data countries. However, in other countries the treatment of this category varies; it is excluded in Belgium and the UK but included in Denmark, Germany, and Ireland.

Temporarily stopped

All countries but two for which information is reported in table 3.4 - and this includes all S countries, except Japan - include the temporarily stopped as part of unemployment. The exceptions are Belgium and the UK, both of which record separately the number of temporarily stopped.

DIFFERENCES IN TREATMENT OF LABOUR FORCE

In an earlier section it was noted that the definition, and thus the measurement, of labour force affects the calculation of the unemployment rate. Over the last decade or so there have been changes in both the definition of labour force and the terminology employed. During the 1970s all those countries that derived unemployment data from surveys also derived estimates of civilian labour force from the same surveys and used this as the denominator for the unemployment rate. In recent years the concept of the civilian labour force has been replaced by that of the economically active population (or total labour force), and as a consequence all S countries but Australia include members of the armed forces as part of their labour force, although for some - Canada, Finland, Italy, and Norway - this does not extend to conscripts. (It should be added that in the USA and France all members of the armed forces have been included in labour force since 1972 and 1975 respectively.) Irrespective of their former practice all S countries now also include employers, self-employed, unpaid family workers, and students as part of the labour force, although in the case of unpaid family workers the minimum number of hours that has to be worked by such workers is seven in Finland, ten in Norway, and fifteen in Sweden and Australia.

For those countries that rely on employment-office data there have also been changes, although information on these countries is not up to date. In Belgium the labour force is assumed to be equal to the total number of workers insured against unemployment in June each year. In Denmark the total labour force concept was introduced in 1979 and prior to that the labour force was equated with the total number of employees (both employed and unemployed). In the Netherlands the number of wage and salary earners has been replaced by the total labour force, including members of the armed forces. Finally, in the UK members of the armed forces are now included, whereas formerly the labour force was assumed to be equal to the mid-year estimate of the number of employees (including students employed during vacations).

TRENDS IN UNEMPLOYMENT IN OECD COUNTRIES

The data discussed in this section are those published by the ILO and the OECD (see Sources). In gathering its data the ILO asks reporting agencies to supply information that conforms as closely as possible to the international definition adopted by itself and the OECD. Before publishing the data the ILO does not adjust it to achieve conformity with that definition and therefore it is essential to bear in mind the main differences in definitions discussed above when comparing unemployment rates across countries. Because of these differences precise comparisons are not valid, although comparison of broad trends in individual series can be made with caution.

Table 3.5 shows, wherever possible, the ILO rates for all OECD countries for the period 1972-86. It also shows the absolute level of unemployment at the beginning and the end of the period. In 1972 the unemployment rate in most countries was in the range 1-3 per cent. The exceptions were Canada, where the rate was over 6 per cent, and a group of geographically dispersed countries, Iceland, Luxemburg, New Zealand,

and Switzerland, all of which had a rate of around 0.5 per cent. By 1986 rates generally were in the range 5 to 12 per cent, although Ireland and Spain had rates around 20 per cent, while that for Switzerland was still below 1 per cent. The rates in Iceland, Luxemburg, Norway, and Sweden were around 2 per cent.

Although the cyclical pattern in each country varied over this period, most experienced rising unemployment in the early or mid 1970s, and again in the early 1980s. The most notable exception to this pattern was Spain where unemployment increased each year over the period 1974-86; with the exception of a 0.1 per cent dip in one year, Italy experienced the same relentless increase over the same period. Belgium and France similarly experienced increases in each successive year over the period 1973-84, and likewise New Zealand over the period 1974-83.

For Norway, Spain, and Sweden table 3.5 shows unemployment rates derived from both survey and registration data. In all three cases the survey data records a higher rate, although the relative gap tends to narrow as unemployment increases.

Table 3.6 summarizes the increase in rates for the periods covered in table 3.5. If Switzerland and Turkey are ignored, it is clear that, on average, the increase in unemployment rates generated from survey data has been considerably lower than the average increase in other rates. According to survey data, Sweden experienced no deterioration in its unemployment rate over the period covered, while the rate in Norway and the USA increased by only 20 per cent compared with a 760 per cent increase in Spain. The registration data show the largest percentage increases in Spain (over 1200 per cent) and New Zealand (900 per cent), with Denmark and Germany following closely behind.

For those countries with data from two sources - Norway, Spain, and Sweden - the deterioration in unemployment as recorded by the survey measure is in each case less severe than that recorded by the measure based on registration data, hence the narrowing of the gap referred to above.

The OECD publishes annual data on unemployment for all member countries (see OECD, Labour Force Statistics, part I, table 5.1). Although it admits to some adjustments in the data, these are not sufficient to make the data conform to the international definition. Furthermore, all rates are computed on the basis of total labour force. For most countries the resulting 'unadjusted' OECD series is fairly close to that published by the ILO, although for both Belgium and the UK there are some surprising differences.[6]

For sixteen of its member countries the OECD also publishes standardized unemployment rates. As far as possible the adjustments preserve comparability over time and conform to the international definition discussed in an earlier section. These adjustments affect mainly those countries which derive their unemployment statistics from registration data gathered by employment offices. Table 3.7 shows the OECD-adjusted series for the period 1971-86.

Inspection of the data in table 3.7 confirms the broad trends in ILO data that have already been commented upon. However, there are some differences in the two sets of data and these can best be seen by comparing them for two different years, one (1974) when unemployment generally was relatively low, the other (1984) when it was somewhat higher. The comparisons are shown in table 3.8.

Table 3.8 suggests that for Australia, Canada, France, Japan, Norway, Sweden, Switzerland, Italy, and the USA, the two series are fairly close. A

Table 3.5 Total unemployment in OECD countries: unadjusted

	1972	*1972*	*1973*	*1974*	*1975*	*1976*	*1977*	*1978*	*1979*	*1980*	*1981*	*1982*	*1983*	*1984*	*1985*	*1986*	*1986*
	Absolute	%	%	%	%	%	%	%	%	%	%	%	%	%	%	%	Absolute
Australia (S)	150.1	2.6	2.3	2.7	4.9	4.7	5.7	6.2	5.8	5.9	5.6	6.7	9.9	9.0	8.3	8.1	609.9
Austria (EO)	49.1	1.9	1.6	1.3	2.0	2.0	1.8	2.1	2.0	1.9	2.4	3.7	4.5	4.5	4.8	5.2	152.0
Belgium (EO)	105.2	. .	. .	3.1	5.2	6.6	7.6	8.4	8.4	9.1	11.1	13.0	14.0	14.1	13.3	12.3	516.8
Canada (S)	552.0	6.3	5.6	5.4	6.9	7.1	8.1	8.3	7.4	7.5	7.5	11.0	11.9	11.3	10.5	9.6	1,236.0
Denmark (EO)	32.9	. .	0.9	2.1	5.1	5.3	6.4	7.3	6.1	7.0	9.2	10.0	10.5	10.2	9.3	8.0	217.3
Finland (S)	55.0	2.5	2.3	1.7	2.6	3.9	5.9	7.3	6.0	4.7	5.1	5.9	6.1	6.2	6.3	5.4	138.0
France (EO)	595.3	2.7	2.6	2.8	4.1	4.4	4.9	5.2	5.9	6.3	7.3	8.1	8.3	9.7			2,516.6
Germany FR (EO)	246.4	1.1	1.2	2.6	4.7	4.6	4.5	4.3	3.8	3.8	5.5	7.5	9.1	9.1	9.3	9.0	2,228.0
Greece (EO)	23.8	. .	. .	. .	3.0	2.3	2.1	2.3	2.2	2.4	2.7	3.2	3.8	4.2	5.1	6.1	49.4
Iceland (EO)	0.5	0.5	0.4	0.4	0.7	0.5	0.4	0.4	0.5	0.3	0.4	0.8	1.0	1.2	. .	. .	
Ireland (EO)	66.6	. .	. .	. .	. .	. .	. .	. .	. .	. .	10.1	12.1	14.8	16.4	17.8	18.2	236.4
Italy (S)	1,297.0	6.4	6.4	5.4	5.9	6.7	7.2	7.2	7.7	7.6	8.4	9.1	9.9	10.0	10.3	11.1	2,611.0
Japan (S)	730.0	1.4	1.3	1.4	1.9	2.0	2.0	2.2	2.1	2.0	2.2	2.4	2.6	2.7	2.6	2.8	1,670.0
Luxemburg (EO)	0.04	. .	. .	. .	0.2	0.3	0.5	0.8	0.7	0.7	1.0	1.3	1.6	1.8	1.7		2.3

Netherlands (EO)	107.9	2.8	2.8	3.5	5.0	5.3	5.1	5.0	5.1	5.9	9.1	12.6	17.1	14.1	12.9	12.0	710.7
New Zealand (EO)	5.7	0.5	0.2	0.1	0.4	0.4	0.6	1.8	2.0	2.9	3.6	3.9	5.7	5.0	4.0	5.0	67.2
Norway (EO)	14.8	1.0	0.8	0.7	1.3	1.3	1.1	1.3	1.4	1.3	1.7	2.4	3.8	3.2	2.5	1.8	36.2
Norway (S)	28.0	1.7	1.5	1.5	2.3	1.8	1.5	1.7	2.0	1.7	2.0	2.6	3.3	3.2	2.6	2.0	42.0
Portugal (S)	. .	. .	. .	1.8	4.5	6.4	7.5	8.1	8.2	7.8	8.2	7.4	7.7	8.3	8.5	8.4	381.6
Spain (S)	. .	. .	2.5	2.9	5.0	4.9	5.8	7.8	9.6	12.6	15.4	17.1	18.4	20.6	21.9	21.5	2,960.7
Spain (EO)	190.9	1.5	1.1	1.1	1.9	2.8	4.1	6.2	7.9	9.9	12.1	14.2	16.5	18.4	19.5	20.0	2,758.7
Sweden (S)	107.0	2.7	2.5	2.0	1.6	1.6	1.8	2.2	2.1	2.0	2.5	3.1	3.5	3.1	2.8	2.7	117.0
Sweden (EO)	48.2	2.0	1.9	1.5	1.4	1.2	1.2	1.6	1.5	1.4	1.9	2.5	2.8	2.8	2.5	2.5	84.2
Switzerland (EO)	0.1			0.0	0.3	0.7	0.4	0.4	0.4	0.2	0.2	0.4	0.9	1.1	1.0	0.8	25.7
Turkey (EO)	43.9	. .	. .	. .	. .	. .	. .	. .	. .	. .	. .	. .	. .	. .	. .	. .	1,054.6
United Kingdom (BC)				2.6	4.0	5.5	5.8	5.7	5.3	6.8	10.4	10.9	11.6	11.7	11.9	11.8	3,289.1
United States (S)	4,882.0	5.6	4.9	5.6	8.3	7.6	6.9	6.0	5.8	7.0	7.5	9.5	9.5	7.4	7.1	6.9	8,237.0

Notes S Survey data
EO Employment-office data
BC Unemployment Benefit Claimants

Table 3.6 Increase in unemployment, 1972-86, as indicated by ratio of 1986 rate to 1972 rate[1]

Australia (S)	3.1	Luxemburg (EO)	8.5
Austria (EO)	2.7	Netherlands (EO)	4.3
Belgium (EO)	4.0	New Zealand (EO)	10.0
Canada (S)	1.5	Norway (EO)	1.8
Denmark (EO)	8.9	Norway (S)	1.2
Finland (S)	2.2	Portugal	4.7
France (S)	3.6	Spain (EO)	13.3
Germany (EO)	8.2	Spain (S)	8.6
Greece (EO)	2.0	Sweden (EO)	1.3
Iceland (EO)	2.4	Sweden (S)	0.0
Ireland (EO)	**	Switzerland[2] (EO)	257.0
Italy (S)	1.7	Turkey[3] (EO)	24.0
Japan (S)	2.0	United Kingdom (BC)	3.1
		United States	1.2

Source: Table 3.5

Notes

1 Where the beginning and terminal years are not 1972 and 1986, the ratio refers to the years shown in table 3.5
2 Since the rate in 1972 was negligible, the ratio shown reflects the absolute levels of unemployment in 1986 and 1972
3 Since no rates are recorded, the ratio reflects the absolute levels of unemployment in 1986 and 1972

more detailed inspection of tables 3.5 and 3.7 shows that for all countries in this group, except Australia and Italy, the ILO and standardized OECD rates are all within one-tenth of one percentage point of each other. In the case of Australia and Italy, while this has also been true for most years, there have been occasional years when the discrepancy has been greater. For the other seven countries in the group of sixteen the nature and the magnitude of the discrepancy varies, both from country to country and through time.

In Australia the standardized OECD rate was lower than the ILO rate in the early 1970s; this gap disappeared in the late 1970s but reappeared again in the 1980s. For Belgium the OECD rate was only 0.2 lower in the late 1970s but by 1983 had increased to 2.0. For Finland the gap increased from 0.1 in the late 1970s to 1.3 in 1985, declining to 0.1 again in 1986. In Germany the gap increased steadily and by the mid-1980s exceeded 2.0; in Spain the opposite happened. In both the Netherlands and the UK there was considerable fluctuation. For the former the OECD rate was lower than the ILO rate in the early 1970s, but from 1975 onwards the gap was reversed, only to be reversed yet again after 1980. For the UK the OECD rate was above the ILO rate by about 0.3 until 1978 and thereafter the gap reversed itself every two to three years. In 1985-86 the OECD rate lagged by about 0.7.

CONCLUDING COMMENTS

There are considerable differences in the measurement of unemployment in OECD countries and a good deal of caution must be exercised in comparing unemployment across countries. When international comparisons are attempted, analysts should use the adjusted data of the OECD rather than unadjusted ILO data. Individual country data on unemployment are most useful in assessing whether the national labour market situation has changed in that country; they are less useful in forming judgements about the absolute level of hardship or economic loss at a particular point in time.

Unemployment data (particularly unemployment rates) are subject to periodic revisions and users must be aware of these. Also in recent years the many small changes in national definitions have resulted in further official revisions in national series, thereby making it even more difficult to obtain a consistent series over a long period of time.

It is quite clear from the data examined in this chapter that all countries have suffered an increase in unemployment between the early 1970s and the mid-1980s. Notwithstanding the above comment on the need for caution in making international comparisons, it is also clear that the burden of unemployment is not shared equally among member countries.[7]

NOTES

1 Julius Shiskin (1976) 'Employment and unemployment: the doughnut or the hole', Monthly Labor Review, vol. 99, February.

2 See, for example, John Craven (1984) Introduction to Economics: An Integrated Approach to Fundamental Principles, Oxford: Blackwell: 93.

3 While this definition has the advantage that part-time workers are included and automatically weighted according to their hours or work, it also implies that workers who feel themselves to be overemployed at the hours they actually work will have the effect of reducing unemployment.

4 See Sources 1, 515. Also I. Chernyshev (1988, 3) 'ILO -Comparable annual employment and employment estimates', Bulletin of Labour Statistics, Geneva: ILO.

5 See Sources 6, 183-5.

6 For example, for Belgium and the UK the 1974 ILO rates were 13.1 and 2.6 respectively, compared with unadjusted OECD rates of 2.4 and 2.1. In contrast, the 1974 adjusted (i.e. standardized) rates were 3.0 and 2.9 respectively.

7 For a discussion of recent differential unemployment experience (and some possible causes) for a number of individual OECD countries see Economica, vol. 53, 1986 (Supplement) and Joyanna Moy (1985) 'Recent trends in unemployment and the labor force, 10 countries', Monthly Labor Review, vol. 108, August.

SOURCES

Statistics

1 ILO (1986) Year Book of Labour Statistics (and earlier issues back to 1981), Geneva.
2 ILO (1987) Bulletin of Labour Statistics, Parts I, II, III and IV, Geneva.
3 OECD (1986) Labour Force Statistics, 1964-84, Paris.
4 OECD (1987) Economic Outlook, vol. 42, December.

Table 3.7 Standardized unemployment rates in sixteen OECD countries, 1971–86 (percentage of total labour force)

	1971	*1972*	*1973*	*1974*	*1975*	*1976*	*1977*	*1978*	*1979*	*1980*	*1981*	*1982*	*1983*	*1984*	*1985*	*1986*
	%	%	%	%	%	%	%	%	%	%	%	%	%	%	%	%
USA	5.8	5.5	4.8	5.5	8.3	7.6	6.9	6.0	5.8	7.0	7.5	9.5	9.5	7.4	7.1	6.9
Japan	1.2	1.4	1.3	1.4	1.9	2.0	2.0	2.2	2.1	2.0	2.2	2.4	2.6	2.7	2.6	2.8
Germany[a]	0.9	0.8	0.8	1.6	3.6	3.7	3.6	3.5	3.2	3.0	4.4	6.1	8.0	7.0	7.2	7.0
France	2.6	2.7	2.6	2.8	4.0	4.4	4.9	5.2	5.9	6.3	7.4	8.1	8.3	9.7	10.2	10.4
UK[a]	3.6	4.0	3.0	2.9	4.3	5.6	6.1	5.9	5.0	6.4	9.8	11.3	12.5	11.7	11.2	11.1
Italy[b]	5.3	6.3	6.2	5.3	5.8	6.6	7.0	7.1	7.6	7.5	8.3	9.0	9.8	10.2	10.5	* *
Canada	6.1	6.2	5.5	5.3	6.9	7.1	8.0	8.3	7.4	7.4	7.5	10.9	11.8	11.2	10.4	9.5
Major 7 countries	3.7	3.8	3.4	3.7	5.4	5.4	5.4	5.1	4.9	5.5	6.4	7.8	8.2	7.4	7.3	* *

Australia	1.9	2.6	2.3	2.6	4.8	4.7	5.6	6.2	6.2	6.0	5.7	7.1	9.9	8.9	8.2	8.2
Austria	1.3	1.2	1.1	1.4	1.7	1.8	1.6	2.1	2.1	1.9	2.5	3.5	4.1	3.8	3.6	* *
Belgium	2.1	2.7	2.7	3.0	5.0	6.4	7.4	7.9	7.9	8.2	8.8	10.8	12.6	12.1	11.2	10.8
Finland	2.2	2.5	2.3	1.7	2.2	3.8	5.8	7.2	5.9	4.6	4.8	5.3	5.4	5.2	5.0	5.3
Netherlands[a]	1.3	2.2	2.2	2.7	5.2	5.5	5.3	5.3	5.4	6.0	8.5	11.4	12.0	11.8	10.6	9.9
Norway	1.5	1.7	1.5	1.5	2.3	1.8	1.5	1.8	2.0	1.6	2.0	2.6	3.4	3.1	2.6	2.0
Spain	3.1	3.1	2.5	2.6	3.6	4.6	5.2	6.9	8.5	11.2	13.9	15.8	17.2	20.0	21.4	21.0
Sweden	2.5	2.7	2.5	2.0	1.6	1.6	1.8	2.2	2.1	2.0	2.5	3.2	3.5	3.1	2.8	2.7
Switzerland	—	—	—	—	0.4	0.7	0.4	0.3	0.3	0.2	0.2	0.4	0.9	1.1	0.9	* *
Total of above countries	3.5	3.6	3.2	3.5	5.1	5.2	5.2	5.1	5.0	5.7	6.6	8.0	8.5	7.9	7.8	* *
Memorandum item																
EEC[c]	2.9	3.2	2.9	3.0	4.3	5.0	5.4	5.6	5.7	6.4	8.3	9.6	10.7	10.9	11.1	* *

Source OECD (1987) *Economic Outlook*, vol. 42, December, 190

a New series based on EEC Labour Force Surveys (see *Quarterly Labour Force Statistics*, no. 3, 1987)

b The existing series is no longer being updated pending the receipt of new data based on EEC Labour Force Surveys

c EEC countries shown (Germany, France, United Kingdom, Italy, Belgium, Netherlands, and Spain) are included in the area totals

Qualitative information (on definitions etc.)

5 ILO (1980) Technical Guide, vol. 2, Geneva.
6 ILO (1986) Statistical Sources and Methods, vol. 3, Economically Active Population, Employment, Unemployment And Hours of Work (Household Surveys), copyright 1986, International Labour Organisation, Geneva.

Table 3.8 Comparison of OECD (adjusted) and ILO (unadjusted) unemployment rates, 1974 and 1984

	1974		1984	
	ILO	OECD	ILO	OECD
	%	%	%	%
Australia	2.7	2.6	9.0	8.9
Austria	1.3	1.4	4.5	3.8
Belgium	3.1	3.0	14.1	12.1
Canada	5.4	5.3	11.3	11.2
Finland	1.7	1.7	6.2	5.2
France	2.8	2.8	9.7	9.7
Germany (FR)	2.6	1.6	9.1	7.0
Italy	5.4	5.3	10.0	10.2
Japan	1.4	1.4	2.7	2.7
Netherlands	3.5	2.7	14.1	11.8
Norway	1.5	1.5	3.2	3.1
Spain	2.9	2.6	20.6	20.0
Sweden	2.0	2.0	3.1	3.1
Switzerland	-	-	1.1	1.1
United Kingdom	2.6	2.9	11.7	11.7
United States	5.6	5.5	7.4	7.4

Source: ILO data from table 3.5
OECD data from table 3.7

4 WAGES AND EARNINGS

K. Holden

INTRODUCTION

This chapter examines the different ways in which the incomes from employment of workers are measured in official statistics and looks at recent international trends in these data. The major sources of international data on incomes are Main Economic Indicators, published monthly by the Organization for Economic Co-operation and Development (OECD), Paris, the Bulletin of Labour Statistics, published quarterly by the International Labour Office, Geneva, and the Monthly Bulletin of Statistics, published monthly by the United Nations, New York. The OECD has, until recently, published special supplements entitled Main Economic Indicators: Historical Statistics which include monthly, annual, and quarterly data for twenty years for OECD countries. The corresponding publications from the other two organizations, which include data for several years for a wider range of countries and for more detailed topics, are The Year Book of Labour Statistics (ILO, Geneva) and The Statistical Yearbook (UN, New York), both of which are published annually. Each year the ILO publishes, in a separate issue of the Bulletin of Labour Statistics, the results of its 'October Inquiry' - a major world-wide survey of wages and hours of work relating to 159 occupations in 49 industry groups, for more than 200 countries (as well as retail prices of 93 food items). A substantial revision and expansion of the Inquiry was introduced in 1985.

The two main areas of interest in this chapter are wage rates, which are the minimum agreed levels of cash payments in national collective agreements for one hour (or week, or month) of normal work, and earnings, which are basic wages plus any extra remuneration received by the workers. In the OECD literature the term 'pay rate' is sometimes used to denote what is more commonly called the wage rate. We adopt the term 'wage rate' here. From these definitions it will be obvious that, in cash terms, for any particular worker, the level of earnings will generally be higher than that of the wage rates. In practice this may not be apparent if index numbers are used to measure each of them.

Both ways of measuring incomes have their uses. Wage rates give a good indication of the minimum cash entitlements of adult workers, as stated in collective agreements. They are particularly relevant for industries where labour is not well organized and unions are weak, or for smaller countries where national agreements have a big impact on incomes. However, it is likely that few workers will actually receive the minimum indicated by the wage rate. Earnings are a more accurate guide to the total value of a worker's remuneration since they include overtime pay and any cash supplements receivable by groups of workers. For any individual worker, earnings are likely to vary from week to week, especially if there is an element of payment-by-results included in the pay structure, and they will also vary between individuals and with the number of hours worked.

Neither wage rates nor earnings are, in themselves, good indicators of the welfare of workers. This is because they ignore employer contributions to fringe benefits (pensions, reduced-price goods, etc.), deductions, and the effect of price changes. Deductions of taxes, health insurance, and social security contributions vary greatly between countries, between individuals, with the level of income and over time. In the United Kingdom a special index, known as the tax and price index,[1] is produced with the intention of measuring the increase in gross taxable income needed to compensate workers for any increase in prices, and so takes account of changes in direct taxes. There are no corresponding series for other countries. Similarly, international data on deductions is not easily available. However, there was a general tendency for deductions to increase in the 1960s and 1970s but the impression is that, with the tighter monetary control of the 1980s, the rate of increase has declined.

Also, wage rates and earnings are not a good guide to the costs of employing labour, since employers generally have to pay various taxes and health and social security contributions for their employees, as well as providing facilities at the workplace. The subject of labour costs is considered in detail in chapter 6.

Price changes affect the value of incomes. A rise in income of, say, 5 per cent may be balanced by a rise in prices of the same amount, leaving the worker no better or worse off. As data on consumer prices is easily available (see chapter 5 for details) it is possible to attempt to adjust wage rates and earnings to take account of price changes. This is normally done by 'deflating' incomes by dividing the index by an index of consumer prices in order to give a measure of 'real income' or spending power. However, the basic problem with index numbers, that is, whether they are appropriate for the purpose they are intended, still remains and any measure of real income is, at best, only an approximation to a measure of welfare.

The concept of 'wage drift' is also of interest. This is obtained as the difference between the annual percentage increase in earnings and the percentage increase in wage rates and it reflects the pressures which occur in the labour market. We return to this later in the chapter.

The group of countries covered in this chapter is Australia, Austria, Belgium, Canada, Denmark, Finland, France, Germany, Greece, Ireland, Italy, Japan, the Netherlands, New Zealand, Norway, Portugal, Spain, Sweden, Switzerland, the United Kingdom, the United States, and Yugoslavia.[2] While for most countries either wage rates or earnings are available, there are four countries (Austria, Belgium, Germany, and the UK) for which both series are published. This allow comparisons to be made to see if the differences between the two ways of measuring incomes appear to be important, and also for wage drift to be examined.

WAGE RATES

The definition of wage rates adopted by the OECD is the minimum cash entitlement of adult wage earners for one hour of normal work as laid down in collective agreements.[3] The countries for which data are available on wage rates are Australia, Austria, Belgium, France, Germany, Italy, the Netherlands, New Zealand, and the UK. In each case the data are for the whole country and refers to hourly wage rates in manufacturing industry, except for Austria (which also includes mining and from 1977 covers weekly rates), New Zealand (which records weekly wage rates for all industries), and Italy (which covers all industries from 1983). The series on wage rates go back at least to 1967 for most of our selection of countries and are monthly for Australia, Austria, Italy, the Netherlands, and the UK, and quarterly for Belgium, France, Germany, and New Zealand. The figures refer to the end of the month or quarter, with the exceptions of France (beginning of quarter) and Germany (end of first month of quarter). In our tables we limit consideration to the annual averages.

For each country, except France, the data are derived from collective agreements and so tend to omit the smallest firms and those sectors where labour is not well organized. The index is a weighted average of wage rates for different groups of workers, with the weights usually reflecting the total number of employees covered. The data on wage rates for France are based on records of establishments with ten or more employees. A sample, stratified by industry and by the number of employees, of establishments is selected and data on hourly wage rates for two successive quarters are collected for seven skill levels. Included with basic wages are bonuses paid to all workers and directly linked to basic rates. Other supplements, such as overtime premiums and expenses are omitted. Employment weights are used to obtain the aggregate figures.

There are slight variations in how wage rates are defined in the different countries. Skill premiums, cost-of-living allowances, and years-of-service payments are generally included, except for Belgium where even supplements paid to all workers are excluded. All countries exclude overtime payments. The treatment of retrospective agreements varies: for France and Italy they are ignored whereas, for the other countries, indices of pay rates for previous periods are subject to revision when the new agreement comes into force. New Zealand is the only country to include benefits in kind, such as free accommodation and cheap produce. Holiday pay, called 'vacation bonus' by the OECD, is specifically excluded by Australia but is included by Italy and the Netherlands. Germany includes the investment bonus, a special payment intended to promote investment in shares.

INTERNATIONAL COMPARISONS OF WAGE RATES

Our data on wage rates are given in table 4.1. The sources are the OECD publications Main Economic Indicators: Historical Statistics, 1964-83, and Main Economic Indicators, May 1987. There are no consistent figures for Australia before 1977 or for the United Kingdom after 1983. All the figures are index numbers with the common base of 1980 as 100. This does not mean that wage rates in these countries were all equal in 1980. Rather, it means that for convenience the values for each country are measured relative to the value in 1980. Valid comparisons can be made only by moving down a column and not across the table. Here we will limit discussion to broad trends. For most of the countries we examine, over the period shown in table 4.1 there are minor changes in the definitions of the industries covered and the weights used in forming the index numbers. However, since the data are the best that can be found on any sort of consistent basis, we will ignore these changes and take care not to place too much reliance on small differences when any conclusions are being discussed.

From table 4.1 we can immediately see that wage rates grew substantially in all the countries covered over the period 1970 to 1986. For each country the values for successive years always increase. The lowest value in 1970 is for Italy and, since this country also has the highest value

Table 4.1 Wage rates (1980=100)

	Australia	Austria	Belgium	France	Germany	Italy	Netherlands	NZ	UK
1970	**	37.8	32.0	26.7	45.8	15.8	39.0	26.2	22.7
1971	**	42.0	35.0	29.7	51.9	18.0	44.0	32.1	25.6
1972	**	47.0	40.0	33.0	56.3	19.8	49.0	35.1	29.1
1973	**	52.3	46.0	37.8	61.8	24.6	56.0	39.1	32.9
1974	**	58.8	56.0	45.2	69.3	30.2	66.0	44.6	38.5
1975	**	70.5	66.0	53.0	75.5	38.2	74.0	50.6	50.0
1976	**	77.4	75.0	60.4	79.7	46.2	81.0	56.6	59.9
1977	78.6	84.4	82.0	68.1	85.7	59.1	87.0	64.0	62.8
1978	83.9	89.4	87.0	76.9	89.6	68.6	92.0	73.0	74.2
1979	90.1	94.3	92.0	86.9	94.3	81.7	96.0	84.5	85.3
1980	100.0	100.0	100.0	100.0	100.0	100.0	100.0	100.0	100.0
1981	111.3	107.3	109.0	114.5	105.5	123.7	103.0	119.3	109.8
1982	127.5	115.3	117.0	131.9	110.2	144.1	110.0	133.4	117.6
1983	136.7	121.6	124.0	146.7	113.9	172.3	113.0	133.8	124.2
1984	147.0	126.9	130.0	158.0	117.0	192.0	114.0	136.9	**
1985	153.8	134.1	134.0	167.1	123.0	212.9	120.0	152.2	**
1986	161.5	141.3	136.0	174.0	127.5	223.1	122.0	176.0	**

Source: See text

Table 4.2 Annual growth of wage rates

	Australia	Austria	Belgium	France	Germany	Italy	Netherlands	NZ	UK	Mean
	%	%	%	%	%	%	%	%	%	%
1971	**	11.1	9.4	11.2	13.3	13.9	12.8	22.5	12.8	13.4
1972	**	11.9	14.3	11.1	8.5	10.0	11.4	9.3	13.7	11.3
1973	**	11.3	15.0	14.5	9.8	24.2	14.3	11.4	13.1	14.2
1974	**	12.4	21.7	19.6	12.1	22.8	17.9	14.1	17.0	17.2
1975	**	19.9	17.9	17.3	8.9	26.5	12.1	13.5	29.9	18.2
1976	**	9.8	13.6	14.0	5.6	20.9	9.5	11.9	19.8	13.1
1977	**	9.0	9.3	12.7	7.5	27.9	7.4	13.1	4.8	11.5
1978	6.7	5.9	6.1	12.9	4.6	16.1	5.7	14.1	18.2	10.0
1979	7.4	5.5	5.7	13.0	5.2	19.1	4.3	15.8	15.0	10.1
1980	11.0	6.0	8.7	15.1	6.0	22.4	4.2	18.3	17.2	12.1
1981	11.3	7.3	9.0	14.5	5.5	23.7	3.0	19.3	9.8	11.5
1982	14.6	7.5	7.3	15.2	4.5	16.5	6.8	11.8	7.1	10.1
1983	7.2	5.5	6.0	11.2	3.4	19.6	2.7	0.3	5.6	6.8
1984	7.5	4.4	4.8	7.7	2.7	11.4	0.9	2.3	**	5.2
1985	4.6	5.7	3.1	5.8	5.1	10.9	5.3	11.2	**	6.4
1986	5.0	5.4	1.5	4.1	3.7	4.8	1.7	15.6	**	5.2
Mean	8.3	8.6	9.5	12.4	6.6	18.0	7.4	12.6	14.0	10.8

Source: Table 4.1

for 1986, it is clear that, in money terms, wage rates have increased most for Italy over this period.

As the values in 1970 all differ it is not immediately clear where the largest changes have occurred and it helps if the annual percentage rate of growth is calculated. This enables the year-to-year fluctuations to be seen and details are given in table 4.2. The final column gives the average for each year. Taking this first, we can see that the annual growth in wage rates was particularly high in 1974 and 1975, with a further minor peak in 1980, but it reduced considerably by 1986.

In chapter 5 we discuss prices and find that there were large increases in oil prices in 1973-4 and 1979-81 which led to high inflation at these times. Since in negotiations workers normally attempt to maintain (or increase) real wages, the reaction to an increase in inflation is an increase in wage rates. However, during the 1970s many governments intervened in the wage-determination process in the hope of reducing inflation.[4] More recently wages have been squeezed by governments adopting generally tight monetary and fiscal policies, by restricting the effects of wage indexation agreements, and by limiting public-sector pay awards.[5]

The country with the highest rate of growth of wage rates is Italy, with an average value of 18 per cent per annum for 1970-86. Thus wage rates grew by a factor of 14 over this period. High values occurred throughout the period 1973-83, with a declining trend since then. For Italy, the highest rate for any individual year is 27.9 per cent for 1976-7.

The UK is the country with the next highest growth rate, averaging 14 per cent per annum, but notice that this is because of the high values attained before 1980 and that for 1980-3 it is down to 7.5 per cent per annum which is smaller than the averages for Australia, France, Italy, and New Zealand. This is the consequence of the Thatcher government's economic policy.[6]

The general ranking of countries, from highest to lowest average growth of wage rates, is Italy, the UK, New Zealand, France, Belgium, Austria, Australia, the Netherlands, and Germany. Thus the smallest increase was for Germany where wage rates rose by a factor of almost 3 between 1970 and 1986. For each country the average of the values since 1980 is always smaller than the value to 1980, showing the more recent general reduction in the growth of wage rates. In fact, the smallest growth rate in the later period is for the Netherlands which averages 3.4 per cent per annum. When the annual changes are considered for particular countries, rather surprisingly it is New Zealand which has the smallest figure. This is 0.29 per cent for 1982-3 which was during a period of strict wage restraint.[7]

Next, we make an allowance for the effect of price changes by dividing the index of wage rates by an index of consumer prices to give real wage rates. The results are presented in table 4.3. Again the base in 1980 equals 100 and so values over 100 indicate that real wage rates are higher than in 1980. For all the countries (except Australia where data are not available before 1977) there is an increase in real wage rates between 1970 and 1980 despite the inflation following the oil price rises of 1973-4 and 1979. Interestingly, real wage rates in New Zealand reached a peak in 1974 before declining for three years and it was not until 1981 that the 1974 value was exceeded. Since then the wage freeze has resulted in a decline, so that by 1986 real wage rates were still 12 per cent below the level of 1980. In fact, five countries, Australia, Belgium, the Netherlands, New Zealand, and the UK all show declines since 1980. In addition to the reasons already mentioned for New Zealand and the UK, possible explanations for

Table 4.3 Real wage rates (1980=100)

	Australia	Austria	Belgium	France	Germany	Italy	Netherlands	NZ	UK
1970	**	69.5	65.2	67.1	75.5	58.7	78.9	85.1	81.4
1971	**	73.3	68.2	70.7	81.2	63.6	82.9	94.4	83.7
1972	**	77.7	73.9	74.0	83.5	66.4	85.5	96.4	89.0
1973	**	80.3	79.6	79.1	85.7	74.8	90.5	99.2	92.9
1974	**	82.5	85.9	83.1	89.8	76.8	97.3	102.1	93.9
1975	**	91.2	89.8	87.2	92.3	82.9	99.1	100.8	98.2
1976	**	93.4	93.5	90.6	93.2	86.0	99.6	96.4	101.5
1977	101.9	96.0	95.5	93.4	96.7	93.2	100.5	95.4	91.8
1978	100.8	98.7	96.9	96.7	98.5	96.2	102.1	97.2	99.5
1979	99.2	100.3	98.1	98.6	99.5	98.9	102.2	98.9	100.9
1980	100.0	100.0	100.0	100.0	100.0	100.0	100.0	100.0	100.0
1981	101.5	100.5	101.3	101.0	99.2	104.2	96.5	103.4	98.1
1982	104.6	102.3	100.0	104.0	98.5	104.3	97.3	99.6	96.9
1983	101.9	104.6	98.4	105.5	98.5	108.5	97.2	93.0	97.7
1984	105.6	103.3	97.0	106.0	98.8	109.3	95.0	89.6	**
1985	103.4	105.7	95.4	105.8	101.7	111.6	97.8	86.3	**
1986	99.4	109.5	95.6	107.3	105.6	110.3	99.3	88.2	**

Source: Tables 4.1 and 5.3

this are the wage freeze of 1982-3 and the Accord between the government and the unions in Australia, the suspension of wage indexation in Belgium, and the agreement to reduce working hours instead of increasing wages in the Netherlands.[8] The remaining countries, Austria, France, Germany, and Italy have increases of 5 to 10 per cent by 1986.

Wage rates reflect the minimum that workers are paid for a normal week. As stated above, they do not directly measure the standard of living of the workers since this depends inter alia on earnings, taxes, and other deductions and prices. In the rest of this chapter we examine what has happened to earnings and in the next chapter we consider consumer prices.

EARNINGS

Data on earnings are available in cash values from the ILO and as index numbers from the OECD. We will consider the former briefly before devoting the rest of this section to the latter. In table 4.4 the level of earnings for manufacturing industry in 1984 in twelve countries is given in units of the national currency, together with the separate values (when published) for male and female workers. From these we can see that earnings are higher for males than for females. However, it is obvious that information on exchange rates is needed in order to be able to make comparisons between countries. Even with this information care must be taken in interpreting cash values and we defer to chapter 6 a more detailed consideration of the difficulties of comparing earnings levels in different countries. For the present, it is useful to turn to index numbers before examining the data on earnings in more detail.

Table 4.4 Cash value of earnings in manufacturing industry in 1984

Country	Per hour (h) or per month (m)	Value	Males	Females	Units
Austria	m	18,631.00	**	**	schillings
Belgium	h	281.78	299.66	223.25	francs
Canada	h	11.16	**	**	dollars
Finland	h	29.72	32.00	24.69	markkaa
Germany	h	15.49	16.50	12.00	marks
Greece	h	262.21	292.59	222.87	drachmas
Ireland	h	3.90	4.36	2.98	punts
Japan	m	292,255.00	365,561.00	152,519.00	yen
Norway	h	**	58.59	49.15	kroner
Sweden	h	49.33	**	**	kronor
United Kingdom	h	3.43	3.68	2.53	pounds
United States	h	9.19	**	**	dollars

Source: ILO (1987, 2), Bulletin of Labour Statistics, table 8, copyright 1987, International Labour Organisation, Geneva

The definition of earnings adopted by OECD is average cash remuneration paid per employed wage earner and per hour,[9] which can be abbreviated to hourly earnings. Data on earnings are published for Austria, Belgium, Canada, Denmark, Finland, Germany, Greece, Ireland, Japan, Norway, Portugal, Spain, Sweden, Switzerland, the United Kingdom, the United States, and Yugoslavia. Compared to wage rates, there is more scope for variation in the way in which earnings are defined and measured. However, there are some aspects where a common approach has been adopted for each country. The income covered includes basic pay, overtime pay (except for Switzerland), and bonuses, and, apart from Austria and Norway, benefits in kind are always excluded. Both full-time and part-time workers are included in the statistics with the exceptions of Germany, where only full-time workers are included, and Switzerland, where all workers employed more than twenty-five hours are included. There are no deductions of taxes except in the case of Yugoslavia where the series is total cash earnings after payments of direct taxes and social security contributions.

To simplify the discussion, table 4.5 presents a summary of the main differences between the definitions adopted by the various countries. Column 1 indicates whether monthly, weekly, or hourly earnings are measured, and in most cases it is hourly. Column 2 gives the frequency of publication, which is either monthly or quarterly. The ways in which earnings are measured are given in column 3. These generally correspond to the frequency of publication so that the monthly index for Denmark, for example, is measured over calendar months. There are a number of special cases listed of which we note that for Belgium the quarterly index is measured by the data for the third month of the quarter, for Germany by the data for the first month, and for Ireland by a week in the third month.

The industrial coverage of the earnings index is generally intended to be the manufacturing sector. Additional industries included are listed in column 4, with the most common one being mining. For some countries particular parts of manufacturing industry are omitted and these are given in column 5. The only ones which merit comment are 'handicraft' for Austria, where the handicraft sector is defined to include those areas 'where skilled labour has a priority over equipment'[10] and the fact that Northern Ireland is excluded for the UK.

The earnings index covers both male and female workers, except in the case of Norway where separate series are produced for males and females. We consider only the series for males here. In the period 1980-5 the index for males rose from 100 to 154, while that for females rose to 157 which suggests that the two series move closely together.

The data used in compiling the earnings index for each country are from surveys of establishments, with the exceptions of Belgium, where enterprises are sampled, and Switzerland, where the source is information concerning workers involved in accidents. In general a sample of establishments above some minimum size is selected, stratified by industry, region, and by number of employees, and all large firms are included. The information on earnings and hours worked is converted into hourly earnings and then aggregated, using the number of workers as weights. As with wage rates, there are a number of minor changes in the coverage and weights used in the earnings indices over the periods considered below. Again, we will assume that the series we have are the best that can be found in the circumstances and we will not place any importance on small changes in the values of earnings.

Back-pay is treated in different ways. Austria, Belgium, Japan,

Table 4.5 Earnings definitions across countries

Country	1 Definition	2 Published	3 Timing	4 Manufacturing plus	5 Excludes
Austria	monthly	monthly	month	mining, gasworks	handicraft
Belgium	hourly	quarterly	3rd month	mining, transport	-
Canada	hourly	monthly	last week	-	-
Denmark	hourly	monthly	month	mining	-
Finland	hourly	quarterly	quarter	mining, electricity	-
Germany	hourly	quarterly	1st month	-	pottery
Greece	hourly	quarterly	7th week	-	-
Ireland	hourly	quarterly	*	-	-
Japan	monthly	monthly	month	-	-
Norway	hourly	quarterly	quarter	-	dairy, females
Portugal	daily	quarterly	quarter	-	-
Spain	hourly	quarterly	quarter	construction, commerce	-
Sweden	hourly	monthly	2 weeks	mining	-
Switzerland	monthly	quarterly	quarterly	-	-
UK	weekly	monthly	last week	-	N. Ireland
USA	hourly	monthly	2nd week	-	-
Yugoslavia	monthly	monthly	month	mining	direct taxes

Source: Derived from OECD (1978) Main Economic Indicators: Sources and Methods, no. 29, May

* A week in the third month of each quarter

Norway, Spain, and the UK count it at the time when it is received, whereas the other countries include it only for the period for which it was due. This results in some of the published series being revised as back-pay is allocated over earlier periods.

Before examining the data on earnings we will consider briefly the factors which determine earnings. While the general level of activity in the economy and the conditions in the labour market of the particular industry are important, it is useful to focus on two factors which affect earnings: one relates to prices and the other to productivity. In wage negotiations, the workers usually argue for increases because of current (and expected) price increases. This link with prices may be institutionalized by indexation agreements. Therefore any external shocks, such as the oil-price rises in 1973-4 and 1979-81, which result in an increase in inflation, lead to attempts to increase earnings. Productivity is also relevant but, as it is determined mainly by investment in capital goods and the skill of management, it is unlikely to fluctuate much from year to year.

COMPARISONS OF EARNINGS

Data on the earnings index for seventeen countries are given in table 4.6 for 1970-86. There are no consistent figures for Portugal before 1973 and for Switzerland after 1983. As with table 4.1, the base year is 1980 and this value is set at 100. Again, comparisons are strictly only valid going up and down the columns and not across them, so that it is rates of growth which are of interest. These are presented in table 4.7. The first point to note is the fact that for Austria there was a decline in earnings in 1986.

The highest growth of earnings between 1970 and 1986 is for Yugoslavia, Greece, Portugal, and Spain, which all averaged 20 per cent or more per annum. For Yugoslavia and Greece there is an increase for 1981-6 as compared with 1971-6. This is in contrast to all the other countries covered which show a decline in the average growth rate of earnings after 1981. The growth rate of Yugoslavia is particularly high for the years 1983-6 when it takes the values 45.3 per cent, 76.9 per cent, and 105.4 per cent. While we discuss real earnings below, it is worth noting here that these four countries had high rates of inflation between 1970 and 1986 (see table 5.4). They also have a large labour force in agriculture and their tourist industries have benefited from the world-wide boom in tourism since the 1960s.

The remaining countries can be conveniently split into those which have the lowest growth rates of earnings (averaging below 8 per cent) and the rest. The countries in the first category are Switzerland, Germany, the USA, and Austria. They are characterized by generally restrictive monetary policy since the mid-1970s and, in the cases of Germany and the USA, are large countries whose policies have important implications for the rest of the world. The earnings growth rate for Switzerland is fairly constant throughout the data period, while there is a marked decline in the period since 1980 for the other three. The countries in the middle group, with growth rates varying between 8 per cent and 16 per cent are, in increasing order of average, Canada, Japan, Sweden, Belgium, Norway, Denmark, Finland, the UK, and Ireland. According to the OECD[11] the main reason for the general reduction in earnings growth in the 1980s was the way monetary policies did not accommodate the 1979-81 oil-price increases. Instead, unemployment rose and other commodity prices fell.

Next we compare the data on wage rates (table 4.1.) with that on earnings (table 4.6) for Austria, Belgium, Germany, and the UK. For

Table 4.6 Earnings (1980=100)

	Austria	Belgium	Canada	Denmark	Finland	Germany	Greece	Ireland	Japan
1970	37.3	30.0	37.0	26.6	26.0	46.0	16.0	18.0	29.4
1971	42.4	34.0	40.0	30.4	30.0	52.0	17.0	21.0	33.5
1972	47.3	39.0	43.0	34.3	34.0	56.0	19.0	25.0	38.7
1973	53.3	45.0	47.0	40.7	40.0	62.0	22.0	29.0	47.8
1974	61.8	55.0	54.0	49.4	49.0	69.0	27.0	35.0	60.2
1975	70.0	65.0	62.0	58.9	59.0	74.0	34.0	45.0	67.2
1976	76.4	73.0	70.0	66.4	68.0	79.0	44.0	53.0	75.4
1977	82.9	79.0	78.0	73.2	74.0	85.0	53.0	63.0	81.9
1978	87.6	85.0	84.0	80.7	79.0	89.0	65.0	72.0	86.7
1979	92.7	92.0	91.0	89.9	89.0	94.0	79.0	83.0	93.0
1980	100.0	100.0	100.0	100.0	100.0	100.0	100.0	100.0	100.0
1981	106.2	110.0	112.0	109.5	113.0	105.0	127.0	116.0	105.6
1982	112.7	117.0	125.0	120.3	125.0	110.0	170.0	133.0	110.7
1983	117.8	122.0	130.0	128.3	136.0	114.0	203.0	149.0	115.0
1984	123.7	128.0	136.0	134.4	150.0	117.0	256.0	164.0	120.3
1985	125.9	133.0	142.0	141.0	163.0	122.0	307.0	176.0	125.1
1986	119.0	136.0	146.0	147.7	173.0	126.0	346.0	188.0	128.0

	Norway	Portugal	Spain	Sweden	Switzerland	UK	USA	Yugoslavia
1970	34.0	**	12.1	36.6	54.6	23.8	46.0	16.0
1971	38.0	**	13.8	39.3	59.9	26.5	49.0	20.0
1972	41.0	**	16.1	45.2	65.2	29.9	53.0	23.0
1973	45.0	22.3	19.3	49.0	71.2	33.7	56.0	27.0
1974	53.0	32.4	24.5	54.4	81.1	39.5	61.0	35.0
1975	64.0	43.1	32.1	62.4	87.1	49.9	66.0	42.0
1976	74.0	51.1	41.7	73.6	88.5	58.2	72.0	48.0
1977	82.0	59.5	54.1	78.5	90.0	64.2	78.0	57.0
1978	89.0	69.3	68.9	85.3	93.1	73.4	85.0	68.0
1979	91.0	80.4	85.2	91.9	95.1	84.9	92.0	82.0
1980	100.0	100.0	100.0	100.0	100.0	100.0	100.0	100.0
1981	110.0	121.7	122.6	110.5	105.1	113.3	110.0	137.0
1982	121.0	143.5	142.0	119.2	111.6	125.9	117.0	175.0
1983	132.0	169.1	163.4	128.6	119.2	137.2	121.0	223.0
1984	143.0	199.7	182.5	140.9	**	149.2	126.0	324.0
1985	154.0	240.5	200.7	151.5	**	162.8	131.0	573.0
1986	169.0	**	222.7	162.7	**	175.3	134.0	1177.0

Source OECD (1987) Main Economic Indicators, May, and its special supplement, Historical Statistics, 1964–83

Table 4.7 Annual growth of earnings

	Austria	Belgium	Canada	Denmark	Finland	Germany	Greece	Ireland
	%	%	%	%	%	%	%	%
1971	13.7	13.3	8.1	14.3	15.4	13.0	6.3	16.7
1972	11.6	14.7	7.5	12.8	13.3	7.7	11.8	19.0
1973	12.7	15.4	9.3	18.7	17.6	10.7	15.8	16.0
1974	15.9	22.2	14.9	21.4	22.5	11.3	22.7	20.7
1975	13.3	18.2	14.8	19.2	20.4	7.2	25.9	28.6
1976	9.1	12.3	12.9	12.7	15.3	6.8	29.4	17.8
1977	8.5	8.2	11.4	10.2	8.8	7.6	20.5	18.9
1978	5.7	7.6	7.7	10.2	6.8	4.7	22.6	14.3
1979	5.8	8.2	8.3	11.4	12.7	5.6	21.5	15.3
1980	7.9	8.7	9.9	11.2	12.4	6.4	26.6	20.5
1981	6.2	10.0	12.0	9.5	13.0	5.0	27.0	16.0
1982	6.1	6.4	11.6	9.9	10.6	4.8	33.9	14.7
1983	4.5	4.3	4.0	6.7	8.8	3.6	19.4	12.0
1984	5.0	4.9	4.6	4.8	10.3	2.6	26.1	10.1
1985	1.8	3.9	4.4	4.9	8.7	4.3	19.9	7.3
1986	-5.5	2.3	2.8	4.8	6.1	3.3	11.4	6.8

	Japan	Norway	Portugal	Spain	Sweden	Switzerland	UK	USA	Yugoslavia
	%	%	%	%	%	%	%	%	%
1971	13.9	11.8	**	14.0	7.4	9.7	11.3	6.5	25.0
1972	15.5	7.9	**	16.7	15.0	8.8	12.8	8.2	15.0
1973	23.5	9.3	**	19.9	8.4	9.2	12.7	5.7	17.4
1974	25.9	17.8	45.3	26.9	11.0	13.9	17.2	8.9	29.6
1975	11.6	20.8	33.0	31.0	14.7	7.4	26.3	8.2	20.0
1976	12.2	15.6	18.6	29.9	17.9	1.6	16.6	9.1	14.3
1977	8.6	10.8	16.4	29.7	6.7	1.7	10.3	8.3	18.8
1978	5.9	8.5	16.5	27.4	8.7	3.4	14.3	9.0	19.3
1979	7.2	2.2	16.0	23.7	7.7	2.1	15.7	8.2	20.6
1980	7.5	9.9	24.4	17.4	8.8	5.2	17.8	8.7	22.0
1981	5.6	10.0	21.7	22.6	10.5	5.0	13.2	10.0	37.0
1982	4.8	10.0	17.9	15.8	7.9	6.2	11.1	6.4	27.7
1983	3.9	9.1	17.8	15.1	7.9	6.8	9.0	3.4	27.4
1984	4.6	8.3	18.1	11.7	9.6	**	8.7	4.1	45.3
1985	4.0	7.7	20.4	10.0	7.5	**	9.1	4.0	76.9
1986	2.3	9.7	**	11.0	7.4	**	7.7	2.3	105.4

Source: Table 4.6

Belgium and Germany the figures for 1970 and 1986 hardly differ between the two measures of income, while for Austria and the UK the differences are more substantial. The growth of earnings exceeds the growth of wage rates by 29 per cent for the UK, but for Austria it is wage rates which grow by 55 per cent more than earnings over the seventeen-year period. The conclusion from this is that the differences between wage rates and earnings do not follow a simple pattern. We return to this below in our discussion of wage drift.

In tables 4.8 and 4.9 the index of real earnings and its rate of growth are given. As with table 4.3, the nominal index has been divided by an index of consumer prices to take account of changes in prices. The prices data are given in table 5.3. From table 4.8 it can be seen that the countries with a more or less steady increase in real earnings between 1970 and 1986 are Finland, Greece (up to 1985), Japan, Spain, and the UK. The USA, Canada, and Denmark reached peak values rather earlier than the remaining countries, where the highest points are generally between 1979 and 1982. The three countries with particularly marked declines since 1980 are Austria, Portugal, and Yugoslavia, but in the last two of these there is a recovery to 1986.

Table 4.9 shows, in the pattern of minus signs, when the recessions hit the various countries. Coinciding with the oil price rises of 1973-4 and 1979-81 there were severe recessions in the USA, which were followed, at varying intervals, by sharp declines in the real-earnings growth in all the other countries. The most noteworthy negative values are for Portugal and Yugoslavia, with Austria and Greece having sharp drops in 1986. Spain is the only country for which all the values are positive, but even here there is evidence of sharp fluctuations in real-earnings growth. The general conclusion from this table is that there are large differences in the growth of real earnings in these countries over this period.

WAGE DRIFT

As was mentioned earlier in the chapter, wage drift is defined as the difference between the annual percentage increase of earnings and that of wage rates. At times when there is a surplus of labour, employers desiring to attract new staff have no need to offer workers anything above the minimum rates that are nationally agreed, and so there will be little or no wage drift. In contrast, if there are shortages of labour, an employer can make employment more attractive by offering special incentives, such as payment rates above the agreed minimum, longer holidays, or shorter hours. The higher the demand for labour, the greater is wage drift expected to be. There are, however, statistical problems in measuring wage drift since it is unlikely that the industries covered by an earnings index will be precisely the same as those covered by a wage-rate index. This is particularly so because wage-rates data are derived from collective agreements, whereas earnings data are obtained from surveys of firms.

We are able to observe wage drift for Austria, Belgium, Germany, and the UK, using the data presented in tables 4.1 and 4.6. For Belgium the wage-rates data cover manufacturing industry, whereas the earnings data also include mining and transport. In the case of the United Kingdom, the earnings data are for Great Britain, but the wage-rates data include Northern Ireland.

The wage-drift series are presented in table 4.10. Just under half of the figures are negative which, assuming it is not the result of the data problems previously mentioned, indicates that the demand for labour was low during this period and that wage rates were increasing faster than earnings. There are only two years, 1979 and 1980, for which all the values have the same sign. It is surprising that there are positive values for the UK for 1981-3, when the economy was going through the worst recession for fifty years. One possible explanation, put forward by Nickell,[12] is that an increase in the number of long-term unemployed does not result in a downward pressure on wages because the long-term unemployed are marginal participants in the labour market.

NOTES

1 See UK Central Statistical Office (1987) Sources and Methods for details.

2 There are no easily available data on pay rates or earnings for Iceland, Luxemburg, or Turkey. See OECD (1978) Main Economic Indicators: Sources and Methods, no. 29, May, for details of the data definitions for the countries listed in the text. More recent issues of the same publication contain up-to-date information for Australia (no. 30), Germany (no. 33), Netherlands (no. 35), and Spain (no. 38).

3 See OECD (1978), op. cit., 8.

4 For a review of incomes policies see K. Holden, D.A. Peel, and J.L. Thompson (1987) The Economics of Wage Controls, London: Macmillan.

5 See W. van Ginneken (1987) 'Wage policies in industrialized market economies from 1971 to 1986', International Labour Review, vol. 126, July-August: 395-6.

6 See T. Barker (1985) 'Forecasting the economic recession in the UK 1979-1982: a comparison of model-based ex ante forecasts', Journal of Forecasting, vol. 4: 133-52.

7 See Holden, Peel, and Thompson, op. cit., 21-2.

8 See van Ginneken, op. cit., for details.

9 See OECD (1978), op. cit.

10 See OECD (1978), op. cit., 22.

11 OECD (1987) Economic Studies, no. 8, Spring: 122.

12 S. Nickell (1987) 'Why is wage inflation in Britain so high?', Oxford Bulletin of Economics and Statistics, vol. 49; 103-27.

Table 4.8 Real earnings (1980=100)

	Austria	Belgium	Canada	Denmark	Finland	Germany	Greece	Ireland	Japan
1970	68.6	61.1	80.1	68.2	74.3	75.8	60.6	64.7	69.5
1971	74.5	66.3	84.2	74.1	81.1	81.4	62.7	69.3	74.4
1972	78.2	72.1	86.5	78.0	87.2	83.1	67.1	76.0	82.0
1973	81.9	77.9	87.9	84.8	90.9	86.0	67.3	79.2	90.7
1974	86.7	84.4	90.9	88.2	96.1	89.4	65.1	81.8	92.6
1975	90.6	88.4	94.2	96.6	98.3	90.5	72.2	86.9	92.6
1976	92.2	91.0	99.0	100.6	98.6	92.4	82.6	86.7	95.0
1977	94.3	92.0	102.1	98.9	96.1	95.9	88.6	90.8	95.3
1978	96.7	94.7	101.0	99.6	95.2	97.8	96.6	96.4	96.9
1979	98.6	98.1	100.2	101.0	98.9	99.2	98.6	98.1	100.2
1980	100.0	100.0	100.0	100.0	100.0	100.0	100.0	100.0	100.0
1981	99.4	102.2	99.6	100.3	100.9	98.8	102.0	96.3	100.7
1982	100.0	100.0	100.3	100.2	102.5	98.3	112.9	94.3	102.7
1983	101.3	96.8	98.6	99.8	102.3	98.6	112.2	95.6	104.7
1984	100.7	95.5	98.8	98.0	105.6	98.8	119.4	96.9	107.1
1985	99.2	94.7	99.2	98.1	107.9	100.8	120.0	98.6	109.2
1986	92.2	95.6	98.0	99.3	110.9	104.4	108.7	101.5	111.0

	Norway	Portugal	Spain	Sweden	Switzerland	UK	USA	Yugoslavia
1970	75.6	**	50.2	86.9	88.6	85.3	97.7	88.9
1971	79.2	**	52.9	90.8	91.3	86.6	99.6	100.0
1972	80.4	**	56.9	98.0	93.1	91.4	104.3	95.8
1973	81.8	92.9	61.3	100.2	93.6	95.2	103.9	93.1
1974	88.3	104.5	67.1	97.8	97.1	96.3	101.8	100.0
1975	95.5	115.5	75.4	102.8	97.8	98.0	101.1	97.7
1976	101.4	115.1	83.1	110.0	97.6	98.6	104.2	100.0
1977	102.5	105.3	86.6	106.1	98.0	93.9	106.1	101.8
1978	103.5	100.1	96.0	103.6	100.3	98.4	107.5	106.3
1979	101.1	93.7	98.4	103.1	99.0	100.5	104.4	106.5
1980	100.0	100.0	100.0	100.0	100.0	100.0	100.0	100.0
1981	96.5	101.4	107.0	99.5	98.7	101.3	99.8	97.2
1982	95.3	97.8	108.3	97.9	99.2	103.7	100.2	94.1
1983	96.4	91.8	111.2	97.0	102.8	107.9	100.5	85.4
1984	97.9	83.8	111.6	101.0	**	112.1	101.2	80.6
1985	100.0	84.6	112.8	101.5	**	115.1	101.6	82.0
1986	102.4	**	115.0	103.3	**	119.9	102.4	89.5

Source: Tables 4.6 and 5.3

Table 4.9 Growth of real earnings

	Austria	Belgium	Canada	Denmark	Finland	Germany	Greece	Ireland
	%	%	%	%	%	%	%	%
1971	8.7	8.5	5.1	8.7	9.1	7.4	3.5	7.0
1972	4.9	8.8	2.7	5.1	7.5	2.1	7.0	9.6
1973	4.7	8.0	1.5	8.8	4.3	3.5	0.2	4.3
1974	5.9	8.4	3.5	4.0	5.7	3.9	-3.3	3.2
1975	4.5	4.8	3.6	9.5	2.3	1.2	11.0	6.2
1976	1.8	2.9	5.1	4.2	0.2	2.1	14.4	-0.1
1977	2.3	1.0	3.1	-1.7	-2.5	3.8	7.4	4.7
1978	2.5	2.9	-1.1	0.7	-1.0	1.9	9.0	6.2
1979	2.0	3.6	-0.7	1.4	3.9	1.4	2.1	1.8
1980	1.4	2.0	-0.2	-1.0	1.1	0.9	1.4	1.9
1981	-0.6	2.2	-0.4	0.3	0.9	-1.2	2.0	-3.7
1982	0.6	-2.2	0.8	0.0	1.6	-0.5	10.7	-2.1
1983	1.3	-3.2	-1.8	-0.4	-0.2	0.3	-0.6	1.5
1984	-0.6	-1.3	0.3	-1.8	3.3	0.2	6.5	1.3
1985	-1.4	-0.9	0.4	0.1	2.2	2.0	0.5	1.8
1986	-7.0	1.0	-1.3	1.2	2.7	3.5	-9.4	3.0

	Japan	Norway	Portugal	Spain	Sweden	Switzerland	UK	USA	Yugoslavia
	%	%	%	%	%	%	%	%	%
1971	7.1	4.8	**	5.3	4.4	3.0	1.5	2.0	12.5
1972	10.1	1.5	**	7.6	8.0	2.0	5.6	4.8	-4.2
1973	10.6	1.8	**	7.7	2.2	0.4	4.1	-0.4	-2.8
1974	2.1	8.0	12.5	9.6	-2.4	3.8	1.2	-2.0	7.4
1975	-0.1	8.1	10.6	12.3	5.1	0.6	1.8	-0.8	-2.3
1976	2.6	6.1	-0.4	10.2	7.0	-0.2	0.6	3.1	2.4
1977	0.4	1.1	-8.5	4.2	-3.6	0.5	-4.9	1.8	1.8
1978	1.6	1.0	-4.9	10.9	-2.3	2.3	4.8	1.3	4.4
1979	3.5	-2.3	-6.4	2.5	-0.5	-1.4	2.1	-2.8	0.2
1980	-0.2	-1.1	6.7	1.6	-3.0	1.1	-0.5	-4.2	-6.1
1981	0.7	-3.5	1.4	7.0	-0.5	-1.3	1.3	-0.2	-2.8
1982	2.0	-1.3	-3.6	1.2	-1.6	0.5	2.4	0.4	-3.2
1983	2.0	1.1	-6.1	2.6	-1.0	3.7	4.1	0.3	-9.2
1984	2.3	1.7	-8.7	0.4	4.1	**	3.8	0.7	-5.7
1985	1.9	2.1	0.9	1.1	0.5	**	2.6	0.4	1.7
1986	1.7	2.4	**	2.0	1.7	**	4.2	0.7	9.2

Source: Table 4.8

Table 4.10 Wage drift

	Austria	Belgium	Germany	UK
	%	%	%	%
1971	2.6	4.0	-0.3	-1.4
1972	-0.4	0.4	-0.8	-0.8
1973	1.4	0.4	0.9	-0.3
1974	3.5	0.5	-0.8	0.2
1975	-6.6	0.3	-1.7	-3.5
1976	-0.6	-1.3	1.2	-3.2
1977	-0.5	-1.1	0.1	5.5
1978	-0.3	1.5	0.2	-3.8
1979	0.3	2.5	0.4	0.7
1980	1.8	0.0	0.3	0.6
1981	-1.0	1.0	-0.5	3.5
1982	-1.3	-1.0	0.3	4.0
1983	-0.9	-1.7	0.3	3.4
1984	0.6	0.1	-0.1	**
1985	-3.9	0.8	-0.9	**
1986	-10.8	0.8	-0.4	**

Source: Tables 4.2 and 4.7

5 CONSUMER PRICES

K. Holden

INTRODUCTION

In this chapter we consider the ways in which consumer prices are measured and we compare the rates of inflation in a number of countries over the period since the early 1970s. Most of the available data on prices comes originally from the government statistical offices in each country, and generally their publications include the widest and most detailed sets of information. However, collections of international statistics are published by the Organization for Economic Co-operation and Development (OECD), Paris, in the monthly issues of Main Economic Indicators and in its special supplement, Historical Statistics; by the United Nations, New York, in the Monthly Bulletin of Statistics and the annual Statistical Yearbook; by the International Monetary Fund, Washington, in the monthly International Financial Statistics; and by the International Labour Office, Geneva, in the quarterly Bulletin of Labour Statistics and the annual Year Book of Labour Statistics. In some cases the same information is duplicated, but in others the timing of the series differs or the series are processed (for example, by seasonal adjustment, or by using alternative information on exchange rates) so that the final results can differ.

The major non-governmental sources of prices data are the market-research publications of different countries. In general, these consist of specially commissioned studies of the market for particular products and usually include prices charged in the shops. By their nature, these studies are one-off publications and, as well as being difficult to find, can be expensive to buy. However, some examples of regular marketing publications, each published by Euromonitor Publications Ltd, London, are the monthly Market Research Great Britain and, with more emphasis on cross-country comparisons, the annual International Marketing Data and Statistics and European Marketing Data and Statistics. Much of the market research information is also included in on-line marketing databases, such as MAID (by Market Analysis and Information Database Systems Ltd, London) and the Dialog Data Base (by Dialog Information Services Inc., Palo Alto, Calif., USA). As these cover a wide range of other information we do not examine them further here.

Before looking at the data we will review some of the complications that make price comparisons difficult. There are major problems in trying to measure prices at different times or in different countries. It is not enough simply to find out the price of, say, bread in two countries and to use that, converted at the current exchange rate, as a guide to prices. This is because not only does the price of most products vary at any particular time in different parts of a country (say in different shops or between city and rural areas) but also we know that exchange rates vary over time and that, when prices in two countries are compared, some products can be relatively cheap in one country, while others are relatively expensive because of differences in, for instance, tastes and climate. Additionally, as time passes, the pattern of spending changes as new goods become available. For example, sales of candles are much lower now than they were one hundred years ago, while sales of electricity have increased.

What is required is some overall measure of the price level in each country so that valid comparisons can be made. This is done by compiling an index of consumer prices which effectively measures the price of a 'shopping basket' of goods. Before discussing the details of this, we consider the nature of a price index. By definition, a price index is an average of the prices of a number of products and is usually standardized by taking a base-year value of 100. It is intended to indicate how the price of a group of typical products varies over time. It does not necessarily give a good representation of the price of every product it covers. When two periods of time are compared, some prices will have risen, some will be unchanged, while others will have fallen. This is particularly true of seasonal foods such as fresh fruit and vegetables. Including different selections of products in the index or using different methods of calculation will produce different results. An index number is not a precision tool. It is an attempt at an approximation to some concept which is difficult to quantify and so is to some extent subjective, relying on the judgement of the person compiling it.

MEASURING CONSUMER PRICES

Consumer prices are the prices of those goods purchased by individuals or households, rather than by institutions, governments, or firms. The basic problem in measuring consumer prices is deciding which goods to include in any index and what importance to give to each item. The methods used by OECD countries are explained in Consumer Price Indices: Sources and Methods and Historical Statistics (special issue, March 1984, OECD, Paris). Summarized information for 146 countries is presented in Statistical Sources and Methods, vol. 1, Consumer Price Indices (second edition 1987, International Labour Office, Geneva). As stated above, the approach generally adopted is to compare the cost of a 'shopping basket' of goods in successive months. That is, a list of products which are typically purchased by families is identified (from a household survey) and their prices are recorded at different times. The two steps are usually separated: a survey of households is used to find out what products people buy and in what quantities (the weights), and then each month or quarter a survey of shops is undertaken to determine the prices. While the first survey covers different households as it progresses, the same shops are usually included in each prices survey.

For any country, the first step in measuring consumer prices is to decide on the extent of the geographical coverage. For most of the OECD countries the intention is to cover the whole population. However, in some cases it is prices in the cities which are of interest. This is partly because of their importance in size, relative to the rest of the country, and partly because many products are not easily available in rural areas. Thus, Iceland limits coverage to Reykjavik; Turkey, France, and Portugal to urban areas, and Australia to the eight state capitals, while small towns are excluded in the USA (below 2,500), Greece (below 10,000), and Canada (below 30,000).

Expenditure patterns vary with household composition and so this is a factor in the choice of which households are covered. Initially, interest in consumer prices arose from concern about the cost of living for workers.[1] This concern focused on the effects of poverty on workers' families and so information relating to particular household sizes was collected. In many cases single-person households were ignored since they were not thought to have problems. Households of at least two persons are covered by the consumer prices data for Iceland, Japan, the Netherlands, and Spain. The remaining OECD countries attempt to cover all sizes of household. For the USA, the old consumer-price index was compiled for use in wage negotiations and covered only urban households with their main income from the employment of wage earners. These made up 32 per cent of the non-institutional population. In 1978 this was replaced by the 'all urban' consumer-price index which covers 80 per cent of that population.[2]

Another relevant factor is the size of income. To avoid the distorting effects of including a small number of highly paid workers, Australia, Luxemburg, the Netherlands, Portugal, Spain, and the UK limit coverage to low- and middle-income groups. Portugal requires the head of the household to be in the labour force. In the UK pensioner households with at least three-quarters of their income from state benefits are excluded. Australia, France, Luxemburg, the Netherlands, and Portugal include only wage and salary earners, while Japan excludes agricultural workers. The rest of the OECD countries cover the whole population and so include pensioners, the self-employed, and those with high unearned incomes.

Once the scope of the coverage is defined, a survey of consumers' expenditure is conducted to determine which items are purchased and what the relative importance of each item is. These surveys typically involve the household members filling in diaries showing their purchases over the period of the survey (usually 10-14 days) and/or being interviewed on their expenditure patterns. An alternative approach, adopted by Italy, is to use national accounts data to determine the relative weights of food, durable goods, transport, etc. Thus, for example, if all the petrol used in a country is imported, then expenditure on petrol can be estimated from data on stocks, quantities of imports, and taxation paid by motorists, rather than by surveys of consumers. This method is thought to be more reliable than a survey in the case of expenditure on alcoholic drink, where the consumers may be reluctant to admit their true expenditure. Denmark, France, and Sweden combine surveys and national accounts data.

The result of these procedures is that a list is obtained of items which are purchased by households and also details of how important each item is in the household budget. These lists are updated at regular intervals (usually each year) because of the changing composition of purchases over time. For example, expenditure on motor cars has risen dramatically since 1950, while (relative) expenditure on bread has fallen. By adjusting the weights frequently there are no abrupt jumps in the consumer price index and gradually changing consumption patterns are accommodated. In the UK the weights for the retail-prices index are formed from the average weights found by the Family Expenditure Survey over the past three years.[3]

The number of items on the list varies between 105 for Australia and 770 for Norway. For most OECD countries the prices of these items are collected each month by a survey. There is a minor problem over what to do about special reductions in prices, such as discounts and sales. Belgium, Italy, Japan, and Luxemburg ignore these, while Switzerland includes them only if they are permanent. The other OECD countries use the actual prices in the shops, taking account of any reductions. Taxes on expenditure paid by the consumer are usually included.

Rather than combine the actual prices together, they are transformed into index numbers with a common base, and these are then combined using the weights from the household survey. The composite index number formed is a Laspeyres price index, which weights the prices by the base-year quantities. Since the base year is continually changing, this procedure is thought to give a reasonably good measure of current consumer prices. The only exception is Belgium, where the aggregate index is an arithmetic average of the item indices. In this case there is an implied weighting in the way in which terms are selected for inclusion in the index.

There are a number of problems over the treatment of certain items of expenditure. Most countries make adjustments so that there are no strong seasonal variations in the index. In the case of fresh fruit and vegetables, where the prices fluctuate seasonally, either varying monthly weights are used or the products are excluded from the index. With seasonal clothing and other products which may not be available throughout the year, the usual method is to carry forward the last normal price during the off-season, except for Norway which carries forward the average price for the season.

The treatment of owner-occupied dwellings is also a problem since the occupier does not pay rent to himself, whereas a tenant in an identical house will pay rent to the landlord. That is, even though their consumption of housing services is the same, their expenditure on housing differs. Half of the OECD countries exclude the owner-occupers' rent from consumers' expenditure, while the remainder take account of the imputed rent as a charge on the owner.

All forms of saving are excluded from consumers' expenditure. In particular, expenditure on house purchase, life insurance premiums, and contributions to pension funds are omitted. The only insurance that is included is that concerning motor cars.

A final problem concerns changes in quality. If a new version of a product goes on sale, it may be possible for the statisticians to decide how a price change can be allocated to a quality component and a pure price component. This is easily done if both versions are on sale simultaneously. The quality effect can then be incorporated into the base price so that the index remains unchanged, while the price effect changes the value of the index. In other cases the new version simply replaces the old item in the index.

The result of all these differences in definitions and measurement methods is that the price-index numbers for different countries are not reliable measures of the impact of changes in prices on particular households. Any international comparisons must be made with care.

PENSIONER HOUSEHOLDS IN THE UK

To illustrate some of these points we present in table 5.1 the values for 1986 of three consumer price indices for the United Kingdom, with the base 15 January 1974=100. These are the general index of retail prices, which is the commonly accepted measure of the overall price level, and two special indices, for one-person and two-person pensioner households. These are defined as households with the members receiving at least three-quarters of their income from national retirement or similar pensions. The reason these households have been identified for special treatment is the general concern about poverty and the effects of inflation on pensioners. The weights change each year and in table 5.1 we include the weights allocated for 1980, which is half-way through our data period. For

Table 5.1 Price variations between households in the UK: weights for 1980 and values for 1986 with 15 January 1974 = 100

	General index		Pensioner households			
			One-person		Two-person	
	Weights	Value	Weights	Value	Weights	Value
All items (excluding housing)	876	371.5	1000	382.0	1000	379.2
Food	214	347.3	409	340.1	416	334.6
Alcoholic drink	82	430.6	23	428.4	44	445.3
Tobacco	40	584.9	32	587.2	52	584.4
Fuel and light	59	560.0	182	510.4	142	511.3
Durable household goods	69	266.7	46	281.3	44	281.2
Clothing and footwear	84	229.2	70	231.0	71	239.5
Transport and vehicles	151	390.1	32	472.1	63	428.5
Miscellaneous goods	74	409.2	89	468.4	84	456.0
Services	62	400.5	96	357.0	72	368.4
Meals bought and consumed outside the home	41	439.5	21	432.7	12	432.9

Source: Employment Gazette, vol. 95 (1987) July: table 6.7; and vol. 88 (1980) April; 381-2, 448-9.

pensioners, the items which have high weights relative to the general index are food, fuel and light, miscellaneous goods, and services. These reflect the differences in spending patterns between the groups. The pensioners' indices are calculated quarterly and exclude housing, since recipients of state pensions normally qualify for allowances which cover housing costs. As well as the 'all items' index, indices for ten categories of expenditure are given.

Since the base is 15 January 1974 = 100, table 5.1 shows the effects of price changes over thirteen years. The all-items figures indicate that prices rose more for pensioners than for the general public over this period, but not by much. The average annual rates of inflation are 10.6, 10.9 and 10.8 per cent. When the detailed categories of expenditure are considered there is more variation. The pensioners' inflation rates are lower than the general rate for food, fuel and light, services, and meals bought and consumed outside the home, but are higher for durable household goods, clothing and footwear, transport and vehicles, and miscellaneous goods. The largest differences are for transport and vehicles where the index for one-person pensioner households increased by an average of 12.7 per cent per annum, while the value for two-person pensioner households was 11.8 per cent and for the general index 11.0 per cent. This category has a low weight for pensioners. However, despite these wide variations for the detailed categories of expenditure and the differences in weights, our general conclusion is that, over this thirteen-year period, there was little difference in the inflation rates for pensioner households compared to the general index of retail prices in the UK. This is some consolation when comparisons of index numbers are made.

CROSS-COUNTRY COMPARISONS

From our discussion of how consumer prices are measured it will be apparent that there are problems in making comparisons within countries over different periods and these will be more serious when comparisons are made across countries. The different ways of defining the coverage by geographical location, and household size and income levels mean that, strictly, no valid comparisons can be made. However, it is important to remember that the peculiarities of consumer-price measurement arise for each country because the statisticians are trying to get as good a measure as possible. Their estimates of inflation can have important political implications at the time of elections and, through their effects on wage negotiations (especially where there is index-linking of wages[4]), can have important consequences for the future of the economy. The adjustments they make, such as ignoring those workers with high incomes, or omitting agricultural and self-employed workers, are made for good reasons and it is sensible to take their data as being the best that can be compiled in the circumstances. In view of this, we can make use of the data on consumer prices as a general guide to trends between countries while being careful about putting too much emphasis on minor differences.

All the discussion about consumer prices concerns index numbers. That is, there are no measures of absolute prices but only of prices relative to the price level in the base year. Also, an index number is an average and so is not intended to represent individual behaviour. This means that it is not possible to make direct comparisons of the cost of living in different countries using index numbers. The way in which the definitions differ between countries and what is included in the items which make up the 'basket' of commodities examined should also lead us to be suspicious of any comparisons. The best that can be done is to compare the rate of change of consumer prices (or the rate of inflation) across countries. Such comparisons show broad trends and can be a good guide to the state of the economy and the well-being of the people.

Our first international comparison of prices is for the disaggregated price indices for twenty-five countries given in table 5.2. These are taken from the Year Book of Labour Statistics, 1986 (International Labour Office, Geneva). As well as the general index of consumer prices for each country, indices for food, fuel and light, clothing and rent are included. From what was said above it is not surprising that there are minor differences in the ways these categories are defined and measured. Perhaps the biggest of these is in the way 'rent' includes repairs and maintenance for Austria, Australia, Ireland, and Sweden but not for the other countries.

The data in table 5.2 are for the years 1975 and 1984, and have as the common base 1980=100. Therefore a low value for 1975 implies a high rate of inflation to 1980, and similarly a high value for 1984 shows there has been a high rate of inflation since 1980. For the general index the lowest value in 1975 is for Turkey, which indicates a rise in prices by a factor of 7.5 to 1980. The highest value is for Switzerland, where prices rose by only 12 per cent over the same period. The corresponding countries for 1980 to 1985 are Iceland, with prices rising by a factor of 7.2, and Japan where prices rose by a total of 14.4 per cent.

Turning now to the data on food prices, since food is an important component of household budgets, taking typically 20-30 per cent of total expenditure, and possibly more for lower income households (see table 5.1), we see that the food index moves closely with the general index. In contrast, except for Finland, prices of fuel and light have all increased by more than the general index over the period 1975-85, as a direct result of the various disruptions in the international oil market. The remaining two categories, clothing and rent, do not show any consistent pattern between countries, with some increases being below and others above the general index. It is also interesting to notice that two countries with almost identical values for the general index, Australia and Denmark, have quite different price changes for the various sectors.

CONSUMER PRICES AND INFLATION

The data on consumer prices for twenty-five countries are given in table 5.3 as index numbers with 1980=100 as base. The wide variations between the values for 1970 and those for 1986 indicate different experiences of inflation over this period. Taking 1970 to 1980, a low value for 1970 shows a high price increase to 1980, the base year. The countries with the highest increase are Iceland and Turkey, where the price level changed by more than a factor of 16, and those with the lowest increase are Switzerland and Germany, where the change is just over 60 per cent. The other countries with large price increases are Yugoslavia, Spain, Greece, Italy, the UK and Ireland. For the period since 1980, a large increase is indicated by a high value for 1986, and those countries with the highest increases are Yugoslavia, Iceland, Turkey, Portugal, and Greece. Those with the lowest increases are Japan, Germany, the Netherlands, Switzerland, Austria, and the USA.

The annual percentage rates of change of prices, or inflation rates, are given in table 5.4. There is just one negative value - for Germany in 1986 - when prices actually fell. Otherwise all the changes are positive, with the largest individual value being for Turkey in 1980, where prices more than doubled in a single year. The table also includes the mean value for each country, and for each year. As we saw in table 5.3, the highest inflation rates are for Iceland and Turkey, and the lowest are for Germany and Switzerland. The annual averages show peaks in 1974 and 1980, with fluctuations between these years and a general decline to 1986.

One possible explanation of these changes in inflation is the way oil prices have varied. Because of the importance of oil to developed economies and the delays between the change in crude oil prices and this change reaching the final consumer, an increase in oil prices feeds through to general inflation with a lag of up to two years. Between 1970 and 1974, oil prices rose by a factor of 6, mainly because of the Middle East war of 1973 and its repercussions. After 1974 oil prices remained relatively stable until 1979 when successive increases led to a peak in 1981. Since then they have declined.[5]

However, the explanation of why inflation occurs is complex and any link between oil prices and consumer prices is likely to be modified by changes in other commodity prices and monetary and fiscal developments.[6] From table 5.4 it is clear that the experience of inflation differs between the various countries, and so care must be taken in reaching general conclusions.

Table 5.2 International disaggregated price indices (1980 = 100)

Country	General Index		Food	
	1975	1985	1975	1985
Australia	60.5	148.9	56.8	145.1
Austria	77.3	126.9	80.1	122.5
Belgium	73.5	140.5	79.8	140.6
Canada	65.8	143.1	62.1	134.5
Denmark	60.9	146.4	73.7	148.0
Finland	60.3	150.5	59.8	157.3
France	60.8	158.0	62.0	158.9
Germany	82.0	121.0	84.9	116.9
Greece	47.0	255.9	44.4	262.7
Iceland	17.5	719.9	17.6	788.0
Ireland	51.8	178.3	52.8	160.2
Italy	46.4	190.3	48.4	180.3
Japan	72.9	114.4	76.6	114.4
Luxemburg	74.5	139.8	75.5	143.2
Netherlands	74.5	122.7	79.4	117.8
New Zealand	50.2	176.3	46.1	165.7
Norway	66.8	155.0	70.2	163.9
Portugal	37.3	284.3	37.9	285.5
Spain	42.6	178.0	47.5	178.3
Sweden	60.7	153.8	61.3	172.9
Switzerland	89.1	123.3	86.9	128.9
Turkey	13.3	337.9*	14.3	380.4*
UK	51.1	141.5	52.1	131.4
USA	65.3	130.6	69.4	121.8
Yugoslavia	43.4	694.0	41.3	720.8

Source: ILO (1986) Year Book of Labour Statistics, tables 23-27, copyright (1986), International Labour Organisation

* Value for 1984

Fuel, light		Clothing		Rent	
1975	1985	1975	1985	1975	1985
59.1	177.9	61.1	138.0	62.0	154.2
69.0	141.8	79.5	117.7	69.1	141.3
58.4	165.9	78.6	131.8	**	146.3
53.2	178.4	70.0	123.8	76.4	136.5
38.9	151.0	69.3	134.0	62.3	147.0
58.7	137.1	62.1	141.9	72.2	150.7
51.0	176.2	62.8	157.8	64.4	155.9
67.7	133.4	80.1	118.4	82.6	123.9
43.9	244.4	47.2	292.5	53.8	191.4
22.0	975.7	16.7	708.6	18.7	627.6
43.9	181.5	56.0	150.8	69.3	168.2
34.6	219.8	44.5	190.4	51.3	207.9
59.8	110.6	76.0	116.1	69.3	120.8
62.2	155.0	70.0	131.8	**	**
63.2	160.1	73.6	113.8	67.8	138.8
32.8	156.7	51.2	158.3	59.2	197.0
49.2	186.4	66.9	143.3	72.3	151.3
23.0	342.0	61.1	256.0	61.4	**
**	**	36.8	177.2	55.6	155.3
43.1	173.1	72.0	132.9	61.1	144.4
64.8	118.7	92.9	120.0	93.4	127.4
**	**	12.7	328.9*	**	**
47.1	166.1	61.2	108.5	46.6	167.8
52.6	139.7	79.8	115.5	71.7	138.1
37.3	726.8	46.5	742.0	48.1	500.6

Table 5.3 Consumer prices (1980 = 100)

	Australia	Austria	Belgium	Canada	Denmark	Finland	France	Germany
1970	37.1	54.4	49.1	46.2	39.0	35.0	39.8	60.7
1971	39.4	56.9	51.3	47.5	41.0	37.0	42.0	63.9
1972	41.7	60.5	54.1	49.7	44.0	39.0	44.6	67.4
1973	45.6	65.1	57.8	53.5	48.0	44.0	47.8	72.1
1974	52.6	71.3	65.2	59.4	56.0	51.0	54.4	77.2
1975	60.5	77.3	73.5	65.8	61.0	60.0	60.8	81.8
1976	68.7	82.9	80.2	70.7	66.0	69.0	66.7	85.5
1977	77.1	87.9	85.9	76.4	74.0	77.0	72.9	88.6
1978	83.2	90.6	89.8	83.2	81.0	83.0	79.5	91.0
1979	90.8	94.0	93.8	90.8	89.0	90.0	88.1	94.8
1980	100.0	100.0	100.0	100.0	100.0	100.0	100.0	100.0
1981	109.7	106.8	107.6	112.5	109.2	112.0	113.4	106.3
1982	121.9	112.7	117.0	124.6	120.0	122.0	126.8	111.9
1983	134.1	116.3	126.0	131.9	128.5	133.0	139.0	115.6
1984	139.4	122.9	134.0	137.6	137.1	142.0	149.3	118.4
1985	148.8	126.9	140.5	143.1	143.7	151.0	158.0	121.0
1986	162.4	129.0	142.3	149.0	148.7	156.0	162.2	120.7

	Greece	Iceland	Ireland	Italy	Japan	Luxemburg	Netherlands	NZ
1970	26.4	5.6	27.8	26.9	42.3	52.6	49.4	30.8
1971	27.1	6.0	30.3	28.3	45.0	55.0	53.1	34.0
1972	28.3	7.0	32.9	29.8	47.2	57.9	57.3	36.4
1973	32.7	8.0	36.6	32.9	52.7	61.4	61.9	39.4
1974	41.5	12.0	42.8	39.3	65.0	67.3	67.8	43.7
1975	47.1	18.0	51.8	46.1	72.6	74.5	74.7	50.2
1976	53.3	23.0	61.1	53.7	79.4	81.8	81.3	58.7
1977	59.8	30.0	69.4	63.4	85.9	87.3	86.6	67.1
1978	67.3	44.0	74.7	71.3	89.5	90.0	90.1	75.1
1979	80.1	64.0	84.6	82.6	92.8	94.1	93.9	85.4
1980	100.0	100.0	100.0	100.0	100.0	100.0	100.0	100.0
1981	124.5	152.0	120.5	118.7	104.9	108.1	106.7	115.4
1982	150.6	226.0	141.1	138.1	107.8	118.2	113.1	134.0
1983	181.0	421.0	155.8	158.8	109.8	128.4	116.2	143.9
1984	214.4	552.0	169.3	175.6	112.3	134.3	120.0	152.8
1985	255.8	728.0	178.5	190.7	114.6	139.8	122.7	176.3
1986	314.7	889.0	185.2	202.3	115.3	140.2	122.9	199.6

Table 5.3 (cont.)

	Norway	Portugal	Spain	Sweden	Switzerland	Turkey	UK	USA	Yugoslavia
1970	45.0	18.2	24.1	42.1	61.6	6.1	27.9	47.1	18.0
1971	48.0	19.7	26.1	43.3	65.6	7.1	30.6	49.2	20.0
1972	51.0	21.5	28.3	46.1	70.0	8.0	32.7	50.8	24.0
1973	55.0	24.0	31.5	48.9	76.1	9.4	35.4	53.9	29.0
1974	60.0	31.0	36.5	55.6	83.5	11.1	41.0	59.9	35.0
1975	67.0	37.3	42.6	60.7	89.1	13.3	50.9	65.3	43.0
1976	73.0	44.4	50.2	66.9	90.7	15.4	59.0	69.1	48.0
1977	80.0	56.5	62.5	74.0	91.8	19.7	68.4	73.5	56.0
1978	86.0	69.2	74.8	82.3	92.8	29.5	74.6	79.1	64.0
1979	90.0	85.8	86.6	89.1	96.1	46.2	84.5	88.1	77.0
1980	100.0	100.0	100.0	100.0	100.0	100.0	100.0	100.0	100.0
1981	114.0	120.0	114.6	111.0	106.5	136.0	111.9	110.2	141.0
1982	127.0	146.8	131.1	121.7	112.5	172.8	121.4	116.8	186.0
1983	137.0	184.3	147.0	132.6	115.9	221.2	127.1	120.4	261.0
1984	146.0	238.3	163.6	139.5	119.3	337.9	133.1	124.5	402.0
1985	154.0	284.3	178.0	149.2	123.3	481.6	141.5	128.9	699.0
1986	165.0	317.4	193.7	157.5	124.2	707.7	146.2	130.9	1315.0

Source: OECD (1987) Main Economic Indicators: Sources and Methods May, and Historical Statistics, 1964–83

Table 5.4 Annual inflation rates

	Australia	Austria	Belgium	Canada	Denmark	Finland	France	Germany
	%	%	%	%	%	%	%	%
1971	6.2	4.6	4.5	2.8	5.1	5.7	5.5	5.3
1972	5.8	6.3	5.5	4.6	7.3	5.4	6.2	5.5
1973	9.4	7.6	6.8	7.6	9.1	12.8	7.2	7.0
1974	15.4	9.5	12.8	11.0	16.7	15.9	13.8	7.1
1975	15.0	8.4	12.7	10.8	8.9	17.6	11.8	6.0
1976	13.6	7.2	9.1	7.4	8.2	15.0	9.7	4.5
1977	12.2	6.0	7.1	8.1	12.1	11.6	9.3	3.6
1978	7.9	3.1	4.5	8.9	9.5	7.8	9.1	2.7
1979	9.1	3.8	4.5	9.1	9.9	8.4	10.8	4.2
1980	10.1	6.4	6.6	10.1	12.4	11.1	13.5	5.5
1981	9.7	6.8	7.6	12.5	9.2	12.0	13.4	6.3
1982	11.1	5.5	8.7	10.8	9.9	8.9	11.8	5.3
1983	10.0	3.2	7.7	5.9	7.1	9.0	9.6	3.3
1984	4.0	5.7	6.3	4.3	6.7	6.8	7.4	2.4
1985	6.7	3.3	4.9	4.0	4.8	6.3	5.8	2.2
1986	9.1	1.7	1.3	4.1	3.5	3.3	2.7	-0.2
Mean	9.7	5.6	6.9	7.6	8.8	9.9	9.2	4.4

Table 5.4 (cont.)

	Greece	Iceland	Ireland	Italy	Japan	Luxemburg	Netherlands	NZ	Norway
	%	%	%	%	%	%	%	%	
1971	2.7	7.0	9.0	5.2	6.4	4.6	7.5	10.4	6.7
1972	4.4	16.7	8.6	5.3	4.9	5.3	7.9	7.1	6.3
1973	15.5	14.3	11.2	10.4	11.7	6.0	8.0	8.2	7.8
1974	26.9	50.0	16.9	19.5	23.3	9.6	9.5	10.9	9.1
1975	13.5	50.0	21.0	17.3	11.7	10.7	10.2	14.9	11.7
1976	13.2	27.8	18.0	16.5	9.4	9.8	8.8	16.9	9.0
1977	12.2	30.4	13.6	18.1	8.2	6.7	6.5	14.3	9.6
1978	12.5	46.7	7.6	12.5	4.2	3.1	4.0	11.9	7.5
1979	19.0	45.5	13.3	15.8	3.7	4.6	4.2	13.7	4.7
1980	24.8	56.3	18.2	21.1	7.8	6.3	6.5	17.1	11.1
1981	24.5	52.0	20.5	18.7	4.9	8.1	6.7	15.4	14.0
1982	21.0	48.7	17.1	16.3	2.8	9.3	6.0	16.1	11.4
1983	20.2	86.3	10.4	15.0	1.9	8.6	2.7	7.4	7.9
1984	18.5	31.1	8.7	10.6	2.3	4.6	3.3	6.2	6.6
1985	19.3	31.9	5.4	8.6	2.0	4.1	2.3	15.4	5.5
1986	23.0	22.1	3.8	6.1	0.6	0.3	0.2	13.2	7.1
Mean	17.0	38.5	12.7	13.6	6.6	6.4	5.9	12.4	8.5

	Portugal	Spain	Sweden	Switzerland	Turkey	UK	USA	Yugoslavia	Mean
	%	%	%	%	%	%	%	%	
1971	8.2	8.3	2.9	6.5	16.4	9.7	4.5	11.1	6.7
1972	9.1	8.4	6.5	6.7	12.7	6.9	3.3	20.0	7.5
1973	11.6	11.3	6.1	8.7	17.5	8.3	6.1	20.8	10.0
1974	29.2	15.9	13.7	9.7	18.1	15.8	11.1	20.7	16.5
1975	20.3	16.7	9.2	6.7	19.8	24.1	9.0	22.9	15.2
1976	19.0	17.8	10.2	1.8	15.8	15.9	5.8	11.6	12.1
1977	27.3	24.5	10.6	1.2	27.9	15.9	6.4	16.7	12.8
1978	22.5	19.7	11.2	1.1	49.7	9.1	7.6	14.3	11.9
1979	24.0	15.8	8.3	3.6	56.6	13.3	11.4	20.3	13.5
1980	16.6	15.5	12.2	4.1	116.5	18.3	13.5	29.9	18.9
1981	20.0	14.6	11.0	6.5	36.0	11.9	10.2	41.0	15.7
1982	22.3	14.4	9.6	5.6	27.1	8.5	6.0	31.9	13.8
1983	25.5	12.1	9.0	3.0	28.0	4.7	3.1	40.3	13.7
1984	29.3	11.3	5.2	2.9	52.8	4.7	3.4	54.0	12.0
1985	19.3	8.8	7.0	3.4	42.5	6.3	3.5	73.9	11.9
1986	11.6	8.8	5.6	0.7	46.9	3.3	1.6	88.1	10.7
Mean	19.7	14.0	8.6	4.5	36.5	11.0	6.7	32.3	12.7

Source: Table 5.3

NOTES

1 See G.S. Simpson and K. Taswell (1986, 2) 'Revision of the ILO October Inquiry: Retail Prices Part', Bulletin of Labour Statistics, ILO, p. IX.

2 See Monthly Labor Review (1987), vol. 110, no. 7, July: 55.

3 See UK Central Statistical Office (1987) Sources and Methods or 'A short guide to the retail prices index', Employment Gazette (1987), vol. 95, August: 393-406 for details.

4 See H. Suzuki (1980) 'Wage indexation in industrialized market economies', International Labour Review, vol. 119: 455-66.

5 Statistics on oil prices are included in the United Nations Monthly Bulletin of Statistics and in the monthly International Financial Statistics. For a discussion of the oil market see P.R. Odell (1987) 'The prospect for oil prices and the energy market', Lloyds Bank Review, July: 1-14.

6 For a detailed discussion of recent developments in commodity prices and international inflation see 'Costs, prices and profits' in OECD (1987), Economic Outlook, June: 37-9.

6 LABOUR COSTS

George F. Ray

In this chapter we discuss various aspects of labour costs: what is the true cost to the employer - that is, the take-home pay of the employee, plus all kinds of additional, social, and other charges; how can these costs be compared internationally; what is the significance of labour costs in the international competitiveness, and what other factors influence the latter?

SOURCES OF INFORMATION

The national statistical service in all developed countries provides the basic statistical information on wages and earnings in the various sectors of the national economy, although the details and the frequency of publication vary. Usually earnings in industry are the most detailed. In the United Kingdom, the Employment Gazette (Department of Employment) is the basic source of most details, many of which are included in the Monthly Digest of Statistics as well as, on an annual basis, in the Annual Abstract of Statistics. In the United States, the Bureau of Labor Statistics publishes Employment and Earnings, and similar publications exist in other countries.

Whilst not as up to date as the national sources, a convenient service is provided by the Statistical Office of the European Communities in Luxemburg in the form of two of their regular publications: Eurostat - Hourly Earnings and Eurostat - Labour Costs in Industry. The International Labour Office in Geneva also publishes useful summary statistics, though with a longer delay, as does the Statistical Office of the United Nations in its Monthly Bulletin of Statistics and annual statistical yearbook, although this is restricted to the most important indicators.

A valuable and convenient source of information is the annual publication of the Swedish Employers' Confederation (SAF) in Stockholm, Wages and Total Labour Costs for Workers - International Survey. The main task of this nationwide Swedish organization is to conduct collective wage bargaining and to support employers' associations and individual companies in their negotiations. The pay statistics complied by it are accepted by all parties concerned, including the trade unions, as bases for their negotiations; the statistics comprise comprehensive data for sixteen advanced countries in comparable forms. This publication has been used as the main source of the international comparisons in this chapter and the permission given by SAF to use its data for this purpose is gratefully acknowledged.

There are, of course, several other secondary or tertiary sources for the relevant statistics. One of these is, for example, the quarterly National Institute Economic Review published in London by the National Institute of Economic and Social Research (NIESR), which gives in its statistical appendix annual (for a period of about ten years), quarterly (for the most recent years), and monthly (recent months, UK only) information on weekly earnings by employees in the UK economy, hourly earnings in UK manufacturing, and average earnings in the six largest industrial countries (USA, Canada, Japan, France, Germany, and the UK).

Definition of labour costs

Two basic concepts of labour costs are distinguished in what follows. Wages for time worked covers time rates, piece rates, shift supplements, overtime payments, regularly paid bonuses, and premia, in fact all that constitutes 'take-home pay' before tax.

Total labour costs include, apart from wages for time worked, all additional costs to the employer. These latter are considered as social charges; they vary greatly from country to country and represent the following:

pay for time not worked (annual leave, public holidays, etc.);

other cash payments and payments in kind;

employers' social security expenses; these can be statutory or collectively agreed, contractual and non-obligatory social security contributions for schemes covering pensions, sickness, injuries at work, unemployment, and family allowances;

cost of vocational training;

cost of welfare services;

taxes of a social nature (for example in Italy);

taxes regarded as labour costs (for instance, the building-research contribution in Sweden);

any other labour costs carried by the employer and not classified elsewhere.

Whilst information on wages and earnings is fairly readily available in the national statistical sources mentioned above, the compilation of costs of a non-wage nature is less straightforward; these have been evaluated and determined after processing material that is partly available in the sources mentioned, and partly from the producers of national or international statistics.

LABOUR COSTS IN BRITAIN

Table 6.1 presents selected indicators: weekly earnings in the whole UK economy and hourly earnings in manufacturing, social charges, the average weekly hours worked, and retail prices, as well as the exchange rate of the pound sterling. With the exception of social charges, all indicators are shown in the form of an index, taking 1976 as equalling 100. The summary message of the table is this: earnings (that is, wages) more than doubled from 1971 to 1976 and then just about trebled in the following ten years to 1986. In the whole period, with the exception of one or two years, wages rose faster than inflation, as measured by the retail-price index, indicating the real increase in earnings. The number of actual hours worked per week has not changed markedly, apart from downward fluctuations in the years of recession.

Table 6.1 Labour costs in Britain: selected indicators, 1971 and 1976-86 (1976=100)

	Weekly earnings in the whole economy[a]		In manufacturing: Hourly earnings[a]		In manufacturing: Social charges[b]	In manufacturing: Average weekly hours worked[a]	Retail prices[a]		$/£[a]	£ effective rate IMF index[a]
		%		%	%			%		
1971	41.7		44.6		21	102.2	51.8		134.8	150.8
1976	100.0		100.0		27	100.0	100.0		100.0	100.0
1977	109.1	(9.1)	109.5	(9.5)	29	100.8	115.7	(15.7)	96.7	94.9
1978	123.2	(12.9)	126.5	(15.5)	31	100.5	125.3	(8.3)	106.1	95.3
1979	142.4	(15.6)	146.6	(15.9)	33	100.4	142.3	(13.6)	117.1	102.2
1980	171.8	(20.6)	176.7	(20.5)	35	97.1	167.8	(17.9)	128.7	112.2
1981	194.0	(12.9)	202.3	(14.5)	43	95.8	187.8	(11.9)	112.2	111.0
1982	212.2	(9.4)	222.1	(9.8)	43	97.6	203.9	(8.6)	96.7	105.7
1983	230.1	(8.4)	240.6	(8.3)	43	98.5	213.3	(4.6)	84.0	97.3
1984	244.2	(6.1)	258.8	(7.6)	43	99.7	223.8	(4.9)	74.0	91.9
1985	264.8	(8.4)	281.8	(8.9)	**	100.2	237.4	(6.1)	71.8	91.5
1986	285.7	(7.9)	304.1	(7.9)	**	99.8	245.5	(3.4)	81.2	85.2

Source: For column 3: wages and total labour costs for workers, Swedish Employers' Confederation, Stockholm; for exchange rates: National Institute Economic Review; for others: Employment Gazette (Department of Employment)

a 1976=100 (in brackets: percentage change on previous year)
b As percentage of earnings

EXCHANGE RATES

As the last two columns of table 6.1 indicate, the exchange rate of pound sterling fluctuated appreciably between 1971 and 1986. In the table the rate is shown in two ways: against the US dollar and in the form of an index (produced by the International Monetary Fund) which shows its movements against the trade-weighted rates of the currencies of the UK's main trading partners. Both measures indicate the significant fall in the value of the pound between 1971 and 1977, the sharp increase in its rate in 1978-81 - years when oil production in the British section of the North Sea rose rapidly - and the gradual erosion that followed until 1986 when the parity of the pound improved vis-à-vis the weakening dollar, though not against other currencies.

The exchange rate has been included in this table because of its importance from the point of view of international trade. British exports - indeed, any country's exports - compete in international markets on the basis of exchange rates. Therefore, if labour costs are to be compared internationally, they first have to be converted into some common denominator, some common currency, applying the appropriate exchange rate. The already quoted Swedish publication offers just such a comparison: the labour-cost data of all countries covered there are shown in national currencies, as well as converted into Swedish currency, using official exchange rates. The consistent method of this type of conversion into a common currency makes possible the international comparison of labour costs.

THE LIMITATIONS OF THE COMPARISON

Whilst such a comparison is legitimate for analysing, on a comparable basis, the differences in total hourly labour costs, its limitations should be borne in mind. First, although the exchange rates in financial markets provide a common standard of measurement, they relate strictly to international trade, that is, the export markets where the products or services embodying the local labour input of the exporting country meet and compete with other countries' similar products or services; they may not be an accurate reflection of competitive domestic purchasing power, because of the differences in the national price structures. Thus, the domestic purchasing power of wages for time worked may not be assessed accurately on the basis of these data; any more precise comparison -aimed, for example, at comparing standards of living or the local purchasing power of wages in different countries - requires much more elaborate data stemming from detailed exercises which apply country A's prices to country B's consumption pattern (and/or vice versa), thereby estimating 'purchasing power parities'.

The usefulness of the international comparison of labour costs that follows is limited, however, from other angles too. It shows how much one hour of labour in manufacturing industry, or elsewhere, costs the employer. It does not show the output achieved (in other words, the production performed, the value added) during that hour. The latter depends on the level of labour productivity, usually measured by output per person or output by person-hour worked. This varies a great deal by country even in the very same industry or activity. Whilst changes in productivity are generally fairly easy to find in national statistics, the comparison of the levels of productivity is again a complex and difficult procedure. Later in this chapter we will present an attempt to demonstrate the importance of productivity-level differences and their impact on the interpretation of labour-cost comparison.

There are further components of the price of competing products or services, the costs of primary-material input, other production costs (such as transportation), and of course profits. These vary from country to country too; no allowance has been made for them in this chapter, which concerns labour costs alone. Similarly, no allowance has been made for differences in non-price factors. Apart from the price, many other factors are taken into consideration before any international transaction is concluded, particularly a major one, such as product design, technical performance, delivery dates, after-sales service, the supply of parts and components, and so forth. In their aggregate, these non-price factors may be as important as the price of the product; because of their complex nature they defy quantification but can be decisive in the ever sharpening sphere of international competition.

Table 6.2 Hourly wages in manufacturing, 1971-84 (UK=100)

	1971	1974	1976	1978	1980	1982	1984
United States	226	185	199	177	126	167	205
Canada	206	187	223	173	122	163	193
Japan	73	110	121	150	92	104	132
France	74	87	107	109	91	88	90
Germany	121	145	157	169	127	119	122
Italy	74	79	85	94	77	80	90
Austria	64	82	101	109	82	81	85
Belgium	97	127	159	172	132	112	111
Denmark	149	189	227	226	160	147	150
Finland	89	106	133	110	92	100	110
Ireland	**	**	87	90	81	85	92
Netherlands	104	132	155	166	121	114	114
Norway	135	160	206	194	140	147	156
Sweden	167	172	213	179	128	122	123
Switzerland	114	148	176	201	141	150	158

Source: Wages and total labour costs for workers: International Survey, Stockholm: Swedish Employers' Confederation.

General notes to the international tables Data in national currencies have been converted at annual average exchange rates (see text). Finnish data include mining and electricity; Japanese data represent total cash earnings. Germany means the Federal Republic (West Germany) throughout.

LABOUR COSTS INTERNATIONALLY COMPARED

By means of the method described above - national data converted into a common denominator - labour costs in the countries covered can be compared. This comparison is shown in table 6.2 for hourly wages (that is, take-home pay before personal income tax) and table 6.4 for total hourly wage costs including social charges; in these two tables the costs are indicated in relation to the UK, that is, in the form of an index taking the UK data as 100 in each year. The social charges, which link employees' earnings to employers' costs, are given in table 6.3, expressed as percentages of earnings. These three tables cover the countries in North America, Japan, and Western Europe (though, with the exception of Italy, not Southern Europe). Detailed figures are given for selected years in the period 1971-84, with a provisional 1986 estimate for the most important indicator, total labour costs.

In 1971, hourly wages in seven (out of fifteen) countries were lower than in the UK; in 1984 in only four of them: France, Italy, Austria, and Ireland. In three countries, Belgium, Finland, and particularly Japan, wages in these terms were below the British level in 1971 but had risen above it by a later date. However, when allowance is made for social charges, the situation changes markedly because of the very different extent of social charges. The higher charges in France, Italy, and Austria - where social charges are about twice as high as in the UK (table 6.3) - make total labour costs more than 20 per cent higher than in the UK. Indeed, as indicated in table 6.3, whilst social charges in the UK are higher than those in North America and Japan, they are lower than in most West European countries.

The combined effect of the differences in hourly wages and social charges is reflected in relative total hourly labour costs. The comparison in table 6.4 indicates that since the early 1970s, total hourly labour costs in the UK have been the lowest among this group of the sixteen most important industrial countries, with the exception of Ireland (and Japan in the early 1980s, due entirely to exchange rate movements). Total labour costs in Germany, the USA, the Scandinavian and Benelux countries (and probably also Switzerland) were about 50 per cent or more higher than in the UK; French, Italian, and Japanese costs exceeded the UK level by less, 20-30 per cent. Thus, in these terms, the UK has become the 'cheap labour' country in the industrial camp.

UNIT LABOUR COSTS

So far the analysis has been aimed at hourly labour costs. However, as already explained above, output during that hour - the value added in the manufacturing process - differs in the various countries depending on the level of productivity. Although labour costs are relatively low in the UK, so is the level of productivity as compared with other leading industrial countries. If low labour costs offer an advantage in international competitiveness, low productivity offsets it. The combination of the two indicates the labour cost of one unit of production. Table 6.5 shows how productivity level differences affect the comparison of labour costs per unit of output.

The table starts with total hourly labour costs in the manufacturing industries of five leading industrial countries, the USA, Japan, and the three largest European countries. This is followed by the estimated level of output per hour worked in 1980, the year for which the original

Table 6.3 Social charges, 1971-84: percentages of hourly wages

	1971	1974	1976	1978	1980	1982	1984
United States	27	30	33	34	35	36	36
Canada	20	22	24	26	25	28	28
Japan	16	15	17	19	18	19	18
France	67	74	79	81	80	80	80
Germany	51	61	68	74	76	78	81
Italy	91	101	102	95	89	86	86
Austria	76	80	84	86	87	90	92
Belgium	63	70	74	80	81	82	82
Denmark	17	21	21	21	25	26	29
Finland	30	43	53	56	60	60	59
Ireland	**	**	30	29	33	35	35
Netherlands	69	73	77	79	79	79	79
Norway	36	43	41	45	48	48	50
Sweden	29	42	50	61	66	67	70
UK	21	23	27	31	35	43	43

Source: As for table 6.2. Switzerland not available.

Table 6.4 Total hourly labour costs in manufacturing,[a] 1971-86 (UK=100)

	1971	1974	1976	1978	1980	1982	1984	1986[b]
United States	236	195	209	182	126	158	194	161
Canada	204	186	217	167	113	146	173	134
Japan	69	103	112	137	80	86	109	129
France	102	123	151	151	121	110	114	122
Germany	151	191	208	223	165	147	153	173
Italy	116	129	136	141	108	104	117	127
Austria	93	120	146	155	106	108	115	127
Belgium	130	176	219	236	176	142	140	149
Denmark	144	186	217	210	148	129	135	144
Finland	95	139	161	131	109	112	123	132
Ireland	**	**	89	82	80	80	87	95
Netherlands	145	186	217	227	160	142	142	156
Norway	151	186	230	215	153	152	163	164
Sweden	178	198	253	221	170	142	147	154

Source: As for table 6.2. Switzerland not available

a Including social charges and all other costs to the employers
b Provisional

Table 6.5: Unit labour costs in manufacturing, 1980 (UK=100)

	(1) Total hourly labour costs[a]	(2) Labour productivity (output per hour)[b]	Unit labour costs[c]
United States	126	273	46 (61)
Japan	80	196	41 (75)
France	121	193	63 (68)
Germany	165	255	65 (74)
Italy	108	173	62 (83)

Source: Table 6.4.

a Including social charges
b The estimates of comparable 1980 productivity levels have been taken from the special issue on British comparative productivity of the National Institute Economic Review (1982), issue no. 101, August
c 1:2. The figures in brackets are crude provisional estimates for 1986

calculations, as quoted in the note to the table, were carried out. The estimates indicate that in the USA and Germany hourly productivity in 1980 was more than twice the level in Britain, in Japan and France almost twice that level, and that Italian productivity was also only somewhat lower than that in France. Thus, whilst labour costs in these countries (with the exception of Japan) are considerably higher than those in the UK, much more is produced there in the same time and therefore the eventual labour cost of one unit of production is lower than in the UK. The difference in 1980 was very significant; provisional estimates, given by bracketed figures in the table, seem to indicate that the gap between the British and other unit labour costs had narrowed by 1986, in some cases only marginally (for example, France) but in others (such as Japan or Germany) quite appreciably - the different changes in productivity and movements in the exchange rates have caused the gap to diminish. However, these changes can hardly influence the conclusion that the UK's relative advantage of low labour costs is outweighed by the higher productivity in the other countries shown. Estimates seem to indicate that a comparison with the Benelux and Scandinavian countries would show very similar results.

WOMEN'S EARNINGS

The wage figures discussed above concern adult men and women. Women's average earnings are generally lower than those of men. Statistics in every single country demonstrate this. The difference is mainly caused by the fact that there are many types of work in manufacturing that carry higher pay but are not usually performed by women; another reason might be that women are paid less than men for the same kind of work, a practice that used to be fairly general in the past but has been changing recently in favour of equal pay.

Table 6.6 indicates women's wages in manufacturing, as a percentage of wages paid to men. International comparison is made difficult by the different pattern of women's participation in the activities of various industries within manufacturing which pay different wage levels. Nevertheless, it seems that, as related to men's wages, women's average earnings are lower in each of the countries shown, although the difference varies quite appreciably, from Japan where women earn only half of men's wages, to Sweden where the difference between the two is a mere 10 per cent. The UK is at the lower end of the range for Western Europe - in most European countries women earn more (in relation to men) than in the UK.

Table 6.6 Women's hourly wages in manufacturing, 1971-84, as a percentage of men's wages

	1971	1974	1976	1978	1980	1982	1984
Japan	53	52	51	51	49	49	49
France	76	76	76	76	77	78	78
Germany	70	71	72	72	73	73	73
Italy	76	78	82	84	85	86	86
Belgium	68	69	72	71	70	72	73
Denmark	77	84	84	85	86	85	86
Finland	71	73	73	75	75	77	77
Ireland	**	**	61	64	68	68	70
Netherlands	61	70	75	75	75	75	75
Norway	75	77	79	80	82	83	84
Sweden	83	84	85	87	90	90	89
Switzerland	65	66	66	66	66	67	67
UK	58	64	69	70	68	69	68

Source: As for table 6.2. United States, Canada, and Austria not available.

LABOUR COSTS BY INDUSTRY

The Swedish publication already cited contains comparable information for fifteen industries within manufacturing for all the countries covered. This abundance of detail makes possible further analyses in various directions. Some of them are shown in table 6.7. In part (i) of the table, total (1984) labour costs in these industries are shown in the same way as in previous tables, that is, as related to costs in the UK. The usefulness of this data is obvious: manufacturers/exporters are primarily interested in comparable labour costs in their own industry and not so much in manufacturing generally.

The second part of the table indicates, first, the extent to which total hourly labour costs in each of the industries shown are higher in the continental European countries, and also in the OECD area (which includes North America and Japan), than they are in the UK. Second, the pattern of labour costs is analysed, showing their level in various industrial sectors as related to the average costs in total manufacturing. This is shown for the UK, for the continental European countries, and for the OECD. Finally, the last two lines illustrate the extent to which this pattern differs in the UK

Table 6.7 Total labour costs by industry, 1984

	All manufacturing	*Food*	*Beverages*	*Textiles*	*Clothing*[b]	*Leather*	*Footwear*	*Wood, furniture*	*Paper*	*Printing publishing*	*Chemicals*[d]	*Mineral products*[f]	*Base metals*	*Engineering*	*Shipbuilding*	*Motor vehicles*
	ISIC3	311-2	313	321	322	323	324	33	341	342	35	36	37	38	3841	3843
(i) Britain = 100																
USA	194	191	208	179	183	183	147	174	213	140	191	202	228	212	206	258
Canada	173	164	181	174	161	137	130	182	204	121	151	181	199	179	219	184
Japan	109	98[a]	. .	167	92	119[c]	. .	94	115	94	130	113	138	107	121	113
France	114	116	110	128	138	132	120	110	122	98	107[e]	120	117	114	117	111
Germany	153	133	126	162	172	156	140	157	150	116	141	140	142	152	155	165
Italy	117	130	109	142	155	151	119	118	129	105	110	113	117	115	149	106
Austria	115	134	. .	119	117	104	101	115	122	. .	109	125	124	112	. .	107
Belgium	140	137	120	150	162	158	143	139	156	109	134	145	161	144	144	141
Denmark	135	134	151	163	183	175	. .	137	140	131	117	128	. .	130	. .	. .
Finland	123	123	99	134	148	137	117	121	148	100	102	115	123	115	120	. .
Ireland	87	94	111	103	95	126	84	78	. .	77	90	105	82	83	. .	94
Netherlands	142	. .	135	171	157	. .	. .	135	. .	111	144	138	151	133	136	119
Norway	163	157	149	182	208	178	156	162	154	162	150	159	148	163	161	. .
Sweden	147	156	126	182	211	201	166	154	162	119	130	147	136	140	143	133

	All manufacturing	*Food*	*Beverages*	*Textiles*	*Clothing*[b]	*Leather*	*Footwear*	*Wood, furniture*	*Paper*	*Printing publishing*	*Chemicals*[d]	*Mineralsi products*[f]	*Base metals*	*Engineering*	*Shipbuilding*	*Motor vehicles*
	ISIC3	311-2	313	321	322	323	324	33	341	342	35	36	37	38	3841	3843
(ii) The pattern of costs: averages by industry, excl. UK																
Europe[g]	131	131	124	149	159	152	127	130	143	113	121	130	130	137	141	122
OECD[g]	137	136	135	150	156	151	129	134	151	114	129	138	144	143	152	140
Manufacturing=100																
UK (GB)	100	92	114	72	58	67	75	88	105	136	113	101	117	103	108	115
Europe	100	100	95	114	121	116	97	99	109	86	92	99	99	105	108	93
OECD	100	99	99	109	114	110	94	98	110	83	94	101	105	104	111	102
UK – Europe	. .	−8	+19	−42	−63	−49	−22	−11	−4	+50	+21	+2	+18	−2	0	+22
UK – OECD	. .	−7	+15	−37	−56	−43	−19	−10	−5	+53	+19	0	+12	−1	−3	+13

Source: as for table 6.2

[a]Including beverages and tobacco.

[b]Excluding footwear

[c]Including footwear.

[d]Including petroleum, coal, rubber and plastic products.

[e]Excluding petroluem refineries.

[f]Non-metallic.

[g]All countries listed above. Arithmetic averages.

ISIC 3 International Standard Industrial Classification.

from that in Europe and the OECD: as related to average labour costs in manufacturing, labour costs in the UK are relatively high in the drink, printing/publishing, chemical, base metal, and motor industries. In all other industries the British costs are relatively lower (except in engineering and shipbuilding, where the difference is negligible).

LABOUR COSTS IN CONSTRUCTION

We complete this chapter by adding a brief comparison of labour costs in the building and construction industries (International Standard Industrial Classification Division 5 - this is not included in the manufacturing industries discussed so far). In table 6.8 the first three columns show hourly earnings, compared in the same way as in tables 6.2 and 6.4 for the manufacturing industries, followed by indications of the level of earnings in the construction industries as compared with those in manufacturing. The last three columns give total hourly labour costs in construction, including all social charges (which in some countries are not quite identical with social charges in manufacturing).

The comparison of labour costs in construction confirms the relatively low level already observed in the UK; the message from table 6.8 is similar to that relating to manufacturing - except that here the country with the lowest cost is Japan, where earnings of construction workers, as related to those in manufacturing, are the lowest among the countries covered.

Table 6.8: Labour costs in construction, 1980-4[a] (Britain=100)

	Hourly earnings				Total hourly labour costs[c]		
	1980	1982	1984	RM84[b]	1980	1982	1984
United States	166	227	273	132	168	216	265
Canada	174	236	241	124	169	215	219
Japan[d]	76	88	111	83	72	78	96
France	88	87	89	98	122	113	117
Germany	129	125	131	107	212	156	163
Italy	82	88	100	111	130	129	147
Belgium	133	114	111	99	185	148	143
Denmark	163	154	160	106	160	142	157
Finland	103	116	132	118	**	**	**
Netherlands	134	128	124	108	182	163	157
Norway	162	178	183	117	187	192	200
Sweden	160	142	142	114	203	169	172
Switzerland	139	152	161	101	**	**	**

Source: As for table 6.2

a Converted from national currencies at annual average market exchange rates.
b RM84 = relative to earnings in manufacturing (=100), 1984. UK: 99
c Including social charges
d Total cash earnings

7 HOURS OF WORK

Paul Blyton

INTRODUCTION

The length of the working period has been an issue in relations between employers and employed which predates the process of industrialization itself. After the Industrial Revolution the question of hours acted as a rallying point for reform groups and later, trade unions. In Britain the campaign for a 10-hour working day was active at the beginning of the nineteenth century, though a Ten Hours Act was not finally passed until 1847. Many early trade unions were founded in part to fight for a shorter working day. To take another example from Britain, one of the pressures which led to the formation of what was to become the largest trade union in the mid-nineteenth century, the Amalgamated Society of Engineers, was the discontent over the high level of enforced overtime imposed on engineering workers at that time.[1] Similar feelings were also being expressed outside Britain at this time. For example, the demand for an 8-hour working day was one of the resolutions adopted by the International Workingmen's Association (the First International) in the 1860s.

Periodically, at times of high unemployment, interest in working time has been further stimulated by calls for 'work sharing' to reduce unemployment; that is, shortening the time worked by those in employment so that (in theory), additional jobs may be created to work the remaining hours. In practice, however, the link between hours and level of employment is far from simple and evidence exists on both sides of the argument as to whether reducing hours creates jobs.[2] Yet, whatever the relative merits of long-term work sharing, temporary work-sharing measures - using short-term working provisions to overcome a projected temporary drop in demand - are widely used in recessionary periods; in certain countries, notably West Germany, detailed systems of compensated short-time working have been developed as a means of avoiding temporary lay-offs.

More recently, the issue of working hours has been brought back to centre stage by employers' growing demands for greater flexibility in working time so that capital equipment can be more fully utilized, services provided over a longer period of the day, changes in product markets more rapidly adjusted to, and generally that the productivity of labour time be increased, and unit labour costs reduced. This search for greater flexibility has begun to feed through into a series of working-time developments, including varying the length of shift periods (e.g. in transportation), and establishing annual-hours contracts which allow for variation in work time over the year and also pave the way for a greater individualization of working-time contracts.

This greater visibility of working-time issues has been further increased in recent years by a number of industrial relations disputes over working-time issues. Most prominent of these was the 1984 engineering strike in West Germany (the biggest strike in West Germany's history) which was settled by an average $1\frac{1}{2}$-hour reduction in the working week and the introduction of more flexible hours scheduling (a flexibility which has been taken further in subsequent agreements which bring basic weekly hours in the German metal-working industry down to 37 hours by 1989).[3]

In Britain too, the question of hours and more flexible working time has led to a number of disputes and protracted negotiations. Prominent among these is British Coal's plan to introduce longer shifts and/or 6-day working at thirteen of its pits which has led to a major intra-union disagreement over the acceptability of the employer's proposals, and their long-term implications for employment and for the National Union of Mineworkers. Likewise, recent union-management relations in the engineering industry, post office, and secondary education have focused on working time and its distribution over the working week and year.[4]

The topic of 'hours of work' comprises not only the length of the working day and week - the traditional focus for labour-management negotiations - but also several additional elements which together determine the overall pattern of working time in relation to the length of the working week, the working year, and the working lifetime. Indeed, it is developments in these latter areas, and in particular the extension of paid holidays and the growth of early retirement, which have been among the most prominent changes in working-time patterns in recent years.

DEFINITIONAL PROBLEMS

Cross-national comparisons of statistics on working hours are hampered by variations between individual countries in terms of methods of calculation. This is compounded by further variations between the major international organizations collecting data on hours of work; 'It is difficult', wrote one recent commentator[5] on working hours, 'to find two publications using the same basis of calculation'. In comparing 'weekly hours', for example, care must be taken over whether the comparisons are between 'normal' (or 'standard' or 'basic') hours which exclude any overtime worked, or between 'average' or 'actual' hours, which will usually include overtime.

This definition of weekly hours is part of a broader definitional problem relating to what is included as 'hours of work'. The International Labour Office, for example, distinguishes between hours actually worked (normal work periods plus overtime and short rest periods, but excluding holidays, sick leave, and meal breaks), and hours paid for (which include hours actually worked, plus paid annual vacation, paid public holidays, and paid sick and other leave). In its Year Book of Labour Statistics[6] for 1986 the hours for Canada, Iceland, Luxemburg, Netherlands, New Zealand, Switzerland, the USA, and West Germany are reported in terms of hours paid for, whereas Belgium, France, Italy, Japan, Norway, Portugal, Sweden, Spain, and the UK are shown as hours actually worked. The difference between these two measures will be more significant in some countries than in others but is unlikely to be less than a 15 per cent variation. The picture is yet further complicated in the ILO statistics by the tendency for countries to use slightly different elements of the working population as the basis of hours of work statistics. The ILO figures on 'hours of work per week in non-agricultural activities' seeks to cover the following divisions of economic activity: mining and quarrying; manufacturing; electricity, gas, and water; construction; wholesale and retail trade; restaurants and hotels;

storage and communication; finance, insurance, real estate, and business services; community, social, and personal services. However, in some cases not all these sectors are represented fully in the statistics, either through the exclusion of certain groups (e.g. juveniles) or by some divisions being represented by only certain industries within that division.

Complicating the picture still further is the variation in definitions of part-time work, and those temporarily working short-time due to a lack of demand. Chapter 2 outlined the differences between countries in relation to the maximum hours defined as part-time. One effect of these differences is that those countries which maintain 30 hours or below as the criterion for part-time will treat those working 30-35 hours as full-time. On the other hand, where 35 hours is the cut-off for defining part-time work, the counting of full-time workers will only begin above 35 hours. As a result, the overall average of full-time hours in the former case will be reduced by the inclusion of those workers who in other countries would have been counted as part-time and thus excluded from the full-time statistics.

The potential for confusion in making international comparisons does not end even here. A study undertaken in EEC countries by the European Foundation for the Improvement of Living and Working Conditions also found widespread variation in the recording of breaks, unpaid overtime, changing and washing time, and preparatory and finishing work, all of which were seen to reduce comparability between national surveys.[7]

Yet while these various discrepancies represent sources of error in direct comparability, they are not of sufficient magnitude to prevent a general comparison of hours between countries and the patterns of change over time. What they should deter, however, is a too hasty basing of conclusions on relatively small differences between countries. Caution must also be used in comparing statistics drawn from several sources rather than from a single source, given the variation between organizations on how their statistics on hours are compiled.

WEEKLY HOURS

In general, industrial countries currently operate a basic work week of 40 hours or a little below. Commonly (West Germany is one exception) the basic hours of manual workers are significantly above their white-collar counterparts; at the end of 1986 in Britain, for example, the average basic weekly hours for manual workers were just under 39, compared to 37 hours for non-manual grades.

Basic weekly hours in many countries have developed from a combination of legal definitions and collective agreements, though the relative importance of each varies from country to country. Among the European members of the OECD, for example, only Denmark and the United Kingdom have little or no legislation on working hours (see table 7.1); in Britain the legislation on hours is mainly confined to the maximum hours of certain groups and occupations such as juveniles and road-haulage drivers. Previous restrictions on women's working time originally contained in the Factory Act 1961 and Quarries Act 1954 have recently been abolished in the Sex Discrimination Act 1986 (effective February 1987). Restrictions on women's nightwork in industrial undertakings, however, continued until February 1988.

In a number of countries (e.g. Greece, Luxemburg, and Spain) the collectively agreed work week closely resembles that defined by legislation. In others, however, including Ireland, Italy, the Netherlands

Table 7.1: Statutory work day and work week and the basic week defined by collective agreement: eighteen OECD European countries

	Statutory week (day in brackets) hours		Collective agreements hours
Austria	40	(8)	38 - 38½
Belgium	40	(8)	36 - 40
Denmark	-	(-)	37½ - 40
Germany (FR)	48	(8)	38½ - 40
Finland	40	(8)	37½ - 40
France	39	(10)	35 - 39
Great Britain	-	(-)	35 - 39
Greece	40	(8)	40
Iceland	40	(?)	37 - 40
Ireland	48	(9)	38 - 40
Italy	48	(8)	40
Luxemburg	40	(8)	40
Netherlands	48	(9½)	32 - 40
Norway	40	(8)	37½ - 40
Portugal	48	(8)	35 - 44
Spain	40	(8)	40
Sweden	40	(-)	35 - 40
Switzerland	45	(?)	40 - 45

Source: 'Working time in seventeen countries, Part 1', European Industrial Relations Review (1987) no. 158, March: 18-25. European Trade Union Institute (1984) Collective Bargaining in Western Europe in 1983 and Prospects for 1984, Brussels, ETUI: 77.

and West Germany, collective bargaining has reduced the work week considerably below legal maxima which typically were established several decades ago (1919 in the Netherlands, 1929 in Italy, 1938 in Germany, and 1944 in Ireland).

In many countries, and in particular sectors and/or during certain parts of the year within those countries, the basic work week is significantly extended by the practice of overtime working. There has been little direct comparative analysis of overtime working *per se*. Data are incomplete partly as a result of a lack of recording (or even recognition) of overtime worked by certain groups (e.g. senior managers, self-employed). Yet even allowing for a degree of non-recording among some groups, it is evident that most overtime is worked by prime-age, male manual workers in manufacturing industry (for example, in Britain in July 1987, almost 36 per cent of manual workers in manufacturing worked an average of 9.4 hours per week overtime). Britain has a reputation for maintaining a high level of overtime working but it is not alone in this. Table 7.2 below indicates, for six Western European countries, the extent to which work is continued beyond the basic work week.

Table 7.2: Hours of work and overtime in six European countries (early 1980s)

	Basic hours of work (collective agreements)	Overtime: percentage of workers affected 42h or more	45h or more	51h or more
Belgium	36 - 39	7.0	6.1	2.4
France	36 - 39	33.7	21.7	4.8
Germany (FR)	40	18.1	14.2	4.9
Italy	35 - 40	22.0	12.5	1.6
Netherlands	40	14.8	12.4	5.1
United Kingdom	37½ - 40	27.5	21.3	9.3

Source: EEC and European Trade Union Institute in Manpower Argus (1983) June, cited in P. Weiss, 'From reduction of working time to flexibility of work: trends and their interpretation for Switzerland', Labour and Society (1987) vol. 12, no. 2, May: 255.

In Britain (and the USA) overtime levels have tended to remain comparatively stable or slightly increase over a long period, while in certain other countries, such as the Netherlands, significant reductions in overtime working have occurred. This downward trend may become more common in the future as managements extend their search for lower labour costs through the introduction of greater flexibility; part of the impetus behind new shift-work systems (see below) has been to reduce the amount of overtime worked.

The importance of overtime working is such that, for many purposes, it is more meaningful to examine changes in actual hours worked rather than in basic hours. The OECD has collected information on average hours both on a weekly and an annual basis over a long period, though changes in base years of the index numbers and in sample composition make some of the earlier data not strictly comparable with more recent figures. To provide a backcloth on which to examine more recent changes in working time, table 7.3 reports the trends in average weekly hours in manufacturing in eleven industrial countries since 1960. It is evident from this table that the general trend in average weekly hours in manufacturing was downwards during the 1960s and 1970s. In some cases, such as Belgium, Italy, the Netherlands, and Spain, the average decline over this period has been greater than 1 per cent per annum. Overall this fall in average hours follows reductions in agreed basic hours; this overall picture is complicated slightly, however, by short-term fluctuations which reflect economic cycles and their impact on the amount of overtime worked.

Table 7.3 Trends in average weekly hours in manufacturing, 1960–82: eleven OECD countries (1977=100)

Year	*USA*	*Canada*	*Japan*	*Belgium*	*Denmark*	*France*	*Germany*	*Italy*	*Netherlands*	*Sweden*	*UK*
1960	98.6	103.8	118.8	124.1	125.4	111.9	117.9	128.8	126.0	124.7	114.2
1961	98.9	103.3	116.5	123.4	121.7	112.4	115.5	127.4	120.7	123.6	112.6
1962	99.8	104.3	113.5	121.7	122.6	112.7	112.7	123.5	119.8	122.7	111.4
1963	100.1	104.7	112.6	122.4	120.7	111.7	111.0	124.1	119.5	121.4	111.3
1964	100.8	105.1	112.1	122.3	121.7	111.4	111.4	118.4	118.3	120.2	112.2
1965	102.0	105.1	109.9	121.4	121.5	110.3	110.4	114.6	118.0	119.2	110.4
1966	102.4	104.3	110.6	120.3	119.3	110.7	108.7	118.1	117.0	119.1	108.4
1967	100.9	103.6	111.0	118.3	118.0	109.6	106.5	118.7	116.7	117.2	107.5
1968	101.2	103.8	110.3	118.3	115.3	106.3	108.9	118.7	114.2	114.8	108.3
1969	100.8	103.3	108.7	117.6	113.8	109.1	109.0	113.5	112.7	112.8	108.3
1970	99.0	102.9	107.4	115.0	112.0	107.9	108.6	113.2	110.5	110.4	106.6
1971	99.3	102.2	105.5	112.5	109.8	107.1	106.1	108.8	109.3	110.2	104.1
1972	100.8	102.2	104.9	110.2	107.5	106.1	105.0	105.5	107.7	107.2	102.9
1973	101.0	101.7	104.3	107.4	101.7	105.0	104.6	102.1	105.9	105.2	104.4
1974	99.5	101.0	99.3	105.0	103.7	103.4	101.6	100.9	102.5	104.0	100.4
1975	98.3	99.9	96.3	99.1	100.4	101.0	98.4	95.7	100.6	102.0	99.1

Year	*USA*	*Canada*	*Japan*	*Belgium*	*Denmark*	*France*	*Germany*	*Italy*	*Netherlands*	*Sweden*	*UK*
1976	99.4	100.0	99.7	101.6	100.9	100.9	101.6	99.1	100.3	100.7	99.4
1977	100.0	100.0	100.0	100.0	100.0	100.0	100.0	100.0	100.0	100.0	100.0
1978	100.2	100.3	100.6	100.3	98.8	99.3	98.6	99.8	98.9	97.4	99.8
1979	99.6	99.5	101.7	100.4	98.7	99.1	98.2	98.8	97.7	95.8	99.1
1980	98.5	99.1	101.6	97.9	99.4	98.7	96.8	99.0	98.5	94.7	94.7
1981	98.5	98.6	101.0	95.7	99.4	98.1	95.2	96.6	98.4	94.2	93.0
1982	97.0	97.9	100.8	. .	99.6	93.6	94.6	95.8	. .	95.0	94.8

Source US Department of Labor, Bureau of Labor Statistics
Note The data relate to all employed persons (wage and salary earners, the self-employed, and unpaid family workers) in the USA and Canada, and all employees (wage and salary earners) in the other countries.

In North America, the pattern is rather different. Canada demonstrates only a small decline in average hours over the period as a whole and, for much of the period, average hours remained remarkably stable. The USA demonstrates no overall decline between 1960 and 1980, but rather indicates a series of small fluctuations. Japan too exhibits a different trend in hours from its European counterparts. Having declined significantly between the early 1960s and the mid-1970s, average hours in Japan subsequently stabilized, whereas in Europe the general decline in hours continued.

Table 7.3 relates only to manufacturing industry which, as discussed in chapter 2, now comprises only a minority of the total workforce of industrial countries. However, more recent statistics collected by the OECD indicate the pattern of change in working time in 11 countries for the economy as a whole (table 7.4). This table is also distinct from table 7.3 in that the average is compiled on an annual, rather than a weekly, basis (other differences between the tables are different base years, the appearance of Finland and Norway in table 7.4, and the non-appearance of Belgium and Denmark).

The general picture for the later 1970s and early 1980s is apparent in both tables, many European countries demonstrating a significant decline, particularly in the later 1970s, in the number of hours worked. As in the earlier period, the USA exhibits a much less clear trend, with annual hours increasing significantly in 1985 following a general fall over the previous seven years. However, of the eleven countries in table 7.4 it is not the USA but Japan which represents the most exceptional case, with average annual hours increasing both in the late 1970s and again in the mid-1980s. As we discuss below, part of the explanation for this counter-trend in Japan (and to a lesser extent in the USA) is that paid holiday entitlement has not risen as much as in Western Europe where, in many countries (though not all - Sweden and the UK are exceptions) increased holidays have helped to maintain a continuing reduction in hours, even during periods when weekly hours have been stable or even slightly increasing following the 1980-2 recession.

Just as there is a pronounced difference between the trend in average annual hours in Japan (and to a lesser extent the USA) compared with much of Western Europe, this distinction is also maintained in relation to the actual level of annual hours of work. Problems of comparability notwithstanding, table 7.5 suggests that, on average, Japanese and American industrial workers have substantially longer contractual hours of work than most of their European counterparts. So much so that, based on a notional 40-hour week, Japanese workers have contractual hours which represent the equivalent of an additional 11½ weeks per year compared with industrial workers in West Germany. It is worth noting, however, that, while Japan may be exceptional within the OECD, it is far from exceptional in relation to its immediate neighbours where average hours are even longer -approximately 2,800 per year in Korea and over 2,500 in China and Singapore.[8]

VACATIONS AND PUBLIC HOLIDAYS

In a number of industrial countries, the pattern of annual hours change during the 1980s has reflected two separate trends which at times have run in opposite directions: namely, a slight increase in the actual working week due to higher levels of overtime worked in the post-1982 recovery period, and a significant reduction in annual hours due to an increase in paid-

Table 7.4 Average annual hours worked per person in employment[a] (1975=100)

	1975	1976	1977	1978	1979	1980	1981	1982	1983	1984	1985
Canada	100.0	99.5	97.7	98.3	97.7	97.1	96.1	94.7	94.1	94.5	95.0
Finland	100.0	99.5	99.2	99.3	98.2	97.0	96.7	95.7	94.8	94.2	**
France	100.0	100.2	98.6	98.0	98.2	98.5	97.1	92.7	91.5	**	**
Germany	100.0	101.9	100.3	98.6	97.8	97.2	96.3	96.6	96.2	95.8	94.5
Japan	100.0	101.3	101.4	101.7	102.3	102.0	101.6	101.4	101.5	102.4	**
Italy	100.0	99.9	98.0	97.5	97.2	97.2	96.9	96.5	95.8	95.0	94.3
Netherlands	100.0	100.5	99.2	96.8	94.4	94.5	94.7	95.1	94.6	92.2	**
Norway	100.0	97.8	95.6	94.4	93.4	93.3	92.1	92.1	91.6	90.8	91.4
Sweden	100.0	100.6	98.9	96.4	95.7	94.9	94.4	95.3	95.8	96.0	**
UK	100.0	99.1	98.1	97.0	96.5	94.1	91.1	91.9	91.2	92.0	**
USA	100.0	100.1	100.0	99.7	99.6	98.7	98.4	97.9	97.4	96.8	99.3

Source: OECD, Employment Outlook (1986) Paris: 142.

a These data refer, as far as possible, to the total economy, unless otherwise specified below:
Japan Figures refer to employees in enterprises with 30 or more employees
Netherlands Figures refer to persons employed in the private-enterprise sector, excluding agriculture and fishing
USA Figures refer to employees only

Table 7.5 Annual contractual hours of work, industrial workers (November 1985)

Country	Normal contractual annual hours of work
Germany (FR)	1708
Netherlands	1740
Belgium	1756
France	1763
Italy	1776
UK	1778
Sweden	1800
Austria	1804
Luxemburg	1808
Spain	1808
Denmark	1816
Finland	1816
Norway	1840
Ireland	1864
Greece	1864
USA[a]	1912
Switzerland	1936
Portugal	2025
Japan[a,b]	2166

Source: Internationale Sozialpolitik (Federal Union of German Employers Associations (BDA)) in Social International (1986) February: cited in P. Weiss (1987) 'From reduction of working time to flexibility of work: trends and their interpretation for Switzerland', Labour and Society, vol. 12, no. 2: 254.

a 1984 figures
b Japan: average actual annual hours of work

holiday entitlement (an additional week's holiday is equivalent to almost one hour off the working week).

In 1960, two weeks' paid holiday was the norm in many countries, with three weeks in a minority of cases.[9] This level increased only slowly in the 1960s; in Britain, for example, average paid-holiday entitlement for manual workers had reached 2.3 weeks by 1969.[10] The 1970s and early 1980s saw an acceleration in the growth of paid holidays, particularly in Europe. Currently, almost all employees in Western Europe are entitled to at least four weeks' annual paid holiday. In all but two West European countries,

Italy and the UK, there is general legislation guaranteeing specific minimum paid holidays (in the UK, holidays are fixed either by collective bargaining or statutory Wages Council Orders, whilst in Italy the law recognizes the right of individuals to paid holidays, but the duration is regulated through collective agreements).

In several countries (e.g. West Germany, Ireland, and the Netherlands) a relatively low statutory entitlement has been considerably increased by collective agreements (see table 7.6). In West Germany at the end of 1986, 65 per cent of employees were entitled to at least six weeks' annual leave, and only 6 per cent enjoyed less than five weeks.[11] Elsewhere (e.g. Austria, Denmark, France, Greece, Luxemburg, Norway, Spain, and Sweden) higher statutory minima have been only marginally improved by collective agreement.

Table 7.6 Paid annual leave and public holidays in eighteen OECD countries

	Statutory leave (weeks)	Collective agreement (average levels where different from statutory) (weeks)	Public holidays (no.)
Austria	5		13
Belgium	4	4-5	10
Denmark	5		10
Finland	5	5-6	5
France	5	5-6	10
Germany (FR)	3	4-6	9-14
Greece	4		6-12
Iceland	4		11-12
Ireland	3	4	8
Italy	not specified	4-6	10-11
Luxemburg	5		10
Netherlands	3	4-6	7
Norway	21 days		10
Portugal	3	4	12
Spain	5		14
Sweden	5	5-8	11
Switzerland	4	4-5	8
United Kingdom	-	4-6	8-10

Source: 'Working time in 17 countries, part 2', European Industrial Relations Review, (1987) no. 159, April: 18-24; Council of Europe (1983) Hours of Work, Strasbourg; European Trade Union Institute (1984) Collective Bargaining in Western Europe in 1983 and Prospects for 1984, Brussels: ETUI.

Within individual countries, some groups typically are entitled to longer holidays than others. A common criterion for additional holiday is length of service. In Britain, for example, a third of manual workers receive additional service-related holidays; among non-manual workers the proportion is at least as high. Other countries operate age-related holiday increases. In Norway, for example, workers over 60 years are entitled to an extra week's holiday above the statutory minimum; similarly in the Netherlands, many collective agreements provide for additional vacations for older workers.[12]

While the pattern in Europe is a fairly uniform one of a considerable increase in holiday entitlement in the 1970s and 1980s to a general annual level of four to six weeks, this trend is much less evident in North America or Japan. By the end of the 1970s, the average paid vacation in the United States was only just over two weeks, virtually unchanged from the average level a decade earlier.[13] For a minority of long-service workers, such as in the American steel industry, extended holidays are available, but the average paid vacation available to American workers remains considerably below their European counterparts; one effect of this was a significant growth in the 1970s of American workers taking extra unpaid holidays.[14] In Japan too, paid holidays are shorter than in Europe and this contributes to the longer annual hours worked in Japan. On average, Japanese workers receive 15.1 days of paid holiday per year. However, the average annual work time is further increased by the tendency among Japanese workers not to take all the holiday entitlement. In fact on average they take only 8.7 days - 58 per cent of their entitlement.[15] There are many possible reasons for this, including a desire to earn extra income. Also, as Hanami[16] point out, most Japanese have traditionally shown no strong desire to take long vacations, preferring to take holidays in short, one-to-two day spells.

SHIFTWORK

One definition of shiftwork is 'a situation in which one worker replaces another on the same job within a 24-hour period'.[17] Like overtime, it is a means of extending the productive day. The standard economic and technical arguments in favour of shiftwork - e.g. greater utilization of plant and equipment, avoidance of time-consuming and/or expensive machine shut-downs, less cost than high levels of overtime - are well known and need not be elaborated again here. Yet it is not possible to be economically or technologically determinist in explaining the pattern of shift-working. Different companies in the same industry and different countries with similar industrial sectors and at similar levels of economic and technological development display markedly different patterns of shift-working. Also relevant would appear to be the strength of tradition of shift-working in particular localities and countries.

Overall, however, the level of shift-working appears to be increasing in most industrial countries. This was the conclusion of an International Labour Organization study in the late 1970s,[18] and again more recently in a review of studies of shift-working undertaken for the European Foundation for the Improvement of Living and Working Conditions.[19] In Britain, the rise in shift-working appears to have been vigorous in the 1950s and 1960s, followed by a more gradual rise thereafter. New Earnings Survey data indicate that this rise was temporarily reversed in the recession years of the early 1980s, before recovering its earlier trend after 1983.

Despite this general rise, actual levels of shift-working appear to vary considerably from country to country. Detailed comparative data are scarce, if not altogether absent. One comparison of nine European countries, however, indicates a ratio of almost 3:1 between the countries with high and low levels of shift-working (table 7.7). In the USA, estimates of numbers engaged in shiftwork vary from one in four workers to one in six.[20] Part of the discrepancy is caused by different methods of data collection, for example, how day-shift workers at the time of the survey were recorded.

Table 7.7 Shift-working in nine European countries (service sector not included)

	Involved in shiftwork	Sectors with most shiftwork
	%	
Belgium	26.6	Cars, energy, minerals
Denmark	14	Paper, chemicals
Germany (FR)	20	Energy, chemicals, metals
France	31.3	Metals, paper, textiles
Ireland	18.8	Textiles, chemicals, paper
Italy	22	Metals, paper, non-metallic minerals
Luxemburg	41.5	Metals, chemicals, fibres
Netherlands	10.6	Food products, textiles, metals
UK	30	Cars, metals, chemicals

Source: European Trade Union Institute (1979) Reductions of Working Time in Western Europe, Part 1, Brussels; ETUI: 59.

In conjunction with the general increase in shift-working has come a number of innovations in shiftwork systems, including the introduction of fourth and fifth crews, the reduced reliance on night-working and the gradual extension of compressed shiftwork patterns (e.g. individuals working three twelve-hour shifts per week). It seems likely that this increase in shiftwork and the spread of new shiftwork patterns will continue for the next few years. What is also likely is a growth in shift-working in the service sector as services to the public (such as banking and retailing) extend their hours into the evening and weekend. One effect of this, together with recent sex-discrimination legislation, is likely to be that women will become increasingly represented among those engaged in shiftwork.

RETIREMENT

Just as the working week has been affected by changes in basic hours, and the working year by increases in the amount of holiday entitlement, so too the average working lifetime has been undergoing significant change in most industrial countries in recent years. Partly this reflects changes in the minimum school-leaving age which has been widely raised to 16 years (e.g. in France, Norway, Spain, Sweden, and the UK) and as high as 18 years in Belgium. However, a number of countries retain a 15-year minimum leaving age (Austria, Finland, Greece, Ireland, and Luxemburg) or even 14 years (e.g. Italy, Portugal).[21] More than increases in school-leaving ages, however, it is changes in retirement patterns and in the participation rates of older workers which have contributed to a change in average working lifetimes in recent years. Though only in a handful of cases (e.g. France and Sweden) have formal retirement ages been reduced in the past twenty years (i.e. the age at which a full state pension may be drawn), the wider provision of early retirement schemes has in practice reduced average ages of retirement considerably. Only in North America is there evidence of significant pressure towards increasing the age of retirement.

Across most western industrial industries, the retirement age for men and women ranges between 60 and 65 years (Norway and Denmark being somewhat higher and women in Italy lower) (table 7.8). Despite sex-discrimination legislation and individual court cases ruling in favour of equal treatment in the EEC, a significant minority of countries retain differential retirement ages for men and women.

The most active developments in the field of retirement lie not in changes in the normal retirement age but in the more widespread provision of early-retirement schemes. In recent years, and particularly following the economic downturn after 1979, the availability of national, industry- and company-based early-retirement schemes was increased in most industrial countries, primarily to effect a reduction in total labour supply.

National early-retirement schemes have become increasingly common, with countries such as Austria, Belgium, Denmark, West Germany, Greece, Norway, and Spain operating such schemes; as well as an age criterion these schemes typically also stipulate a minimum level of social-security contributions (measured in terms of length of payment of national insurance); in Austria, for example, early retirement is available at age 60 (55 for women) provided that 420 months' contributions have been paid, while in West Germany early retirement at 63 (60 for women) is available to those who have paid 35 years of social insurance. In practice, this national availability of early retirement has led to a de facto lowering of the retirement age.

More specific early-retirement schemes exist in individual sectors of activity, particularly in those experiencing major economic difficulties. Examples include schemes for workers in the iron and steel industry in Austria and Luxemburg, mining in France and the UK, fishing in Portugal, and the railway industry in France.[22] Other schemes exist in service-sector industries, for example, school-teaching and the civil service in the UK. In a number of countries (for example, Austria, Denmark, Finland, and Sweden) older workers who have been unemployed for a specified period (typically, one year) can also opt for early retirement. In Finland, for example, long-term unemployed aged 55 years and over have been able, since 1980, to opt for an 'unemployment pension'; by 1984 there were over 40,000 such pensioners in Finland.

The rise in company-based early retirement has been closely linked

Table 7.8 Normal retirement ages in twenty OECD countries

	Men (years)	Women (years)
Austria	65	60
Belgium	65	60
Canada	65	65
Denmark	67	67
Finland	65	65
France	60	60
Germany (FR)	65	63
Greece	65	60
Ireland	65	65
Italy	60	55
Japan	65	65
Luxemburg	65	65
Netherlands	65	65
Norway	67	67
Portugal	65	62
Spain	65	65
Sweden	65	65
Switzerland	65	62
UK	65	60
USA	65	65

Source: Mainly, 'Working time in 17 countries, part 2', European Industrial Relations Review (1987) no. 159, April: 18-24.

with redundancy programmes and with the growth of occupational pension schemes. In a study undertaken in Britain in the late 1970s, White[23] found that more than half of the companies undertaking manpower reductions had utilized early retirement as one means of effecting the reduction. In these cases, early retirement may often be little more than a euphemism for redundancy. However, the growth of occupational pension schemes has extended the opportunities for voluntary early retirement. Not all workers are covered by occupational pensions, however; in Britain just over half the total workforce belongs to an occupational pension scheme, while in several other countries the proportion is smaller - in Canada, for example, private pension plans cover two in every five workers. Many of these plans allow for a pension to be drawn before normal retirement age; usually this entails an actuarial reduction in the pension payable, though in situations where early retirement is being encouraged, it is common for employers to compensate for a part or all of this reduction by a lump-sum severance payment.

While the emphasis in Europe has been almost entirely on the provision of early retirement, in North America this same development has also been matched by a counter-claim for the right to continue working after the normal retirement age. The USA recognized this right in a 1978 amendment to the 1967 Age Discrimination in Employment Act which establishes that workers up to the age of 70 years in organizations employing more than twenty people cannot be subject to compulsory retirement on grounds of age alone. Not surprisingly, those who have subsequently taken advantage of this law have disproportionately been non-manual grades rather than those in more physically demanding manual jobs.[24] In Canada, this issue of mandatory retirement is prominent at the time of writing. While Quebec has had provincial legislation since 1982 abolishing mandatory retirement on grounds of age alone, in the other provinces it has been left to the courts to decide whether compulsory retirement at 65 years is discriminatory practice, and contrary to provincial and federal charters of rights. Court decisions in some provinces (e.g. Manitoba) have found in favour of the individual workers bringing the case, while in other provinces (e.g. Ontario) courts have made contrasting decisions in different cases. Hence the picture is somewhat confused, though the general indication is that Canada will follow the United States in giving greater support to older workers who wish to continue working after 65 and can show they are still capable of carrying out the duties associated with their job.[25] In Europe, with fewer prospects of a substantial lowering of unemployment in the near future, it is not anticipated that demands for the right to work after the normal retirement age will gain widespread support. Any discussion of a more flexible retirement age in Europe is likely to involve the 55-65 age range, rather than beyond 65.

Not only North America but Japan too shows a number of distinctive features in its retirement provision, compared with Western Europe. One aspect of this is that while state pensions do not become payable until 65 years (and even then remain small), the normal retirement age in many Japanese companies is 55 years. In practice what tends to occur is that many 'retired' workers continue working for the same company but often in a lower position. One study of this system found that three-quarters of those re-employed experienced a drop in status, while more than half were required to take a drop in salary.[26]

One area where some European countries are showing greater flexibility is in relation to 'phased' retirement schemes, whereby the transition from work to retirement is introduced more gradually than the norm of working full-time right up to the date of retirement. The most developed scheme is in Sweden where, under the provisions of the 1976 Partial Pensions Act, workers aged between 60 and 65 years and who meet certain eligibility conditions (in employment for at least ten years since the age of 45 and for at least five months in the previous twelve) can apply to transfer to part-time hours and receive a partial pension which compensates for the majority of their net reduction in earnings. By the early 1980s the scheme was quite strongly supported with well over one-quarter of those eligible taking part.[27] Recently, similar partial retirement schemes have been introduced in Denmark and Finland (effective from January 1987), though with higher unemployment rates in these countries compared with Sweden, more emphasis and provision has been given to early retirement. Examples of phased retirement schemes also exist in other countries, operating at sector or individual company level. These range from parts of the tobacco and brewing industries in West Germany to printing in the Netherlands, civil servants and teachers in Belgium, and individual engineering companies in Britain. Typically, however, these individual schemes are much less ambitious than the Swedish model and some only provide additional days off in the months immediately prior to retirement. A form of partial retirement also seems to be becoming more widespread among some senior managers whereby, following normal retirement, the executives are being rehired on a part-time consultancy basis, either to see particular projects through to their completion or to provide a depth of experience otherwise lacking among younger managers.[28]

CONCLUSIONS

Since the early 1970s, the average time individuals spend at work has fallen significantly. This reflects not only reductions in the length of the working week, but - particularly in latter years - an increase in paid holiday entitlement, and a widespread reduction in average retirement ages, occasionally through a change in the normal age of retirement but more commonly through the greater availability of early retirement schemes. Not all countries adhere to a single general pattern, however. In particular, a distinction can be drawn between, on the one hand, Western European countries where reductions have been experienced in the working week, year, and lifetime, and on the other hand, North America and Japan where annual hours have remained relatively high, not least because of the markedly lower level of paid holiday entitlement and the common practice in Japan for employees to work part of this vacation time. Fine distinctions between countries in relation to average working time are difficult to draw, given the variation in methods of data collection (e.g. in relation to part-time workers, the recording of sick leave, short breaks, etc.). However, it is evident that within the OECD the hours of work in Japan are significantly greater than most, if not all, other member countries and in the near future this difference may become even more marked if Japan's average annual hours continue to rise in the way they have done during the 1980s.

Looking to the immediate future, a number of trends and developments may be anticipated. Two which are likely to be particularly prominent are a renewed demand for shorter weekly hours, and a greater emphasis by employers on flexibility within the working-time structure. On the first of these, there are already signs from a number of sector agreements and negotiations (e.g. in the German and UK engineering industries) that, following a period of advance on holidays, the working week has now been revived as the focus for working-time reductions. With generally low levels of inflation prevailing in OECD countries at present, trade unions are in a relatively favourable position to pursue a non-wage issue such as weekly hours (since when inflation is higher, maintaining real earnings dominates trade union negotiations). One of the factors which may lead to concessions on weekly hours is the second development mentioned above: the increased emphasis on flexibility. As noted earlier, employers have shown a strong interest in recent years in developing new shiftwork systems and modifying standard work-time patterns to create a greater degree of manpower flexibility, which in turn contributes to lower labour costs, greater productivity, and/or greater utilization of capital equipment. If negotiations in the British and German engineering industries are indicative of possible wider trends, it appears that employers may be willing to offer a cut in weekly hours, in order to secure agreement on new patterns of work arrangements which are likely to more than compensate (in terms of costs and productivity) for the overall hours reduction. One effect of this greater flexibility is likely to be a significant drop in levels of overtime working, which in countries such as France and the UK have risen and remained at a persistently high level throughout the period under discussion.

In the past, hours of work have attracted relatively little detailed analysis and have represented a negotiating 'cinderella' - occasionally prominent but more commonly receding into the background as wage issues claim more of the centre stage in negotiations. However, in recent years, developments such as the spread of new technology have begun to challenge the logic of existing work-time arrangements. This has been further reinforced by, on the one hand, management's renewed emphasis on labour costs and productivity and, on the other, by trade-union members and others seeking working patterns which maximize the utility of non-work time.

NOTES

1 K. Burgess (1975) The Origins of British Industrial Relations: The Nineteenth Century Experience, London: Croom Helm.

2 P. Blyton (1987) 'The working time debate in Europe', Industrial Relations, vol. 26, no. 2: 201-7; G. Bosch (1986) 'The dispute over the reduction of the working week in West Germany', Cambridge Journal of Economics, vol. 10: 271-90.

3 Incomes Data Services (1987) European Report, no. 289, London: Incomes Data Services.

4 P. Blyton, S. Hill, A. Gorham, and A. Poole (1988) 'Flexibility and working time', Cardiff Business School working paper.

5 P. Weiss (1987) 'From reduction of working time to flexibility of work: trends and their interpretation for Switzerland', Labour and Society, vol. 12, no. 2: 239.

6 ILO (1986) Year Book of Labour Statistics, Geneva, ILO.

7 European Foundation for the Improvement of Living and Working Conditions (1981) Official Statistics on Working Time: Methodological Problems and Delimitations of Comparability, Dublin: EFILWC.

8 H. Shimada and H. Hayami (1986) Working Hours and the Revision of the Labour Standards Law in Japan, proceedings of the International Industrial Relations Association 7th World Congress, vol. 3 (New Trends in Working Time Arrangements), Hamburg: 211-22.

9 OECD (1983) Employment Outlook: 39.

10 P. Blyton (1985) Changes in Working Time: An International Review, London: Croom Helm: 79.

11 Incomes Data Services, op. cit.

12 'Working time in seventeen countries, Part 2', European Industrial Relations Review (1987) no. 159: 22.

13 J.N. Hedges and D.E. Taylor (1980) 'Recent trends in worktime: hours edge downwards', Monthly Labor Review, vol. 103, no. 3: 3-11.

14 ibid., 9.

15 Shimada and Hayami, op. cit., 215.

16 T. Hanami (1980) Labor Relations in Japan Today, London: John Martin: 161.

17 A.H. Ingram and P.J. Sloane (1984) 'The growth of shiftwork in the

British food, drink and tobacco industries', Managerial and Decision Economics, vol. 5, no. 3: 168.

18 ILO (1978) Management of Working Time in Industrialized Countries, Geneva: 19.

19 European Foundation for the Improvement of Living and Working Conditions (1986) Shiftwork Review: Research of the European Foundation, 1981-1984, Dublin: EFILWC.

20 P. Lehmann, 'The National Institute for Occupational Safety and Health: expanding the frontiers of knowledge', in J. MacLaury (ed.) (1980) Protecting People at Work, Washington: US Department of Labor; P. Finn (1981) 'The effects of shiftwork on the lives of employees', Monthly Labor Review, vol. 104, no. 10: 31-5.

21 European Industrial Relations Review, op. cit.

22 ibid.

23 M. White (1980) Shorter Working Time, Report no. 589, London: Policy Studies Institute.

24 B. Casey and G. Bruche (1983) Work or Retirement, Aldershot: Gower.

25 P. Blyton (1987) 'Retirement policies in Canada: issues and developments', Cardiff Business School Working Paper Series.

26 K. Yoshio (1980) 'The future of the fixed-age retirement system' in S. Nishikawa (ed.) (1980) The Labor Market in Japan, Tokyo: University of Tokyo Press.

27 P. Blyton (1984) 'Partial retirement: some insights from the Swedish Partial Pension Scheme', Ageing and Society, vol. 4, no. 1: 69-83.

28 P. Blyton, 'Retirement policies in Canada', op. cit.

8 TRADE UNION MEMBERSHIP

R. Price

The aggregate growth and decline of trade union membership, by sector, industry, sex, occupation, and region have been issues of key interest to students of industrial relations since the birth of unionism itself. Despite this intense interest there is surprisingly little cross-national consensus on the measurement of union membership, either in absolute or in relative terms; that is, either measured by the number of members or by that number taken as a proportion of those eligible for membership, a ratio usually referred to as the density of union membership. This lack of consensus stems from the wide range of interpretations placed on the three basic definitions that are involved in the measurement of union growth and decline:

> What is a trade union? Which organizations qualify for inclusion in a membership series?
>
> Who is a union member? What should be taken to constitute a member in 'good standing'?
>
> Who is a potential union member? Which categories of the population should be considered to be potentially unionizable?

Added to these definitional problems are the equally significant practical problems of whether unions actually keep membership records and are prepared to make returns to a collecting agency; whether unions' own definitions of membership are the same as the 'optimal' definition adopted by the external observer; and whether the definition of potential membership can actually be realized in practice from published labour-force data. The three following sections discuss these conceptual and practical problems in more detail.

WHAT IS A TRADE UNION?

The Webbs' classic definition of a trade union as 'a continuous association of wage earners for the purpose of maintaining or improving the conditions of their working lives',[1] provides a good starting point for analysis but presents evident problems of interpretation. 'Continuous' might, for example, be taken to exclude transitory bodies such as the Knights of Labor or the 'Wobblies' in the United States, the Grand National Consolidated Trade Union in the UK or the RGO (revolutionary communist unions) which were formed in Germany after World War I. 'Wage earners' might be taken to exclude salaried white-collar and professional workers; and 'maintaining or improving the conditions of their working lives' might imply the exclusion of organizations with strong political orientations and reflect a narrow economistic view of union functions.

For most practical purposes, the definition adopted by Bain and Price[2] for their historical survey of union growth will provide tolerably clear guidelines. They defined a trade union as 'an organization of employees which seeks to represent the job interests of its members to employers and in some circumstances to the state, but which is not dominated by either of them'. This definition includes all types of employee - professional, agricultural, and service; it allows for the exclusion of employer-dominated unions and staff associations; and it allows for wide variations in the character of employee organizations in relation to political and socio-economic activities.

However there are still difficulties of interpretation with this definition. How are self-employed workers to be treated, for example? Since they are well organized in Scandinavia, Israel, Switzerland - and also in the UK in bodies like the Musicians' Union and Equity - they should clearly be included in many cases. But inclusion of the self-employed in the ranks of union membership carries with it the implication of including all self-employed workers amongst the potential union membership, a proposition that is difficult to sustain with conviction. 'Domination' by an employer or by the state is a highly subjective and relative concept. For example, the main French union confederations would not hesitate to describe the company unions in Citroen and Peugeot as under management's thumb, and many critical European observers would query the genuine independence of some Japanese company unions; but these organizations would strongly resist the suggestion that they were dominated by the employers. How does one deal with the union organizations in many one-party states that are closely tied to the ruling party and the state apparatus for economic and industrial planning?

These are substantial difficulties, and they often have to be settled in fairly arbitrary ways. But however these definitional issues are resolved, there remains the major practical problem of actually implementing the definition selected, and compiling a series which accurately reflects it. Here, the observer is in the hands of the union organizations and the state statistical services. Approximately half the OECD nations collect and publish official union membership series; for the others, we have to go to the unions themselves for membership information or use their publications. In either case, however, there may be major deficiencies in the available and accessible data when measured against the ideal definition of a trade union, such as the one outlined above. In almost every country the most accessible data are those relating to the main recognized confederations. The identification and compilation of membership information on independent unions invariably presents difficulties, and the observer has to take a view as to whether they should be included as a trade union. In the British case for example, organizations like the Headmasters' Conference, the Police Federation, and the many small professional bodies representing local government employees have all been included as unions in the official statistical series, while the British Medical Association and the British Dental Association have not. In the USA, the official BLS series varies from the independently compiled National Bureau of Economic Research (NBER) series due to their differing treatment of unaffiliated unions and quasi-professional bodies such as the American Nurses' Association and the National Education Association. In France and Spain small independent unions exist for many groups of employees, most notably for white-collar groups and workers in the public sector. They present the external observer with frequently insuperable problems in both evaluating their status as 'unions' and compiling membership figures.

WHO IS A UNION MEMBER?

Union 'membership' falls into a variety of different categories, and unions follow widely differing practices as to how they are dealt with in published membership statistics. A 'fully paid up member' can be someone with substantial subscription arrears, since unions vary in the speed with which they strike off members for non-payment, or transfer them to an intermediate category. Many unions also include in their membership categories those who are exempt from payments or make substantially reduced payments - such as apprentices, the unemployed, those conscripted into the armed forces, and the retired. The most significant practical problem here involves the retired membership of trade unions. In most cases it will be appropriate to exclude them from a membership and density series, as they are no longer active members of the labour force, so as to permit the calculation of a density series based on the economically active labour force. This approach presents no difficulties where the retired membership can be separately identified, as is the case, for example, of the Swedish confederations TCO and SACO/SR. However, LO, Sweden's main confederation, does not publish statistics which separate out retired members, so that a density series for Sweden can only be compiled from estimates of total membership excluding LO's retired members. In those countries where substantial numbers of retired members are found in the ranks of the unions, it becomes very difficult to calculate accurate disaggregated (industry- and sector-level) density figures, since it is rare that the individual unions publish the detailed information required. In most countries it is unusual for unions to publish information on their membership composition by category.

Regardless of the composition of a union's membership, it may be unwilling or unable to provide accurate data even at an aggregated level. The quality of a union's membership data depends primarily upon the nature of its internal systems of subscription collection and membership reporting. Where subscription collection and the issuing of membership cards take place centrally, membership data is likely to be tolerably accurate. But where subscriptions are collected at the workplace, and central records are kept more for financial than for membership purposes, membership data may be highly inaccurate. To varying degrees, this situation obtains in France, Spain, and Italy. In these countries local membership records are partial and rarely subject to audit; payment of dues is lax, and claimed membership figures include substantial numbers of non-paying supporters, or people who have paid some subscription money but not enough to be genuine 'full' members. National federations and confederations are obliged to rely on these inadequate records for estimates of their aggregate membership position. Frequently, reported membership data is influenced by competitive unionism; prestige and representational status considerations encourage individual unions and confederations to overstate actual membership, often to the point where trends in absolute and relative size are concealed for lengthy periods. In the USA, for example, the competition between the AFL and the rival CIO in the immediate post-war period made it very difficult to obtain a clear picture of relative membership trends prior to the merger of the two bodies. In France, the claimed membership of the main confederations is subject to major reservations, and wide variations are evident in the estimates made by external commentators.

WHO IS A POTENTIAL UNION MEMBER?

The definition of the potential membership of trade unions in any country is an important question since it is the source of the 'density' figure which provides the most common comparative measure of trade unions' standing between countries. For the purposes of international comparisons, it is clearly necessary for the definition of 'potential' to be consistent between countries. If the armed forces and agricultural workers are excluded in one country, these groups must be excluded from the potential membership figure in all. However, defining potential membership on such a consistent basis is fraught with difficulties; which groups should be excluded to arrive at an acceptable definition of potential?

If the definition of a trade union outlined above is adopted, employers would automatically be excluded. But what about the self-employed? As an earlier section has indicated, these groups are both eligible for, and actually join, unions affiliated to central confederations in a wide range of countries. In practice, since unions generally seek to represent employees, organizations which have a significant number of self-employed members will always be in a small minority and, for the purposes of a meaningful comparative density figure, the self-employed can be excluded from the potential membership figure. This will, however, mean a degree of overstatement of density in those countries like Sweden where self-employed professionals are well organized.

The armed forces should probably also be excluded from the potential membership of unions, since in many countries they are banned from trade-union activity and excluded from the ambit of labour legislation for other employees. While their exclusion does achieve a sensible degree of cross-national consistency of treatment it will also result in a degree of overstatement of union density in countries like Sweden where affiliated unions exist for career officers and NCO's, or West Germany where many union members retain their membership when conscripted into the armed forces.

What about those who are retired? Many retired people do retain union membership, depending on the nature of the benefits offered on a continuing basis by the union. However, there are clear reasons for excluding them from a consistent cross-national definition of union potential. Although they retain an interest in employment-related matters such as pensions, and may have the right to participate in union affairs, they are by definition no longer employees, and are excluded from labour-force statistics. While union practices vary between couintries, it is clear that the majority of unions exclude the retired from the membership data which they return to collecting institutions. Hence, it is probably best to exclude them from potential membership and to seek to calculate accurate density series by, as far as possible, also excluding the retired from the union membership side of the equation.

In contrast, there are good reasons for not excluding the unemployed from potential union membership. Many unemployed workers retain their membership since by doing so they have access to financial benefits or information about job vacancies. In Denmark, for example, unions play a major role in the administration of unemployment benefits, and in many closed or semi-closed trades in the United States and Britain unions have been the main suppliers of labour. Even if economic reasons for retaining membership are weak, some unemployed members will be reluctant to cut their links for social or political reasons. In practice, too, it seems that most unions allow lengthy periods before a lapsing unemployed member is excluded from the membership roll. Hence, if the unemployed were excluded from potential union membership, the density of unionization would tend to increase artificially in periods of unemployment, since, as unemployment increased, potential membership would decrease but actual membership figures would do so only after a considerable lag. Finally, it would be very odd to exclude from union potential a group that is entitled to join unions and actually encouraged to do so in many cases. Indeed, the fact that a significant proportion of the unemployed do not retain membership is one of the important explanatory variables in the analysis of fluctuations in membership and density.

It has been suggested by some commentators that other groups of employees such as managers, domestic staff, clergymen, agricultural workers, and part-time workers should also be excluded from potential union membership on the grounds that they are 'unorganizable', or that their organization was not 'essential' to the trade-union movement. This is unconvincing, since all these groups are unionized to some extent in at least some of the countries covered in this chapter, and only in a very few marginal cases are these groups actually barred legally from taking up union membership. While these and other groups of employees have been, and in some cases continue to be, difficult to unionize they should not be excluded from potential membership. If they were, comparability across countries would be reduced in a wholly unacceptable way, and comparability over time would also be seriously compromised as previously 'unorganizable' groups became union members and the definition of 'potential' was amended to reflect the change in circumstances. In order to avoid conflicting and shifting definitions of potential union membership the approach taken in this chapter is to include all employees, whether employed or unemployed, who are legally entitled to unionize, but to exclude the armed forces and the retired.

SOURCES OF INFORMATION

The wide variations between countries in the structure and historical development of trade unions, and the relationship between trade unions and the state, has meant that there is a very low level of comparability between membership data published by official statistical agencies. Unlike most of the statistical series included in this volume, governments cannot arrange to collect the necessary data at first hand. Unions are independent and voluntary associations of working people, and the state is obliged to rely very largely on the membership information provided from their own records. The state cannot enforce the same degree of rigour in collecting practice that is possible when the state's own officials are responsible for assembling and compiling the data. Even in the USA and Canada, where there are strict requirements laid down by statute for union financial management and the publication of financial information, the state has not felt able to impose a standard system of membership recording and reporting.

In countries where there has been, historically, a relatively harmonious relationship between state and unions, where unions are well established institutions, and where there are no sharp ideological or factional divisions between confederations, official statistical publications normally include a reliable series for aggregate union membership. With some reservations, this can be said to be the case for the UK, the USA, Canada, Australia, New Zealand, Austria, Denmark, West Germany, Norway, Sweden, and Switzerland. It must be stressed, however, that even in these cases, the official series are sometimes incomplete or biased. In virtually every case, small independent unions are excluded (such as the Catholic CGB in West Germany), and in many cases the official data include retired or other 'passive' members. They do not, therefore, correspond directly to the definitions of union membership identified earlier as ideal for comparative analytical purposes.

In countries where there is a divided union movement, or where relationships with the state have historically been tense and antagonistic, such as France, Belgium, Italy, Spain, Greece, and Turkey, membership data is normally only published by the confederations themselves, and often appears on a sporadic and unreliable basis. In these countries, the notion of union membership is often less clearly defined than in countries in the first group, and is frequently 'stretched' in the claims made by confederal leaders to include supporters, sympathizers, or those who vote for the union in a works-council election.

In this chapter, the precise details of the sources of membership information have been noted at the foot of each country table. Due to the definitional problems discussed earlier, and the absence of reliable annual data in a sizeable number of countries, neither the European Commission, nor the International Labour Office publish union membership statistics among their regular statistical indicators. Thus, unlike most of the other data reviewed in this volume, the researcher has to derive information from individual country sources and not from the publications of international institutions.

However, while there are competing views about the accuracy of membership data in most countries - even those where the unions are not divided on ideological or confessional lines - it is only for the USA that two competing and independently calculated membership series exist over a long time period. The National Bureau of Economic Research (NBER) began publishing its own series in 1897, and the official Bureau of Labor Statistics (BLS) series followed later. Initially, the BLS relied extensively on NBER information for the compilation of its series but later began to obtain information directly from the unions. Over the ninety years of publication, the two series have experienced substantial changes in their relationship to each other, reflecting the significance of the definitions of 'union' and 'member' used to arrive at the published figures. Currently, the BLS series is based on information from a population sample survey, not from union membership records, and as such is unique among the officially published series in the countries of the OECD; while the NBER is still using its very elaborate information network of union financial data, combined with other documentary sources from within unions and employee associations.

More extensive discussion of the sources and compilation of union membership series in different countries can be found in three places. Bain and Price[3] provide detailed analysis for eight countries (UK, USA, Canada, Australia, West Germany, Sweden, Denmark, and Norway) from 1892 to 1974. This group of countries offers relatively consistent and reliable data over many decades, and in most of them Bain and Price were able to provide disaggregations of membership by state or province (for the federal countries), by industry or sector, by white-collar and manual groups, and male/female groups for some, if not all, years. The basis for these disaggregations and their reliability are discussed in the text accompanying the country tables. More recently, Visser[4] has compiled aggregate, and, in some cases, disaggregated series for the post-World-War-II period for a group of West European nations (Austria, Denmark, France, West Germany, Italy, the Netherlands, Norway, Sweden, Switzerland, and the UK). This survey provides a comprehensive analysis of available data for each of these countries and is particularly helpful in respect of the three countries where major difficulties exist in compiling consistent series - France, Italy, and the Netherlands. Finally, a shorter, and less sophisticated review of union membership in the countries of the EEC can be found in Walsh.[5] While Walsh's discussion is less detailed than that provided by Visser and Bain and Price, it is useful in that it touches, albeit briefly, on countries for which only fragmentary data are available - Greece, Spain, and Luxemburg.

TRENDS IN UNION MEMBERSHIP, 1970-85

There has been considerable debate and controversy about the analysis of union growth. Four broad sets of factors have been identified as influencing trends in union membership, although there is little agreement as to the relative weights to be attached to them and no consensus on a comparative theory of union growth.

Structural factors

Changes in the occupational, industrial, and sectoral composition of the working population can have a major effect on the course of union membership. In particular, shifts in the post-war period out of manual into white-collar occupations and out of manufacturing into service industries have normally had a depressing effect on union membership by reducing the numbers of employees in well-organized sectors and increasing the numbers in poorly organized sectors.

Economic factors

A substantial econometric literature exists linking pay and price movements, and the level of unemployment to changes in the levels of union membership. The influential comparative work by Bain and Elsheikh,[6] analysing the UK, the USA, Australia, and Sweden, concluded that the rate of change of union membership in these countries could be satisfactorily explained by 'The rate of change of prices, the rate of change of wages, the level and/or rate of change of unemployment' (p.115).

Political factors

State and employer policies on union recognition, union security, and collective bargaining structures can exert a major influence on levels and stability of membership. Clegg[7] in his theoretical comparative essay argues that union membership is associated with the 'extent and depth' of collective bargaining. These, in turn, are, of course, affected by legal systems and employer strategies towards union organizations.

Strategic factors

While the three factors above are exogenous to trade unions, in the sense that they operate on the environment in which unions exist, many writers[8] have argued the need to allow for endogenous union strategies and policies which result in the union(s) being either more or less successful in influencing the environment themselves. It has been a central criticism of theories of union growth which stress exogenous variables that they depict trade unions as essentially passive recipients of the increases or losses imposed upon them by external forces. However, arguments which stress the importance of allowing for internal policy elements in the explanation of the course of union growth are generally ad hoc and not easily generalizable into broad theoretical propositions. Despite this, it must be accepted that there should be a place in a fully satisfactory analysis of union growth for the interrelationship between political factors (state and employer policies), and the unions' own policies, strength, militancy, and character. State and employer policies do not emerge in a vacuum; they are shaped by the economic, political, and industrial environment, and thus union policies may play a key role in influencing the strategies of the other actors in the industrial-relations environment.

The sixteen-year period which we review (1970-85) has been one of unusual turbulence and change in respect of all the factors outlined above. There are two clearly distinguishable and substantially contrasting sub-periods of roughly equal length; 1970-7, and 1978-85. The first sub-period is characterized by the worker militancy and self-confidence that had its origins in the events of the latter half of the previous decade, and which is reflected in the titles of two of the most influential comparative texts of the period: Barkin's Worker Militancy and Its Consequences, 1965-75 (1975) and Crouch and Pizzorno's The Resurgence of Class Conflict in Western Europe (1978). During these years rates of price inflation tended to run at historically high levels and wage increases were also substantial; the Oil Shock of 1973 and the collapse of the Bretton Woods fixed exchange-rate regime led to a major disruption of world trade patterns and stimulated decisive shifts in domestic economic policies in many OECD countries. These shifts often reinforced pre-existing tripartite or 'corporatist' arrangements for economic management and enhanced the status and political influence of trade unions. It was also a period in which a wide range of countries developed new forms of institution to strengthen 'industrial democracy' and to improve the quality of working life by 'humanization' of work. Both these streams of political intervention reflected the concern of employers and the state to respond to, and absorb, the upsurge in militancy by more effectively integrating workers and their representatives into the machinery of state and enterprise decision-making.

The period 1970-7 was thus characterized by trends in the economic and political fields that were generally favourable to the growth of union membership. Inflation and wage movements were relatively high, stimulating the 'threat' and 'credit' effects identified by Bain and Elsheikh;[9] employer and state policies were favourable, seeking to accommodate worker demands and union pressures through appropriate changes in labour-market institutions and changes in the law and in social policies. Unemployment certainly rose above the low levels experienced by most OECD countries in the 1960s, but not by a large enough margin to affect union membership seriously. Negative structural changes were occurring, particularly the growth in the relative size of the non-manual workforce, but again not on a large enough scale to counter the positive influences being derived from the political and economic factors.

Table 8.1 illustrates these trends clearly. Large increases in union membership were recorded between 1970 and 1977 in the majority of OECD countries, and in no country did membership decline. After taking

Table 8.1 Union membership growth and decline in two sub-periods, 1970-85

	1970-7		1978-85	
	Increase in union membership	Increase in density	Increase in union membership	Increase in density
	%	%	%	%
Austria	+6.5	-4	+2.7	+0.4 (1984)
Australia	+20.6	+3.8 (1976)	+13.7	+0.3
Belgium	+7.2	+2 (1978)	+22.7	+6.7
Canada	+24.5	-1.7	+20.1	
Denmark	+28.0	+8.9	+20.1	+5.0[a]
France	+7.8	-0.9	-8.7[a]	-3.2[a]
Germany (FR)	+10.9	+2.2	-0.4	-3.4
Ireland	+15.2	+1.3	-3.5	-8.9
Italy	+49.6	+9.4	-2.4	-4.2
Japan	+7.2	-2.2	+0.3	-3.7
Netherlands	+12.6	+1.6	-14.2	-10.0
New Zealand	+25.1	+3.8	+0.8	-3.6
Norway	+16.5	-1.2	+8.0	+5.1[a]
Sweden	+31.5	+12.5	+10.0	+2.3
Switzerland	+12.8	+5.5	-2.2	-1.8
UK	+14.8	+4.9	-18.3	-10.8
USA (Troy)	+3.0	-3.4	-15.9	-5.4 (1984)
(BLS)	+7.3	-3.4 (1978)	-25.5	-8.1

[a] estimates

labour-force growth into account, there were small falls in density in six of the seventeen countries for which comparative data is available, and moderate to large increases in most of the other eleven. By contrast, the later sub-period, 1978-85, shows only six countries with substantial increases in membership, four where membership was stable, and seven with significant reductions in the level of membership. In density terms the later sub-period is even more sombre for the unions. There are significant increases in only four countries (Belgium and the Scandinavian countries), and major reductions elsewhere, particularly in the USA (-8 per cent), in the UK (-10 per cent), and in the Netherlands (-10 per cent).

This reversal of the positive trends of the earlier period is closely associated with the rapid increase in unemployment across the developed economies, in particular following the 1979 Oil Shock. At the same time, employers were adjusting to the impact of micro-electronic technologies on world competitive markets for manufactured goods, and states were adopting more restrictive economic policies in the place of the Keynesian-inspired policies that had generally dominated economic thinking over the previous two decades.

Unemployment rose to levels that were well above the post-war average in most OECD countries in the later sub-period, but the degree to which individual countries suffered was variable, and thus its impact on union-membership patterns has also been variable. The effects of unemployment on union membership are threefold: the most obvious effect is to exclude from membership the majority of those employees who lose jobs in a unionized sector, and who then remain unemployed or who find jobs in non-unionized sectors; the second effect is to reduce union strength and hence union capacity to attract new groups of potential members; the third effect, and the least quantifiable, is to increase the opportunity for the state and for employers to press forward policies which further weaken union standing and effectiveness.

Unemployment and exclusion of employees from unions' spheres of influence

It should be stressed that in the four countries where membership and density continued to increase post-1978, unions are involved in a variety of ways in the administration of unemployment benefits, the control of job-search activities and training initiatives. This direct involvement in matters that are of direct relevance to unemployed union members provides a clear rationale for maintaining affiliation that is absent in the majority of countries, where union services offered to the unemployed are negligible. It is also clear that the relationship between the sectoral and occupational incidence of unemployment and the distribution of union membership varies from country to country and has thus exercised a variable effect on reductions in membership. This is most obvious in the case of the USA and the UK, where unemployment has been disproportionately fuelled by the collapse of employment in the heavily unionized parts of the manufacturing sector. Similar but less pronounced sectoral reductions in employment, and associated increases in unemployment have affected union membership in France, Ireland, and the Netherlands. By contrast, the rise in unemployment in West Germany has not been associated with cuts in employment in manufacturing on any substantial scale, and there has consequently been a more muted impact on union-membership levels.

Unemployment and new groups of members

The reduction in union effectiveness associated with the rise in unemployment has brought the trend towards increased white-collar unionization in many countries prior to 1977-8 to a halt, except in the Scandinavian countries. Indeed, in the later sub-period under consideration here, there is very little evidence of any extension of union membership into new sectors or previously ununionized areas. This is linked to the third consequence of high unemployment.

Unemployment and state and employer policies

The impact of economic recession and increased levels of unemployment on state and employer policies has been highly variable. The most obviously negative cases are again the USA and the UK. In the USA, the 'new industrial relations', concession bargaining, the drive towards union-free workplaces, government deregulation policies, and unfavourable attitudes towards unions, have all accentuated the negative membership trends that were already evident in the 1970s deriving from occupational and geographical shifts in employment.[10] In the UK the Thatcher government has abandoned the sixty-year consensus on the social value of collective bargaining and collective organization. It has virtually excluded the unions from national consultative forums and downgraded their representative status across a wide range of institutions. The legislative changes have severely undermined union security and reduced union effectiveness in industrial action. Employers have been pursuing policies which, while not generally undermining union positions, have certainly limited the unions' capacity for extension into the areas of the economy, notably services, where employment has been growing.[11] In New Zealand the National Government abolished the long-established system of compulsory union membership shortly before losing the 1984 general election; for eighteen months, therefore, the country operated for the first time since 1936 without compulsory membership to support union security.[12]

Elsewhere, however, state and employer policies have been far more differentiated and accommodative; in Australia, it is argued, state policies have actually boosted membership against the trend that might have been expected in the light of increased unemployment,[13] and a similar view might be taken about Scandinavian experience. The demand by employers for more flexible employment practices and appropriate adjustments to the law to underpin them is a common feature of industrial relations in OECD countries in the 1980s, but so far seems to be exercising little direct influence on union membership.[14]

There seems little doubt that the union movements of the OECD countries have, in a variety of ways, been weakened by the recession of the early 1980s. More intense patterns of international competition, a hardening of market conditions in domestic markets, and, in some cases, hostile state intervention have all set tighter constraints on the exercise of union power. However, there are clear differences in the degree to which they have been weakened. Unions in the highly unionized countries of Scandinavia (Sweden, Norway, and Denmark), together with the Belgian and Austrian unions, have incurred the smallest losses or made gains, while weaker union movements have suffered losses. In the light of the continuing labour and product market changes occurring today and the continuing ambiguity of state and employer policies towards unions, it will be a matter of considerable interest whether the trends of 1978 to 1985 were simply a pause, or hiccup, in a long-term trend towards extended unionization - or whether they marked the turning point towards a general marginalization of unions in the final decade of the twentieth century.

In the remainder of the chapter (Table 8.2) detailed figures are presented, with accompanying data sources, of trade-union membership and density for nineteen countries, over the period 1970-85 wherever possible.

Table 8.2: Union membership and density for nineteen countries, 1970-85

AUSTRIA

	Union membership	Labour force	Density[a]
	000s	000s	%
1970	1,520	2,448	62.1
1971	1,526	2,507	60.9
1972	1,542	2,562	60.2
1973	1,560	2,650	58.9
1974	1,580	2,698	58.6
1975	1,588	2,712	58.5
1976	1,605	2,741	58.5
1977	1,619	2,788	58.1
1978	1,629	2,816	57.8
1979	1,642	2,827	58.1
1980	1,661	2,842	58.4
1981	1,677	2,868	58.5
1982	1,673	2,872	58.2
1983	1,660	2,862	58.0
1984	1,673	2,875	58.2
1985	**	2,899	**

a Calculated from unrounded membership and labour-force series

Sources and notes

Union membership

1970-8 F. Klenner (1979) Die Oesterreichischer Gewerkschaftsbund (OGB) vol. III, Wien: 2358.

1979-85 Wirtschafts- und Sozialstatistisches Taschenbuch 1986 (1986) Wien: Oesterreichisches Arbeiterkammer. Statistisches Handbuch für die Republik Oesterreich 1986 (1986) Wien.

Union membership figures, and hence density, are overstated due to the inclusion of retired members in the returns made to the OGB by, in particular, public-sector unions.

Labour force

Oesterreichisches Statistische Zentralamt (annually) Statistisches Handbuch für die Republik Oesterreich, Wien (employed wage and salary earners plus the registered unemployed).

Recent editions of the annual Statistisches Handbuch für die Republik Oesterreich provide more detailed information on disaggregated union membership. A good summary of these statistics can be found in Visser (1984) Dimensions of Union Growth in Postwar Western Europe, EUI Working Paper no. 89 updated, Florence: European University Institute.

AUSTRALIA

	Union membership	Labour force	Density[a]
	000s	000s	%
1970	2,315	4,583	50.5
1971	2,437	4,737	51.4
1972	2,524	4,762	53.0
1973	2,660	4,864	54.7
1974	2,774	5,161	53.7
1975	2,814	5,179	54.3
1976	2,792	5,139	54.3
1977	2,794		
1978	2,775	5,454	50.9
1979	2,874	5,581	51.5
1980	2,956	5,699	51.9
1981	2,994	5,809	51.5
1982	3,012	5,929	50.8
1983	2,985	6,016	49.6
1984	3,028	6,124	49.4
1985	3,154	6,166	51.2

a Calculated from unrounded membership and labour-force series

Sources and notes

Union membership

Detailed union membership statistics have been published annually in a series of ABS (Australian Bureau of Statistics) publications, entitled Labour Report (for the years 1970-2) and Labour Statistics (for 1973-85). Aggregate information is also published in the Year Book Australia, annually. The data presented in Labour Statistics also include disaggregated membership series by state and sex.

Labour force

1970-6 G.S. Bain and R. Price (1980) Profiles of Union Growth, Oxford: Blackwell: 124. This is an adjusted series based on the official series for employed wage and salary workers but including agricultural and domestic service employment and the unemployed.

1977-85 The Labour Force Australia - Historical Survey 1966-84 (1987) Australian Bureau of Statistics, table 17, p.149, Employed Persons - Wage and Salary Earners, plus the registered unemployed at November of each year. The definition of the labour force is slightly wider in this series than in the earlier series and hence there is a break in the density series between 1976 and 1977.

It should be noted that the official union membership series is published with an 'estimated density' series, which is calculated on the employed labour force *excluding* the unemployed. For 1985, this gives a density of 57 per cent.

BELGIUM

	Union membership				Labour force	Density[a]
	CSC/ ACV	FGTB/ ABVV	CGSLB/ ACLVB	All unions		
	000s	000s	000s	000s	000s	%
1970	996	886	90	1,972	2,940	67.1
1978	1,100	970	107	2,177	3,152	69.1
1982	1,300	1,126	210	2,636	3,354	78.6
1985	1,366	1,098	210	2,672	3,523	75.8

a Calculated from unrounded membership and labour force series

Sources and notes

Union membership

No official publication provides a regular statistical series on union membership; all information has to be obtained directly from the three confederal bodies. These are:

CSC/ACV	Confédération des Syndicats Chrétiens/Algemeen Christelijk Vakverbond (Christian)
FGTB/ABVV	Fédération Générale du Travail de Belgique/ Algemeen Belgisch Vakverbond (Socialist)
CGSLB/ACLVB	Centrale Générale des Syndicats Libéraux de Belgique/Algemeen Centrale der Liberale Vakbonden Van Belgie (Liberal)

The main source of reliable estimates is the Centre de Recherche et d'Information Socio-Politique (CRISP) which publishes a regular bulletin under the title Courriers du CRISP. The data above are drawn from this source.

Some information on membership can be found in G. Spitaels (1967) Le mouvement syndical en Belgique, Brussels: Institut de Sociologie; and in V. Lorwin (1975) 'Labour unions and political parties in Belgium', Industrial and Labor Relations Review, vol. 28, January.

CANADA

	Union membership	Labour force	Density
	000s	000s	%
1970	2,550	7,102	35.9
1971	2,597	7,480	34.7
1972	2,683	7,716	34.8
1973	2,734	8,004	34.2
1974	2,863	8,405	34.1
1975	2,982	8,738	34.1
1976	3,137	9,065	34.6
1977	3,175	9,272	34.2
1978	3,298(2,908)	9,528	34.6(30.5)
1979	2,936	10,130	29.0
1980	3,093	10,465	29.6
1981	3,160	10,654	29.7
1982	3,054	10,764	28.4
1983	3,391	10,930	31.0
1984	3,439	11,195	30.7
1985	3,493	11,466	30.5

Sources and notes

Union membership

1970-8 Basic membership data is published in Labour Organizations in Canada, Ottawa: Canada Department of Labour, annually. These have been adjusted in the series given here to include unions not included in the official series. For details, see G.S. Bain and R.J. Price (1980) Profiles of Union Growth, Oxford: Blackwell: 108.

1979-85 Directory of Labour Organizations in Canada, Ottawa: Labour Canada, annually. Unadjusted returns made under the Corporations and Labour Unions Returns Act.

The basic official sources also provide good disaggregated membership series by industry and by province. See Bain and Price op.cit., for historical series by industry and province, and an aggregate historical series for male and female membership.

The change in the basis of the union membership series in 1979 implies a break in the continuity of the series at this point. For the purpose of comparison, a figure for union membership in 1978, on an unadjusted basis, is shown in the table in brackets, together with the reduced density figure.

Labour force

1970-8 Historical Labour Force Statistics: Actual Data, Seasonal Factors, Seasonally Adjusted Data 1978, Ottawa: Statistics Canada: 78 and 80.

1979-85 The Labour Force, Ottawa: Statistics Canada, annually.

Labour force data represent all paid workers plus the unemployed.

DENMARK

	Union membership	Labour force	Density[a]
	000s	000s	%
1970	1,233	1,918	64.3
1971	1,243	1,936	64.2
1972	1,268	1,992	63.7
1973	1,275	2,005	63.6
1974	1,314	2,050	64.1
1975	1,404	2,053	68.4
1976	1,513	2,104	71.9
1977	1,578	2,156	73.2
1978	1,693	2,227	76.0
1979	1,756	2,322	75.6
1980	1,802	2,395	75.2
1981	1,853	2,416	76.7
1982	1,871	2,452	76.3
1983	1,936	2,476	78.2
1984	1,958	**	**
1985	2,034	**	**

a Calculated from unrounded membership and labour force series

Sources and notes

Union membership

1970-2: J. Visser (1984) Dimensions of Union Growth in Postwar Western Europe, EUI Working Paper no. 89 updated, Florence: European University Institute: 11.
1973-85: Statistisk Aarbog Danmark, Copenhagen, annually.

The membership data given here excludes the self-employed membership of the Akademikernes Centralorganisation (AC), and includes throughout the membership of a number of independent white-collar unions which did not make returns to the national statistical bureau until the mid-1970s. For a detailed discussion of the historical aggregate series see Visser, op.cit., 12-13, and G.S. Bain and R. Price (1980) Profiles of Union Growth, Oxford: Blackwell: ch. 8.

Labour force

1970-85 Statistisk Aarbog Danmark, Copenhagen, annually (economically active population, excluding employers, directors and managers, wives assisting in husbands' trade; from labour force sample surveys). See Visser, op. cit., and Bain and Price, op. cit., for full details.

FRANCE

	Union membership	Labour force	Density[a]
	000s	000s	%
1970	3,850	16,653	23.1
1971	3,910	16,980	23.0
1972	3,980	17,308	23.0
1973	4,040	17,642	22.9
1974	4,090	17,869	22.9
1975	4,150	18,150	22.9
1976	4,160	18,391	22.6
1977	4,150	18,707	22.2
1978	4,050	18,906	21.4
1979	3,880	19,121	20.3
1980	3,750	19,510	19.2
1981	3,710	19,547	19.0
1982	3,785	19,587	19.3
1983	**	20,001	**
1984	**	20,219	**
1985	**	20,287	**

a Calculated from unrounded membership and labour force series.

Sources and notes

Union membership

No official series on trade union membership in France is available. The main confederations publish 'claimed' membership figures on an intermittent basis, although the Confédération Générale du Travail - Force Ouvriére (CGT-FO) failed even to do this before the 1970s. Calculation of membership trends therefore requires careful estimation from financial and related representational data. J. Visser (1984) Dimensions of Union Growth in Postwar Western Europe, EUI Working Paper no. 89 updated, Florence: EUI: 24, has compiled the series presented here for 1970-82, from authoritative estimates by G. Adam (1983) Le pouvoir syndical, Paris, H. Landier (1981) Demain, quel syndicats?, Paris, and J-L Birien (1978) Le fait syndicat en France, Paris. These estimates exclude the retired members which significantly inflate claimed membership figures and seek to include as members only those card holders who pay eight dues per year; this excludes a significant number of 'cotisants' who do not pay regularly, but do take a card. If these are included, total membership would be up to four percentage points greater in this period. In addition to the five nationally recognized federations, the series includes estimates for the Féderation d'Education Nationale (FEN) and the two independent federations, Confédération Genérale des Syndicats Indépendents (CGSI) and the Confédération des Syndicats Libres (CSL).

Labour force

Annuaire Statistique de la France, INSEE, Paris annually. Annual average labour-force figures including the unemployed derived from labour-force sample surveys. There is a break in the series between 1982 and 1983 reflecting a more inclusive definition of unemployment after 1982.

FEDERAL REPUBLIC OF GERMANY

	Union membership[a]	Labour force	Density
	000s	000s	%
1970	8,098	21,890	37.0
1971	8,256	22,000	37.5
1972	8,378	22,586	37.1
1973	8,564	22,757	37.6
1974	8,829	22,929	38.5
1975	8,793	22,732	38.7
1976	8,911	22,778	39.1
1977	8,980	22,923	39.2
1978	9,285	23,148	40.1
1979	9,423	23,428	40.2
1980	9,449	23,967	39.4
1981	9,521	24,410	39.0
1982	9,406	24,845	37.9
1983	9,289	25,000[b]	37.2
1984	9,187	25,022[b]	36.7
1985	9,251	25,232[b]	36.7

a Including retired members
b Estimated

Sources and notes

Union membership

The Statistisches Jahrbuch für die Bundesrepublik Deutschland, Wiesbaden: Statistisches Bundesamt, annually provides annual data for the three main federations (DGB, DAG, and DBB). This official source does not, however, include the full membership of the small Christian federation Christliche Gewerkschaftsbund (CGB); only one of its constituent unions, the Deutscher Handels-und Industrieangestelltenverband (DHV) reports its membership to the Federal Bureau of Statistics. The series presented here includes estimates for the CGB's total membership from H. Bayer, W. Streeck, and E. Treu (1981) Die Westdeutsche Gewerkschaftsbewegung in Zahlen, Koenigstein, and from O. Jacobi and W. Muller-Jentsch 'Germania' in G. Baglioni and P. Santi (eds.) (1983), Il Europa Sindacale nel 1981, Bologna, extended by the present author. The management staff union Union Leitender Angestellte (ULA) has not included; its membership in the 1970s was between 30,000 and 38,000.

It must be noted, however, that most German unions include retired members in their aggregate membership figures: Bayer et al. (1981) is the only authoritative source, and these authors conclude that, between 1970 and 1980, retired membership rose from 10 to 15 per cent approximately of total German union membership. More recent discussions with union officials and academic analysts suggest that this proportion has stabilized during the 1980s. This would suggest that the density figures given above are inflated by between 4 and 6 per cent, rising slightly during the 1970s and settling fairly closely to the latter figure in the mid-1980s.

Labour force

For 1970-7, see G.S. Bain and R. Price (1980) Profiles of Union Growth, Oxford: Blackwell: table 6.2: for subsequent years, the annual Micro Census data was supplemented with information on the unemployed from Wirtschaft und Statistik (monthly, Federal Bureau of Statistics) and on the armed forces from the Statistisches Jahrbuch.

GREECE

Union membership and density

The Greek trade union movement was re-established in 1974 following the downfall of the previous military regime and the re-creation of parliamentary institutions and democracy in July of that year. The Greek General Confederation of Labour (Geniki Synomospondia Ergaton Ellados (GSEE)) seeks to combine all political tendencies in one general organization with a 'multi-tendency' executive board. Currently there are five political groupings within the GSEE, paralleling five political parties. there are 77 national unions and 84 regional labour centres, representing considerable growth over the 43 unions and 77 regional centres existing in 1976.

In addition to the GSEE, which is the only representative organization with the right to conclude collective agreements, there is a relatively strong civil service union (ADEDY) and four very much smaller confederations: GSEE (Christian), PSOCS (Orthodox Christian), New GSEE, and the Hellenic Labour Confederation.

Membership information is sparse, but for 1983 a total membership of 675,000 (555,000 in GSEE and 125,000 in ADEDY) is quoted in The Trade Union Movement in Greece (1984) Brussels: European Trade Union Institute. With a labour force of 1.9 million, this would imply a density rate of 35.5 per cent.

REPUBLIC OF IRELAND

	Union membership	Labour force	Density
	000s	000s	%
1970	407	776	52.4
1971	410	778	52.7
1972	416	785	53.0
1973	424	792	53.5
1974	441	812	54.3
1975	448	845	53.0
1976	451	852	52.9
1977	469	872	53.7
1978	491	891	55.1
1979	513	919	55.9
1980	525	952	55.1
1981	522	980	53.3
1982	517	1,003	51.5
1983	512	1,016	50.4
1984	501	1,021	49.1
1985	474	1,025	46.2

Sources and notes

Union membership

There are three sources of data on the membership of trade unions in Ireland, but none is comprehensive in its coverage. The series published by the Registrar of Friendly Societies does not cover the public-service unions, since they are not required to register, and also excludes the membership of UK-based unions with Irish membership. It includes membership of Irish unions in Northern Ireland. The comparable series published by the Department of Labour covers all unions with a negotiation licence, but this again excludes public-service unions and a number of other 'excepted bodies'. The Irish Congress of Trade Unions is an all-Ireland body which publishes an Irish Republic membership figure, but there are seven non-affiliated organizations. The only reliable and comprehensive data are the private estimates made by the Department of Industrial Relations, University College Dublin, from the primary sources cited above, individual unions' own records, and the comprehensive UK data source held by the Industrial Relations Research Unit, University of Warwick. See, DUES Bulletins 1-4 (1986, 1987) Dublin: UCD Department of Industrial Relations.

Labour force

Estimated by the Irish Central Statistical Office from census data; police, defence forces, and the self-employed excluded.

ITALY

	Union membership[a]	Labour force	Density
	000s	000s	%
1970	4,646	14,029	33.1
1971	5,043	14,187	35.5
1972	5,301	14,391	36.8
1973	5,588	14,664	38.1
1974	6,223	14,858	41.9
1975	6,438	15,167	42.4
1976	6,866	15,530	44.2
1977	6,950	15,905	43.7
1978	7,038	15,934	44.2
1979	7,081	16,309	43.4
1980	7,150	16,506	43.3
1981	6,924	16,739	41.4
1982	6,718	16,953	39.6
1983	6,741[b]	17,067	39.5[b]
1984	6,757[b]	17,107	39.5[b]
1985	6,867[b]	17,168	40.0[b]

a excluding retired members
b author's estimate, based on personal communications from the principal confederations

Sources and notes

Union membership

Italian unions do not operate very stringent systems for the recording of membership income and the maintenance of membership records. There is no official source for union membership data, and while the confederations currently publish claimed membership figures for each year, these include a good proportion of non-paying members. Each confederation publishes total membership series including unemployed and retired members, and the above series, derived from J. Visser (1984) Dimensions of Union Growth in Postwar Western Europe, EUI Working Paper 89, Florence: European University Institute, excludes the retired membership so far as is possible. The impact which this exclusion makes on the membership series is substantial; in 1982, some 2.2 million 'passive' members were included in the aggregate claimed membership of the three confederations (25 per cent of the total). Unemployed members are included in the series above. Details of the individual confederations' membership are included in Visser (1984) which relies heavily on the work of G. Romagnoli (ed.) (1980) La sindicalizzazione tra ideologia e pratica: il caso italiana 1950-77, Rome and G. Romagnoli and G. Della Rocca (1982) 'Il sindicato' in G. Prima Cella and T. Treu Relazioni industriali manuale per l'analisi della esperienza italiana, Bologna. Membership data for the autonomous unions are patchy and unreliable and are not included in the series above. This inclusion would raise density by 2 to 4 per cent at most.

International labour statistics

Labour force

1970-80 Annuario di Statistiche del Lavoro (1981), Vol XXII, nuova serie, Rome: ISTAT.

1981-5 Annuario di Statistiche del Lavoro (annually) Rome: ISTAT.

JAPAN

	Union membership	Labour force	Density
	000s	000s	%
1970	11,604.8	32,770	35.4
1971	11,795.6	33,880	34.8
1972	11,888.6	34,690	34.3
1973	12,097.8	36,590	33.1
1974	12,461.8	36,760	33.9
1975	12,590.4	36,620	34.4
1976	12,508.7	37,100	33.7
1977	12,437.0	37,460	33.2
1978	12,382.8	37,960	32.6
1979	12,308.8	38,990	31.6
1980	12,369.3	40,120	30.8
1981	12,471.3	40,550	30.8
1982	12,525.5	41,020	30.5
1983	12,519.5	42,090	29.7
1984	12,463.8	42,820	29.1
1985	12,417.5	43,010	28.9

Sources and notes

Union membership

The Japanese Ministry of Labour publishes an annual survey of union membership that is accepted to be comprehensive in coverage and generally accurate. See Ministry of Labour (annually) Rodokumiai Kihon Tokei Chosa, Tokyo. For a longer-term analysis of membership and density trends, see N. Shimuzu (1984) 'An analysis of union density in the long term', Monthly Labour Statistics and Research Bulletin, Tokyo: April.

Labour force

From the same sources as the union-membership data.

NETHERLANDS

	Union membership[a]	Labour force	Density
	000s	000s	%
1970	1,448	3,860.0	37.5
1971	1,498	3,846.5	38.9
1972	1,525	3,925.4	38.8
1973	1,540	3,975.1	38.7
1974	1,563	4,050.6	38.6
1975	1,579	4,104.4	38.5
1976	1,593	4,132.0	38.6
1977	1,631	4,167.4	39.1
1978	1,651	4,226.2	39.1
1979	1,658	4,322.8	38.4
1980	1,631	4,395.0	37.1
1981	1,605	4,495.7	35.7
1982	1,593	4,554.8	35.0
1983	1,514	4,657.0	32.5
1984	1,456	4,728.0	30.8
1985	1,417	4,862.0	29.1

a Excludes retired members

Sources and notes

Union membership

The Dutch Central Statistical Office undertakes a biennial survey of union membership for all organizations, whether affiliated to the main confederations or not. Regular quarterly surveys are undertaken by the confederations of their membership. Since 1984 the Monthly Bulletin of Social-Economic Statistics of the Central Statistical Bureau has published quarterly data on affiliated unions.

Labour force

Prior to the establishment of the labour-force sample survey, which was first carried out in 1973 and has been annual since 1975, the Dutch Central Statistical Office use a 'volume of available labour' concept measured in man-years to calculate the labour force. This is not an appropriate series for calculating densities and consequently estimates for the relevant years for which labour-survey data are not available have been included here.

The labour-force series presented here is derived from J. Visser (1984) Dimensions of Union Growth in Postwar Western Europe, EUI Working Paper No. 89, Florence: European University Institute. Visser uses the Statistical Yearbook of the Netherlands, section H, table 2, 'Independent and dependent economically active population', adjusted on the basis of the labour-force survey data (Statistiek Werkzame Personen (annually) CBS). The series nominally represents all wage and salary earners working 15 hours and more per week, together with the unemployed looking for a job of 15 weekly hours and more. However, the definition of unemployment post-1983 has been widened, so that the data for 1984 and 1985 are not entirely consistent with the earlier series.

NEW ZEALAND

	Union membership	Labour force	Density
	000s	000s	%
1970	378.5	955.3	39.6
1971	386.3 (+127.3)	974.7[a]	39.6 (52.7)
1972	394.7	983.5	40.1
1973	427.7	1,007.4	42.5
1974	436.6	1,043.4	41.8
1975	455.0	1,065.9	42.7
1976	464.5 (+165.4)	1,078.8[a]	43.1 (58.4)
1977	473.4	1,091.2	43.4
1978	486.5	1,103.5	44.1
1979	507.0	1,111.6	45.6
1980	516.3	1,127.2	45.8
1981	519.7 (+177.8)	1,149.2[a]	45.2 (60.7)
1982	527.8	1,165.3	45.3
1983	527.5	1,178.0	44.7
1984	485.5 (+188.9)	1,192.3	40.7 (56.6)
1985	490.2 (+187.8)	1,210.1	40.5 (56.0)

a See 'Labour force' notes

Sources and notes

Union membership

Annual membership data for registered unions are published by the Department of Statistics in the New Zealand Official Yearbook. Unfortunately, many unions are not required to register and are therefore not included in the series; most significantly state employees' unions are not included. For 1984 and 1985, official estimates were published for these other unions, and their aggregate estimated membership is shown in brackets in the table above. For 1971, 1976, and 1981, authoritative estimates have been made by David Smith of the University of Wellington, and these estimtes are also shown in brackets.

Labour force

Asterisked figures for 1971, 1976, and 1981 are from census information on employed wage and salary earners plus the unemployed in each census year. Data for inter-censal years are estimates based on the movement in the official labour-force series (from labour-force surveys) which include working proprietors and family workers.

NORWAY

	Union membership		Labour force	Density
	LO	All unions		
	000s	000s	000s	%
1970	594.4	750.8	1,215.2	61.8
1971	601.9	765.9	**	**
1972	603.7	775.7	1,363.0	56.9
1973	613.8	806.2	1,403.0	57.5
1974	635.8	864.7	1,425.0	60.7
1975	655.0	902.2	1,491.0	60.5
1976	673.7	917.9	1,557.0	59.0
1977	692.2	965.4	1,593.0	60.6
1978	712.7	1,003.5	1,627.0	61.7
1979	721.1	1,041.1	1,657.0	62.8
1980	748.0	1,094.7	1,685.0	65.0
1981	755.0	1,115.2	1,702.0	65.5
1982	751.4	1,128.5	1,736.0	65.0
1983	745.1	1,142.2	1,772.0	64.5
1984	759.3	1,162.0	1,784.0	65.1
1985	769.6	1,203.9	**	**

Sources and notes

Union membership

1970-6 G.S. Bain and R.J. Price (1980) Profiles of Union Growth, table 9.1.
1977-85 Statistisk Arsbok Norge (annually), Statistisk Sentralbyra.

The 'all unions' series incorporates membership of all bodies affiliated to the AS (Akademikernes Fellesorganisasjon - Central Organization of Academic Professional Employees) and the YS (Yrkesorganisasjonenes Sentralforbund - Central Organization of Occupational Unions), together with independent unions not affiliated to a central federation. Some unions may not be included in this series.

The series is probably inflated by the inclusion of retired members, but the precise extent of this is not known.

Labour force

1970-6 G.S. Bain and R.J. Price (1980) Profiles of Union Growth, Oxford: Blackwell: table 9.1.
1977-85 Statistisk Arsbok Norge (annually); data for employed persons by status and industry, annual averages (excluding the self-employed and family workers), plus the unemployed.

SPAIN

No official sources of union membership in Spain currently exist. There are several competing confederal organizations, split on ideological and regional lines. The most important are the CCOO (Workers' Commissions) and the UGT (General Federation of Labour). Additionally, there is the syndicalist body, CNT; a progressive catholic federation, USO, which has become progressively less clearly linked to an identifiably confessional ideology; the fascist FNT; and two strong regional bodies in the Basque Country (ELA/STV) and Galicia (INTG). Many staff associations exist for white-collar workers, especially in the public services, which are not federated to a national body. Two estimates are given below from sample surveys reported in H. Rijnen (1984) Industrial Relations and Trade Unions in Spain, (paper presented at EGOS Colloquium, Amersfoort, October 1984). They reflect the accepted view that union membership increased substantially following the end of the Franco dictatorship and then fell. For details of the results of the elections of worker representatives, see The Trade Union Movement in Spain (1986) Brussels: European Trade Union Institute: 19.

	Union membership	Labour force	Density
	000s	000s	%
1978	2,900		
1983	2,068	9,845	21.0

Source

H. Rijnen, op. cit.

SWEDEN

	Union membership[a]			Labour force	Density
	LO	TCO	All unions		
	000s	000s	000s	000s	%
1970	1,680.1	661.7	2,499.6	3,109.3	80.4
1971	1,733.1	769.4	2,664.5	3,288.6	81.0
1972	1,771.5	805.0	2,740.5	3,297.3	83.1
1973	1,807.6	839.8	2,819.0	3,336.0	84.5
1974	1,863.5	881.6	2,918.5	3,391.3	86.1
1975	1,918.1	951.4	3,053.5	3,501.3	87.2
1976	1,961.2	1,006.9	3,165.2	3,520.3	89.9
1977	2,017.8	1,059.4	3,287.0	3,538.0	92.9
1978	2,057.3	1,087.1	3,364.8	3,578.0	94.0
1979	2,089.4	1,012.8	3,434.2	3,626.0	94.7
1980	2,126.8	1,042.8	3,502.6	3,645.0	96.1
1981	2,140.8	1,062.3	3,534.5	3,708.0	95.3
1982	2,161.0	1,080.0	3,504.7	3,796.3	92.3
1983	2,195.8	1,101.7	3,573.4	3,839.9	93.1
1984	2,238.6	1,120.1	3,644.3	3,863.7	94.3
1985	2,263.0	1,203.4	3,762.3	3,905.5	96.3

a Includes retired membership

Sources and notes

Union membership

1970-7 G.S. Bain and R.J. Price (1980) Profiles of Union Growth, Oxford: Blackwell: table 7.1.
1978-85 Statistisk Arsbok for Sverige.

LO Landsorganisationen i Sverige (Swedish Federation of Trade Unions).

TCO Tjanstemannens Central Organisation (Central Organization of Salaried Workers).

'All unions' series includes membership of SACO (Sveriges Akademikers Central Organisation - Central Organization of Professional Employees), SR (Statstjanstemannens Riksforbund - Civil Service Salaried Staff Federation), SAC (Sveriges Arbetares Centralorganisation - syndicalist federation) and SALF (supervisory staffs' union).

Swedish union density is overstated by the inclusion of retired members. TCO and SACO/SR publish information on the numbers of retired members included in their returns, but LO does not provide this information. Bain and Price, op.cit., 139, use data for 1974 for all federations to show that density excluding retired members was 78.1 per cent and membership 2,649,200 in that year, compared with the 86.1 per cent and 2,918,500 members shown above.

Using published data for TCO and SACO/SR and estimates for LO it is possible to make the following estimates for aggregate Swedish membership and density for 1970-85, excluding retired members:

	Union membership	Density
	000s	%
1970	2,287.0	73.6
1971	2,433.6	74.0
1972	2,497.2	75.7
1973	2,553.8	76.6
1974	2,648.7	78.1
1975	2,782.9	79.5
1976	2,875.5	81.7
1977	2,984.0	84.3
1978	3,052.9	85.3
1979	3,138.7	86.6
1980	3,197.6	87.7
1981	3,225.1	87.0
1982	3,195.0	84.2
1983	3,251.6	84.7
1984	3,308.7	85.6
1985	3,423.9	87.7

Labour force

1970-7 G.S. Bain and R. Price, op. cit., table 7.1.
1978-85 Statistisk Arsbok for Sverige (annually) Swedish Central Statistical Bureau.

The labour-force series has been compiled from labour-force sample-survey data which exclude part-time workers working less than 20 hours per week, and the unemployed seeking work for less than 20 hours. This reduces the labour-force series by between 200,000 and 300,000 workers.

SWITZERLAND

	Union membership	Labour force	Density
	000s	000s	%
1970	776.8	2,656.0	29.2
1971	782.2	2,698.0	29.0
1972	793.5	2,723.0	29.1
1973	807.5	2,742.0	29.5
1974	820.2	2,735.0	30.0
1975	870.1	2,606.0	33.4
1976	888.4	2,531.0	35.1
1977	876.3	2,527.0	34.7
1978	870.5	2,540.0	34.3
1979	866.0	2,559.0	33.8
1980	869.9	2,598.0	33.5
1981	868.1	2,634.0	33.0
1982	872.8	2,626.5	33.2
1983	867.8	2,603.9	33.3
1984	860.4	2,602.8	33.1
1985	851.4	2,622.2	32.5

Sources and notes

Union membership

Statistisches Jahrbuch der Schweiz (annually). The membership of each individual federation is included in the official Swiss statistical publications. These are as follows:

SGB *Schweizerischer Gewerkschaftsbund*

CNG *Christlich-Nationaler Gewerkschaftsbund*

SVEA *Schweizerischer Verband Evangelischer Arbeitnehner*

LFSA *Landesverband Freier Schweizerischer Arbeitnehner*

FRom *Fédération Romande des Employés*

VSA *Vereinigung Schweizerischer Angestelltenverbande*.

Aggregate memberships of the independent white-collar and public employees' unions are also provided.

The series above *excludes* the retired membership of the SGB, which amounts to between 20,000 and 30,000 over the period in question.

Labour force

The only official data on the labour force for the period covered here are those for the economically active population *including* the self-employed and unpaid family workers. J. Visser, (1984) *Dimensions of Union Growth in*

Postwar Western Europe, EUI Working Paper no. 89, Florence: EUI: 77-8, calculates a labour force series which excludes these groups by making an assumption about the proportion of the economically active population that are employees (employed and unemployed), based on 1970 census information. Visser's series has been extended here from 1982-5 on the same basis. It is uncertain how much error is introduced into the series in this way, but it seems likely that it will produce a slight underestimate of density in recent years when the proportion of migrant workers in the Swiss labour force has been declining.

UNITED KINGDOM

	Union membership	Labour force	Density
	000s	000s	%
1970	11,187	23,050	48.5
1971	11,135	22,884	48.7
1972	11,359	22,961	49.5
1973	11,456	23,244	49.3
1974	11,764	23,339	50.4
1975	12,026	23,576	51.0
1976	12,386	23,875	51.9
1977	12,846	24,069	53.4
1978	13,112	24,223	54.1
1979	13,289	24,449	54.4
1980	12,947	24,632	52.6
1981	12,106	24,551	49.3
1982	11,593	24,170	48.0
1983	11,236	24,032	46.8
1984	10,994	24,194	45.4
1985	10,716	24,755	43.3

Sources and notes

Union membership

1970-4 Data from G.S. Bain and R.J. Price, (1980) Profiles of Union Growth, Oxford: Blackwell: table 2.1.

1975-85 From the trade-union membership statistics published annually by the Department of Employment from returns to the Department and to the Certification Officer. These statistics are revised in the years following their first publication as further information comes to light: consequently, the data for 1984 and 1985 may be further revised in future years.

Labour force

The labour-force series is derived from the annual census of employment, with the addition of the unemployed (including those completing compulsory schooling) as at June of each year, estimated by the Department of Employment.

UNITED STATES

	Union membership		Labour force	Density	
	Troy/NBER	BLS		Troy/NBER	BLS
	000s	000s	000s	%	%
1970	20,990	21,248	78,100	26.9	27.2
1971	20,711	21,327	79,242	26.1	26.9
1972	21,206	21,657	81,634	26.0	26.5
1973	21,881	22,276	84,194	26.0	26.5
1974	22,165	22,809	86,485	25.6	26.4
1975	22,207	22,298	87,829	25.3	25.4
1976	22,153	22,662	89,633	24.7	25.3
1977	21,632	**	92,245	23.5	**
1978	21,757	22,807	95,728	22.7	23.8
1979	22,025	**	98,697	22.3	**
1980	20,968	22,811	100,784	20.8	22.6
1981	20,647	**	102,178	20.2	**
1982	19,571	**	102,967	19.0	**
1983	18,634	17,717	103,626	18.0	17.1
1984	18,306	17,340	105,694	17.3	16.4
1985	**	16,996	108,376	**	15.7

Sources and notes

Union membership

Two competing series are available for aggregate union membership in the United States. The Troy/NBER series has been compiled since 1897, initially under the auspices of the National Bureau of Economic Research, but in recent years under the control of Professor Troy at Rutgers University. The most recently published series is contained in Leo Troy and Neil Shiflin (1985) Union Sourcebook, Industrial Relations Data and Information Services: table 3.4; 3-11.

The Troy/NBER series represents the 'average annual dues-paying full-time equivalent membership' of every known public- and private-sector labour organization in existence during the period from 1897 onwards. The membership figures used are largely derived from financial information from individual unions and associations; where financial data were not available, the researchers have used membership data supplied by the unions themselves or extrapolated estimates.

The BLS series was derived during most of the 1970s from a biennial postal questionnaire sent to individual unions. Where unions failed to reply to the questionnaire, data were obtained from secondary sources, such as journals, convention proceedings, and financial statements. This series was published in the Directory of National Unions and Employee Associations (biennially) Department of Labor, Bureau of Labor Statistics. More recent BLS figures have, however, been developed by the US Bureau of the Census from the Current Population Survey; this is a survey of wage and salaried workers conducted at places of residence for a variety of statistical series related to population and employments trends. It is, therefore, compiled in a quite different way to the Troy/NBER series. It is also different in the concept of membership used. The CPS data relate to the sole or principal job of full- and part-time workers, thus excluding self-employed members and dual members (of whom there are undoubtedly a not insignificant number, particularly of the self-employed); they also do not relate directly to the relevant calendar year, since they are annual averages for years ending in September.

For a lengthy analysis of the strengths and weaknesses of the NBER and BLS series from 1897 to the late 1970s see G.S. Bain and R.J. Price (1980) Profiles of Union Growth, Oxford: Blackwell: chapter 3; 79-84. A recent study which examines American union reporting practices is Gary N. Chaison (1984) 'A note on the limitations of union membership data', Industrial Relations, vol. 23, no. 1, winter. L. Troy and N. Shiflin, op. cit., 3-2 and 3-3 also present an evaluation of the reliability of their method of data compilation.

Labour force

The main US labour-force series refers to the Civilian Labour Force and thus includes the self-employed, employers, and unpaid family workers. To calculate a potential union-membership series, it is necessary to add together three separate series on non-agricultural employment, agricultural workers, and the unemployed. For 1970-85 these were taken from the following sources:

Non-agricultural workers: Employment and Earnings (1987) US Department of Labor, Bureau of Labor Statistics, vol. 34, no. 10, October, table B1.

Unemployment: Employment and Earnings op. cit., table A1.

Agricultural workers: Handbook of Labor Statistics (1985) US Department of Labor, Bureau of Labor Statistics, Bulletin 2217, June, table 63; with the addition of an estimated figure for 1985.

NOTES

1 S. and B. Webb (1920) History of Trade Unions, London: Longmans: 1.

2 G.S. Bain and R. Price (1980) Profiles of Union Growth, Oxford: Blackwell.

3 ibid.

4 J. Visser (1984) Dimensions of Union Growth in Postwar Western Europe, Florence: European University Institute (EUI).

5 K. Walsh (1985) Trade Union Membership, Brussels: Eurostat.

6 G.S. Bain and F. Elsheikh (1976) Union Growth and the Business Cycle, Oxford: Blackwell.

7 H. Clegg (1976) Trade Unionism Under Collective Bargaining, Oxford: Blackwell.

8 See R.J. Adams (1975) The Growth of White Collar Unionism in Britain and Sweden: A Comparative Investigation, Madison: University of Wisconsin Press, and R. Undy, V. Ellis, W.E.J. McCarthy, and A.M. Halmos (1981) Change in Trade Unions: The Development of UK Unions since 1960, London: Hutchinson.

9 G.S. Bain and F. Elsheikh, op. cit.

10 R. Miller (1987) 'The mid-life crisis of the American labor movement', Industrial Relations Journal, vol. 18.

11 J. Macinnes (1987) Thatcherism at Work, Milton Keynes: Open University Press.

12 R. Harbridge and S. Webber (1987) 'Trends in official union membership, 1983-1985', New Zealand Journal of Industrial Relations, vol. 12.

13 J. Niland (1986) 'Gaining against the tide: Australian unionism in the 1980s', IRRA Proceedings, New York: International Relations Research Association.

14 S. Barkin (1987) 'The flexibility debate in Western Europe', Relations Industrielles, vol. 42.

9 INDUSTRIAL DISPUTES

S. Creigh[1]

> Public Agencies are very keen on amassing statistics - they collect them, add them, raise them to the nth power, take the cube root and prepare wonderful diagrams. But what you must never forget is that every one of these figures comes in the first instance from the village watchman, who just puts down what he damn well pleases. (Attributed to Sir Josiah Stamp)

INTRODUCTION

Most of the quantitative work in the industrial relations field has concentrated on strike action and degree of unionization. The reason for this is simply that these two aspects of industrial relations are often the only ones to which national statistical authorities devote any time or attention. Elsewhere the budding researchers must set about creating their own bases by means of extensive (and expensive) surveys.

Since its creation after World War I, the International Labour Office (ILO) in Geneva has collected information from member countries on industrial disputes which resulted in a stoppage of work. However, the records maintained by several of the leading industrial countries stretch back into the nineteenth century.

As early as 1926 the ILO attempted to achieve some standardization of dispute classification. The 3rd Conference of Labour Statisticians held in that year considered detailed recommendations prepared within the ILO itself relating to both the enumeration and classification of disputes. The Conference recommended that the basic unit, the dispute case, should be defined as a temporary stoppage of work wilfully effected by a group of workers, or by one or more employers, with a view to enforcing a demand. Disputes affecting several establishments should be considered as one case provided they were organized or directed by one person or organization. The distinction between strikes and lock-outs should be preserved as far as possible.[2]

Given the absence of other quantitative data, it is not surprising that industrial dispute activity is often used as an indicator of the 'health' of a country's industrial relations system - either over time or relative to comparable economies. However, it must be noted that recorded disputes are at best only a partial indicator of industrial action, and that in turn the level of industrial action is itself only a partial indicator of the prevailing industrial relations 'health' or 'climate'. Unfortunately, it is usually the only statistical indicator available.

The limitations of dispute activity as a measure of an industrial relations system's health rest upon two issues. In the first place, there is the question of the relationship between 'organized' and 'unorganized' conflict. However, a second issue arises because 'organized' conflict itself can take various forms and is not confined to the all-out stoppages recorded by statistical authorities.

Two views have emerged concerning the relationship between different forms of conflict. The 'additive' hypothesis is that, where there is a high rate of one form of conflict, other forms will likewise be high. This will presumably reflect the general industrial relations climate of the particular location concerned. The 'alternative' hypothesis views industrial conflict as a response to discontents arising in the workplace. Such discontents may be expressed in a variety of ways, ranging from organized forms of collective action (such as strikes) to unorganized forms, such as individual absenteeism and labour turnover. Under these circumstances, if one mode of expression is unavailable, discontent will manifest itself in another form.

Most of the empirical research on this question has been undertaken in the UK. For the most part these analyses have concentrated on the statistical correlations between various measures of organized and unorganized conflict.[3]

On balance, the UK evidence appears to support the additive hypothesis concerning the relationship between organized and unorganized industrial conflict. If this were to hold at the international level, a nation's relative strike-proneness might represent a reasonable proxy for its relative standing in terms of unorganized conflict. However, since no substantial comparative data are available, little more can be done than to note the problem and bear it in mind when using the stoppage data alone as an index of industrial conflict.

The relationships between the various forms of organized industrial conflict themselves have also attracted little research attention, presumably due to the formidable data problems. A few of the OECD countries do make a systematic record of disputes resulting in industrial action which falls short of the criteria required for inclusion in the national official stoppage statistics. So few countries are involved, however, that meaningful cross-section analysis is not possible, but in two cases (Japan and New Zealand) statistics are available on the level of both recorded stoppage activity and other dispute-related action over time.[4]

Creigh and Poland (1983)[3] concluded that in both countries movements over time in stoppages qualifying for inclusion in the official dispute statistics are significantly and positively associated (correlated) with movements in other forms of industrial action coming to the attention of the statistical authorities. This evidence cannot of course be applied directly to cross-section differences in recorded stoppages. However, it does give some indirect support to the additive hypothesis - at least between the various forms of organized industrial action.

STATISTICAL COMPARABILITY ACROSS OECD COUNTRIES

The ILO Conference of 1926 produced a range of recommendations on the collection and presentation of statistics on industrial disputes. For instance, the 'importance' of a dispute was to be indicated by the number of establishments affected, the number of workers involved, the duration of the dispute, and the number of man-days lost. In each case, the Conference suggested detailed classifications, e.g. the recommended classification for the number of establishments affected ranged across five groups, from one establishment to more than a hundred establishments.

The Conference also recommended that all five measures of dispute action (number of disputes, establishments affected, workers involved, duration, and working days lost) should be classified according to their 'principal characteristics'. Disputes were to be classified by the principal industrial sectors, and in addition detailed classifications were recommended by 'matter in dispute' (eight groups), 'result' (seven groups), and 'method of settlement' (six groups).

In fact, the Conference's recommendations seem to have had little practical impact on the various statistical agencies of the twenty-four countries which attended. As noted above, even in 1926 several of the major industrial economies had already been collecting and publishing dispute statistics for a considerable period.[5] Thus few attempts seem to have been made to bring these national practices into line with the Conference's recommendations, although the recommendations have been reprinted occasionally.[6]

For most countries information is published on number of disputes, workers involved (thousands), and working days lost (thousands), for both the whole economy and each of the broad sectors.[7] In addition to these raw data the ILO has produced information on working days lost per 1,000 persons employed (hereafter stoppage incidence) in the mining, manufacturing, construction, and transport industries (hereafter the industrial sector).

In the immediate post-war period international patterns of strike activity attracted little attention from either statisticians or academic researchers. This no doubt reflected the historically rather low levels of strike action found in most industrial nations at the time. Some of the earliest and best of the available descriptive studies are those by Forchheimer in 1948. By the early 1960s, however, the level of research interest in comparative strike activity began to increase. In 1960 Ross and Hartman attempted to account for differences in the measured strike patterns between fourteen countries.[8] In the early 1960s the British Department of Employment began to publish comparative analyses of working days lost per thousand employees in the main industrial countries on a regular basis, using information provided by the ILO.

The British Royal Commission on Trade Unions and Employers' Associations (1968), chaired by Lord Donovan, devoted some time to comparing industrial dispute statistics across sixteen countries using ILO data for the mid-1960s. The Commission felt that the UK suffered from a comparatively large number of stoppages, but that they were of fairly short duration, and did not usually involve large numbers of people.[9] However, the Donovan Commission's use of such international comparisons prompted a vigorous dispute between two leading industrial relations academics. The point at issue was the definition of a stoppage of work of sufficient size to warrant inclusion in the official statistics. Turner argued that comparisons based on stoppage numbers were biased against the UK because British statisticians included a wider range of stoppages in the official statistics than many other countries. The Commission's research director, McCarthy, replied by utilizing Turner's own suggestions to argue that, after compensating for definitional differences, the UK's relevant strike-proneness was less encouraging.[10]

In fact, the classification of certain countries into particular groups is more difficult than either McCarthy or Turner implied. Their debate had occurred against the particular background of the major strike wave which swept through much of the industrialized world in the late 1960s and early 1970s. In fact, the shortage of systematic information on dispute statistics across countries led the OECD to commission an important study of member countries undertaken by Fisher in the early 1970s and published in 1973.

The various subsequent studies, however, all suffer from limitations. Jackson and Sweet, for instance, pay relatively little attention to how data are collected and compiled, while Creigh, Donaldson, and Hawthorn do not review the available information in any detail. Other analyses have looked exclusively at European countries, e.g. Shalev.[11]

STATISTICAL COMPARABILITY ACROSS TWENTY OECD COUNTRIES

The present analysis covers twenty OECD member countries. These comprise Australia, New Zealand, Japan, the European Community (except Greece, Luxemburg, and Portugal), the Nordic nations, Austria, Switzerland, Canada, and the United States. In the 1980s these nations accounted for 98 per cent of total OECD production and around 93 per cent of the overall OECD labour force. There are four other non-Communist members of the OECD. Two of these, Greece and Luxemburg, do not produce stoppage statistics, although in the latter case stoppage activity is believed to be very low. Portugal has only produced stoppage data since 1977 and, while Turkey's data stretch back over a longer period, that nation's low per-capita income and relatively small industrial sector preclude useful comparisons with more developed OECD member countries.

As far as possible the information in table 9.1 relates to the early 1980s, the latest period for which full information was available in some cases. However, recent significant changes in practice are noted. For each country information is provided on the type of stoppages included in the statistical records and the methods by which such records are compiled. The information in the table is primarily derived from the relevant statistical publications of the nations concerned, supplemented in some cases by contacts with the various national statistical agencies and occasionally by information from secondary sources.[12]

The diversity of statistical practice shown in table 9.1 is such that it is perhaps appropriate to begin the discussion by noting some <u>common elements</u>. All the countries covered collect statistical information on stoppages of work resulting from industrial disputes over terms and conditions of employment and related sympathetic stoppages. All twenty countries include both strikes and lock-outs in their statistical records; however, only seven countries (Austria, Canada, the Federal Republic of Germany, Iceland, Japan, New Zealand, and Sweden) follow the original 1926 ILO recommendation and distinguish between the two types of stoppage in their published records.[13]

So far as information collection is concerned, most statistical authorities rely on the voluntary provision of information. Only in West Germany are employers legally obliged to report stoppages, although in Italy employers are under a general legal obligation to report matters of this type to the police. In Australia there is no obligation to report stoppages but, once the Australian Bureau of Statistics hears of a dispute and contacts the organizations concerned, they are legally obliged to provide the information requested, which is then regarded as confidential by the ABS and cannot be disclosed to third parties.

In most countries local officials of the national ministry of employment (or labour) act as the primary channel for dispute reporting and information collection. However, the police appear to play an important role in dispute reporting in Belgium and Italy, while in two of the Nordic countries (Denmark and Sweden) the employers' associations are the

Table 9.1 Recording criteria and data collection methods for work stoppages resulting from industrial disputes

	Criteria for inclusion of stoppage in statistics	Collection methods
Australia[a]	Ten or more days lost	Information on occurrence from newspapers, periodicals, contacts with industrial arbitration authorities, employers and unions. Form sent to employers who are legally obliged to complete and return it
Austria[b]	No known limitation	Trade unions provide information
Belgium[a]	One working day (8 hours) or more	Reports by police received via National Conciliation Service with questionnaire follow-ups from National Institute of Statistics
Canada[a,b]	Ten or more person days lost	Manpower Centres of Canada Employment and Immigration Commission file reports. Provincial Labour Departments and press clippings for additional information. In some cases parties directly involved are contacted by telephone
Denmark[a]	More than 100 working days lost	Information obtained from Danish Employers' Confederation and other major employer organizations
Finland[a]	Four hours or more, unless 100 or more days lost in aggregate	Returns assembled from enquiry mailed to both employer and employees in establishments covered by a dispute
France[b]	No formal limitation	Labour inspectors using standardized form. No statistics collected on Agriculture or Public Administration
Germany (FR)[a,b]	One day and 10 workers involved. All stoppages with more than 100 working days lost are included	Employers legally obliged to report disputes to the local office of the Federal Employment Service

Table 9.1 (cont.)

	Criteria for inclusion of stoppage in statistics	Collection methods
Iceland[b]	Four hours or more, 4 workers or more involved	Reports from trade unions in the various areas
Irish Republic[a]	One day or an aggregate loss of 10 man days	Reports from local employment offices based on standardized recording form
Italy[b]	No formal restrictions	Provincial police send reports to Central Institute of Statistics
Japan[b]	Half of normal daily working hours (shorter stoppages recorded separately)	Interviews with employers or workers' representatives concerned by Prefectorial Policy Section or local Labour Policy Officers
Netherlands[a]	No formal limitations	District employment offices inform Central Bureau of Statistics
New Zealand	Ten or more working days lost	Heavy reliance on Department of Labour District Offices to gather information on stoppages
Norway[a]	One day or more	Questions to employee and employer organizations
Spain[a]	No known limitations	Returns from local provincial delegates of the Ministry of Labour
Sweden[a]	Duration of one hour or more	State Conciliation Office prepares statistics on basis of newspaper reports, these are checked by Swedish Employers' Confederation. Conciliation Office then sends the figures to the Central Statistical Office
Switzerland[a]	One day or more. A separate note is kept of shorter stoppages	Federal office for industry, crafts, occupations, and employment collects information from press reports and inquiries sent to trade unions and employers' organizations

Table 9.1 (cont.)

	Criteria for inclusion of stoppage in statistics	Collection methods
United Kingdom	Ten workers and one day All stoppages with more than 100 working days lost are included	Reports primarily from unemployment benefit offices based on own knowledge, press reports, employer and union contacts, supplemented by returns from some nationalized industries
United States[a]	Six workers or more, or one full day or shift until December 1981. Since than 1,000 or more workers and a full shift. It is estimated that this change has reduced the recorded number of days lost by 30-40 per cent	Press cuttings, reports from employers, unions, and agencies followed up by questionnaires

a Indicates stoppage records known to include political stoppages. In Italy this applies from 1975 only. New Zealand has a separate record of non-industrial stoppages

b Indicates that data are collected only for workers directly involved in stoppages, i.e. those who actually stopped work and who are in dispute with their employer. The other countries collect data for both workers directly involved and those indirectly involved because they are laid-off due to a stoppage elsewhere at the same establishment

See Creigh and Poland,[4] table 1 for a fuller discussion of the statistical publications for each country

major reporting centres. Initial reports are usually followed up by the collection of detailed information on the basis of standardized forms or questionnaires.

Recent industrial relations research studies have underlined the extent to which the same events may be described in different terms by representatives of the various parties concerned.[14] Since the statistical agencies of many countries draw most (if not all) of their information on disputes from the employers concerned or from employers' associations, the resulting statistics will inevitably tend to reflect 'management bias' in their interpretation of events. In contrast, only Austria and Iceland gather information on disputes exclusively from trade unions, although some six other countries explicitly state that they gather information on stoppages from both unions and employers.

All twenty countries collect and publish data on the number of workers actively in dispute with their employer i.e. those directly involved in stoppages. Furthermore, no country systematically collects and publishes information on the secondary effects of stoppages i.e. lay-offs due to shortages of components or lack of orders because of a stoppage at another establishment.

Some further common ground can be found in terms of the indices of stoppage activity produced and published. All twenty countries produce statistics on the number of workers involved in stoppages and the number of working days (or in the cases of Austria, Finland, and Italy the number of working hours) lost. Except for the German Federal Republic, all the countries currently publish information on the number of stoppages recorded. However, only a small minority of countries (i.e. Belgium, Finland, France, and the German Federal Republic) have followed the ILO's recommendation that information be published on the number of establishments affected by stoppages, although the Irish Republic and Switzerland produce data on firms (employers) affected.

Australia and New Zealand are the only countries which publish estimates of the loss of wages due to stoppages. The United Kingdom and Australia both produce statistics on working days lost per thousand employees, and Australia also publishes data on average working days lost per worker involved in stoppages. Iceland produces data on the number of days on which stoppages occurred, and on working days lost as a percentage of potential working time.

As noted above, commentators have devoted considerable attention to the various definitions used, in terms of minimum or threshold levels, to decide whether or not a particular dispute qualifies for inclusion in the national statistics. Such requirements are listed in table 9.1. Among the countries covered one quarter (Austria, France, Italy, the Netherlands, and Spain) do not appear to lay down any formal criteria for the inclusion of stoppages in their official statistics. Another quarter (Belgium, Japan, Norway, Sweden, and Switzerland) have limits on the duration of stoppages included. In three cases (Belgium, Norway, and Switzerland) stoppages lasting one day or more qualify for inclusion, whereas the other two countries have shorter duration limits. A further group of four countries (Australia, Canada, Denmark, and New Zealand) include only stoppages attaining a minimum size (in three cases ten or more working days lost). The remaining countries have more complex additive or alternative multiple criteria, reaching their most complex in the cases of the UK and the German Federal Republic. These countries basically include only those stoppages lasting one day or more and involving ten or more workers - however, all stoppages involving more than one hundred working days are also included.

Other things being equal, the higher the threshold set for inclusion in the stoppage statistics, the more small, or short, disputes will be excluded from the official statistics. Thus, for example, a stoppage involving fifty workers and lasting one day would qualify for inclusion in the official dispute statistics of Australia (where disputes accounting for ten working days or more qualify for inclusion), but not in Denmark (where only disputes accounting for one hundred working days or more are counted).

Statistical comparability problems are, of course, not limited merely to industrial stoppages, and attempts are often made to produce 'adjusted', directly comparable statistics. In the case of stoppage statistics the obvious solution would be to adopt a 'highest common denominator' approach. This would involve producing adjusted figures for each country which included only those stoppages exceeding the limits set by the nation employing the most stringent criteria. Unfortunately, in practice, such adjustment cannot be achieved so readily for several reasons. As noted earlier, countries use up to three different criteria (stoppage duration, the number of workers involved, and the number of working days lost) in deciding whether or not a particular stoppage coming to the attention of the statisticians concerned in fact qualifies for inclusion. Furthermore, the OECD countries have not adopted the standardized approach to dispute classification originally recommended by the ILO in 1926.[15]

In the early 1980s some eleven countries published information on recorded stoppages classified by duration, but no two countries used the same classifications and the diversity was such that any standardized classification would cover only a handful of countries. With respect to workers involved and working days lost, the situation appeared even less promising. Six countries produced information on the distribution of recorded stoppages by workers involved, and only four countries currently published data classified by the number of working days lost.

Thus, it is simply not possible to produce an adjusted set of statistics on stoppage numbers covering an appreciable number of countries based on common criteria for the inclusion of disputes. Moreover, even when two or three countries happen to use the same definition and similar recording methods, comparability problems may still persist. Thus, for example, if two countries both exclude stoppages lasting less than one day, this rule may have little effect in one country where many of the stoppages which actually occur are lengthy, but it may exclude a high proportion of all the stoppages occurring in another country where the typical stoppage lasts only a few hours. However, provided these patterns are relatively stable, com-parisons between countries of trends over time will probably still be valid.

Under-reporting occurs when stoppages which ought, on the published criteria, to be included in the national stoppage statistics in practice escape the attention of the responsible statistical authorities. In terms of Sir Josiah Stamp's remark quoted at the beginning of the chapter, the problem reflects the occasions when the village watchman was otherwise engaged. As noted earlier, very few countries place a legal obligation on employers in terms of initial stoppage reporting. The only exceptions appear to be the German Federal Republic and (to a lesser extent) Italy. Elsewhere information provision is essentially on a voluntary basis, and the parties concerned may if they wish simply ignore requests for information from the various national statistical agencies.

Probably the most impressive work on the extent of the under-reporting problem has been undertaken in the UK. During the winter of 1977-8 a large-scale survey was undertaken by the then British Social Science Research Council's Industrial Relations Research Unit. Some 970 manufacturing establishments were covered and a subsequent analysis, undertaken in collaboration with the Department of Employment's Statistics Division, sought to compare the survey results on industrial action with the Department's own internal records. Such an exercise raises many methodological problems, not the least of which being the implicit assumption that the survey results themselves present the accurate picture against which official statistical records must be judged. However, the results (fortunately) appear to square well with common sense.

In essence the results showed that 68 per cent of eligible stoppages were in fact recorded by the Department of Employment. However, the Department's reporting rate rose strongly with stoppage duration - from 41 per cent of stoppages lasting one day to 98 per cent of stoppages of ten or more days' duration. The Department's detection rate also rose with establishment size - from 55 per cent of eligible stoppages in plants with 50 to 99 employees to 65 per cent in the case of plants with 1,000 or more employees.

This evidence of substantial under-reporting of stoppages in a major OECD country relying (like most nations) on voluntary reporting, together with the (untested) possibility that the degree of underreporting may vary from country to country, raises yet further doubts about the usefulness of international comparisons based on recorded stoppage numbers. In contrast, the Department's success in detecting long stoppages and stoppages occurring in large establishments (where there are more potential strikers) means that no less than 97 per cent of the one million working days lost according to the survey results were actually recorded by the Department of Employment.[16]

BASES FOR INTERNATIONAL COMPARISON

When all the statistical factors are considered, the working days lost measure of stoppage activity is clearly likely to provide the best single comparative yardstick. This is basically because the bulk of days lost in each country are accounted for by a small number of major stoppages which will be recorded irrespective of differences in definitions, collection methods, and underreporting. Also, the use of the working days lost measure of strike activity may have additional advantages quite apart from statistical comparability considerations. Various authors have argued that the working days lost measure reflects bargaining attitudes more comprehensively and is a more useful, but still seriously incomplete, indicator of the impact and economic costs of stoppages.[17]

When comparisons of stoppage action levels are being made, differences in working population size, and hence in those 'at risk' of becoming involved in strikes, must clearly be allowed for since, otherwise, stoppage differences may simply reflect differences in the size of the workforce. However, stoppage incidence comparisons can be undertaken on various bases depending on which industries are included in the analyses.

The 'industrial sector'

Throughout the post-war period ILO data on stoppage incidence have covered the 'industrial sector' - comprising mining, manufacturing, construction, and transport. The ILO argues that this approach improves data comparability. It holds that the exclusion of agriculture, most of the private service sector, and government avoids many of the areas in which government regulations would affect comparisons and covers industries in which the effect of differences in definitions of employees between countries is likely to be minimal. The case of France, which does not collect stoppage data for agriculture and public administration, is usually cited in support.

However, on closer inspection many of these arguments are less convincing. So far as is known, no other OECD country imposes restrictions comparable to those of France. While several countries have restrictions on the right to strike of certain public employees (notably the police and armed forces), industrial action by such groups is very unusual and would in any case qualify for inclusion in the stoppage statistics in the usual way. Furthermore, although it is true that large numbers of self-employed persons and family workers are found in the agricultural sectors of many countries, estimates of agricultural employment are available, at least for the latter part of the post-war period. In fact, even the ILO's data suffer from minor comparability problems simply because it is not possible to

Table 9.2 Stoppage incidence (working days lost per 1,000 persons employed) in mining, manufacturing, construction, and transport and communication

	1970	1971	1972	1973	1974	1975	1976
Australia	1,040	1,300	880	1,080	2,670	1,390	1,490
Belgium	830	720	190	520	340	340	560
Canada	2,190	800	1,420	1,660	2,550	2,810	2,550
Denmark	170	30	40	4,440	330	110	220
Finland	270	3,300	520	2,530	470	310	1,310
France	180	440	300	330	250	390	420
Germany (FR)	10	340	10	40	60	10	40
Irish Republic	490	670	600	410	1,240	810	840
Italy	1,730	1,060	1,670	2,470	1,800	1,730	2,310
Japan	200	310	270	210	450	390	150
Netherlands	140	50	70	330	-	-	10
New Zealand	470	350	300	530	360	390	950
Norway	70	10	-	10	490	10	70
Spain	240	190	120	210	310	370	2,540
Sweden	40	310	10	10	30	20	20
Switzerland	-	10	-	-	-	-	20
UK	740	1,190	2,160	570	1,270	540	300
USA	2,210	1,600	860	750	1,480	990	1,190

Source: 1970-9 Creigh and Poland[4]. 1980 onwards Employment Gazette (1986) vol. 94, no. 6

- indicates less than five working days lost per 1,000 persons employed. A major definition change affects US data from 1981 - see table 9.1

1977	1978	1979	1980	1981	1982	1983	1984
670	960	1,560	1,360	1,700	900	620	510
430	660	360	140	**	**	**	**
830	1,930	1,660	1,510	1,870	1,410	600	930
240	90	140	210	720	100	80	150
2,360	160	270	1,250	560	220	390	690
260	200	360	170	160	260	160	170
-	370	40	10	-	-	-	510
960	1,500	3,470	650	930	630	550	650
1,560	880	2,560	1,630	970	1,930	1,480	730
70	60	40	50	20	20	20	20
150	-	190	30	10	60	40	**
910	890	860	750	810	710	840	960
40	90	10	140	40	390	10	60
3,350	1,820	3,260	**	**	**	**	**
20	10	20	2,240	60	-	10	20
-	-	-	-	-	-	-	-
840	840	2,420	1,150	330	460	330	3,120
1,070	1,070	890	540	470	300	590	160

produce information on the industrial sector for all the countries covered.[18] Stoppage incidence in the industrial sector since 1970 across OECD nations is summarized in table 9.2. Recorded working time lost due to stoppages ranged from an average of over 4 days per employee in Denmark in 1973 (representing some 1.8 per cent of normally available working time) down to zero (e.g. Switzerland in several years). Over the fifteen-year period as a whole the nations covered fall into three broad groups. Eight countries recorded annual average stoppage incidence rates of over 900. This group includes five European countries - Italy, Spain, the UK, Finland, and the Irish Republic - North America, and Australia. A second group comprising New Zealand and three European countries - Denmark, Belgium, and France - exhibit intermediate stoppage incidence rates averaging between 900 and 200 days lost per annum. The remaining six countries covered by the industrial sector data all have average rates below 200 days lost. Except for Japan, all are European economies - Sweden, West Germany, Norway, the Netherlands, and Switzerland.

All industries and services

The main alternative to the 'industrial sector' approach is to produce analyses covering all industries and services.[19]

In the 1970s as a whole the mining, manufacturing, construction, and transport sectors accounted for an average of only about 47 per cent of total employment in OECD member countries, ranging from 37 per cent of total employment in the USA up to 58 per cent in the Federal Republic of Germany. However, the industrial sector was, of course, much more important in terms of stoppage level, being responsible for 84 per cent of all recorded stoppages and 83 per cent of total working days lost. This disparity means that more comprehensively based statistics will inevitably show lower stoppage incidence rates than those which are confined to the industrial sector.

Various academic researchers began to produce comprehensive all-industry analyses in the late 1970s. Clegg produced and analysed comprehensive information on stoppage frequency, stoppage incidence, average involvement, and average duration across six countries (Australia, France, the Federal Republic of Germany, Sweden, the UK, and the USA) in the post-war period.[20] Smith and his colleagues produced information on working days lost per 1,000 persons in the labour force across a wider range of industrial economies.[21]

The Statistical Office of the European Communities also began to produce economy-wide comparative information on stoppage incidence for Community member countries,[22] and the British Department of Employment subsequently began to publish similar information for a wider range of countries in parallel with data for the industrial sector provided by the ILO.[23]

These new developments appear to have sprung from three sources. First, there had been improvements in the quantity and reliability of the labour-force statistics needed to provide the denominator in stoppage-incidence rate calculations. Second, the tertiary or service sector was providing an ever increasing share of total employment and was beginning to experience some industrial action, whereas previously its predominantly non-manual employees had been virtually strike-free. Third, it became clear that the partial coverage of the ILO stoppage incidence data could occasionally result in a distorted picture of a country's relative strike-proneness. Thus during the 1970s, both the Irish Republic and Sweden experienced usually high levels of strike activity outside the industrial sector, and consequently had their relative stoppage incidence understated by the ILO data. In the extreme case, that of Sweden, only 31 per cent of total working days lost during the 1970s were in the industrial sector, since many of the country's major disputes occurred in the forestry industry.[24]

Information on the most accurate measure of the number of persons at risk of involvement in stoppages - the number of wage earners and salaried employees - has been published by the OECD for 1962 onwards.[25] Stoppage-incidence rates in all industries since 1970 are summarized in table 9.3.

There are considerable variations between years in the stoppage incidence figures for any particular country, since a given figure may be dominated by the effects of a few major stoppages. Comparisons over extended periods are thus more appropriate than annual ones. Across the entire period 1970 to 1984 the highest average stoppage incidence figures were found in Italy, Iceland, Canada, Spain, the Irish Republic, and Australia. On the other hand, the lowest average stoppage incidence rates were recorded by Switzerland, Austria, the Netherlands, Norway, Federal Germany, and Japan. The overall ranking of countries is broadly similar to that in the industrial sector for the eighteen countries also covered in table 9.2. The two additional countries included in table 9.3 represent (almost) polar cases. Iceland ranks second only to Italy in terms of average stoppage incidence, while only Switzerland has a lower rate than Austria.

During the fifteen-year period wide variations existed between countries in terms of key economic variables such as unemployment and inflation rates. These variables have been found to be associated with changes in stoppage activity levels both over time and between economies. (See Creigh, Poland, and Wooden for a discussion of the evidence on the factors accounting for international differences in stoppage activity.[26])

SUMMARY AND CONCLUSIONS

Strike activity is necessarily only a partial indicator of industrial conflict, let alone of the wider industrial relations climate within an economy. Unfortunately, the very absence of comprehensive quantitative information on other forms of industrial action, which leads to the exclusive use of stoppage statistics, in itself prevents any full analysis of the problem.

However, recent studies in the UK support the view that 'organized' and 'unorganized' forms of conflict are positively associated, and time-series evidence for Japan and New Zealand indicates that, within the spectrum of organized conflict, movements in all-out stoppages are paralleled by movements in other types of action. The available evidence thus suggests that stoppage activity may provide a useful, though by no means complete, indicator of the level of industrial conflict in an economy, and hence of the climate of the national industrial relations system.

In 1926 the ILO sponsored an attempt to standardize the way in which strike statistics were classified and published. However, even at that time, most industrial countries had their own well-established statistical methods and the recommendations for standardization were mostly ignored. Nevertheless, certain common features are to be found across many of the OECD countries:

(a) All countries collect data on both strikes and lock-outs resulting from disputes over terms and conditions of employment and related sympathetic disputes.

Table 9.3 Stoppage incidence (working days lost per 1,000 employees) - all industries

	1970	1971	1972	1973	1974	1975	1976
Australia	536	668	433	550	1,274	715	770
Austria	12	-	6	70	-	-	-
Belgium	481	408	116	280	183	194	289
Canada	933	399	1,040	732	1,121	1,302	1,358
Denmark	55	11	11	2,006	95	52	107
Finland	144	1,665	284	1,435	239	154	676
France	109	272	229	233	198	228	292
Germany (FR)	-	211	-	25	48	-	25
Iceland	4,478	451	165	190	1,190	781	3,716
Irish Republic	1,405	375	284	279	733	393	1,003
Italy	1,630	1,142	1,502	1,770	1,429	1,968	1,814
Japan	118	176	148	127	265	219	87
Netherlands	68	25	35	151	-	-	-
New Zealand	303	169	116	234	158	158	354
Norway	39	6	9	8	227	8	90
Spain	137	107	70	125	199	205	1,438
Sweden	45	242	-	-	16	98	6
Switzerland	-	-	-	-	-	-	7
UK	488	612	1,080	317	647	264	145
USA	937	668	367	364	613	406	476

Source: As table 9.2.

\- indicates less than five working days lost per 1,000 employees. A major definition change affects US data from 1981 - see table 9.1

** indicates not available

1977	1978	1979	1980	1981	1982	1983	1984
335	432	864	640	780	400	310	240
-	-	-	6	-	-	-	-
208	324	196	69	**	**	**	**
381	827	842	934	899	610	460	390
115	62	82	89	311	50	40	60
1,312	74	133	848	339	100	360	750
211	126	209	95	87	130	80	80
-	203	22	5	-	-	-	260
2,260	587	179	344	878	**	**	**
571	767	1,756	483	508	500	380	470
1,162	714	1,895	1,119	716	1,280	980	610
40	35	24	25	13	10	10	10
60	-	76	14	6	50	30	**
430	378	372	348	380	310	360	400
16	39	-	62	17	170	-	60
1,907	1,361	2,288	790	680	370	590	890
23	9	7	1,149	53	-	10	10
-	-	-	-	-	-	-	-
448	413	1,286	531	201	250	180	1,280
436	425	386	230	190	100	190	90

(b) Almost all countries publish some information on the number of stoppages, the number of workers involved, and the number of working days (or hours) lost.
(c) Initial reporting of stoppages is voluntary in most countries.
(d) Employers provide the basic information on stoppages in most cases. In most cases this information is channelled through the local offices of the ministry of labour.
(e) All countries collect information on the numbers of workers directly involved in stoppages - those actively taking industrial action.

On the other hand, there are very substantial differences between countries with respect to:

(a) The size and/or duration which stoppages must attain before they qualify for inclusion in the national statistics, e.g. France and Italy have no formal limits, whereas in Denmark only stoppages costing more than 100 working days are included.
(b) The exclusion of political stoppages by a minority of countries.
(c) The collection of information on the number of workers laid off as a result of a stoppage elsewhere at the same plant - that is workers indirectly involved. Some countries only produce data on workers directly involved.

The production of adjusted data standardized to a common base is simply not practicable, given the limited amount of information on the distribution of stoppages by size, duration, and cause produced by most countries.

Recent research studies in the UK have disclosed very substantial underreporting of stoppage numbers, due to the obvious problems faced in gathering data on small and short stoppages (especially in small establishments) under voluntary reporting systems. However, the official stoppage statistics relating to working days lost proved to be very accurate, largely because the large and long stoppages which are the most likely to be recorded account for most working days lost.

The various difficulties outlined above make any international comparisons based on the numbers of recorded stoppages very unreliable. On the other hand, the working-days-lost statistics are likely to be the most reliable for comparative purposes simply because most of the days lost in an economy during a year are due to relatively few large stoppages which can hardly escape the attention of the responsible statistical agencies. Comparisons based on workers involved appear to fall between these two extremes in terms of their reliability for comparative purposes.

Shortly after its foundation the ILO began to publish data on industrial disputes in member countries, and since the 1930s it has on various occasions provided information on stoppage incidence (working days lost per 1,000 employees) in mining, manufacturing, construction, and transport (the industrial sector) for selected countries - predominantly the industrialized economies. This decision to limit information to the industrial sector is claimed to improve statistical comparability. This sector accounted for just under half of employment but over 80 per cent of total stoppage activity across the OECD countries during the 1970s.

There are two alternatives to this approach, since data can be produced either on a more narrowly defined, or on a fully comprehensive, basis. Manufacturing is the obvious base for any more narrowly defined comparative statistical analysis.

In the 1970s both statistical agencies, such as Eurostat and the British Department of Employment, and academic researchers began to produce comparative analyses covering stoppages in all industries and services. There were several reasons for these developments. First, the industrial sector had for some time been declining as a percentage of total employment as the private service and government sectors expanded. Second, significant industrial action was beginning to make its appearance in these previously virtually strike-free areas. Third, it had become clear that the partial coverage of the ILO data could produce a distorted picture of relative strike-proneness where an economy experienced exceptionally high levels of stoppage activity outside the industrial sector e.g. Sweden and the Irish Republic.

Comparative data on all three bases were produced by Creigh and Poland (1983). Statistical analysis indicates that the rankings of countries in terms of stoppage incidence are relatively stable over the post-war period on all the bases, and that this degree of stability is unlikely to occur purely by chance.

The comprehensive all-industries approach to stoppage comparisons has major advantages for analytical purposes over both the industrial-sector and manufacturing industry data. This is simply because most potential explanatory variables relate to the economy as a whole rather than particular sectors. Future studies which focus on international variations in disputes will probably concentrate on the most statistically reliable yardstick - stoppage incidence among wage earners and salaried employees in all industries and services.

NOTES

1 Employment Market Research Unit, Department of Employment, London. The views expressed in this paper are personal and do not represent those of the Department. Much of the material used is derived from a project on strike activity undertaken while the author was based at the National Institute of Labour Studies in the Flinders University of South Australia. Thanks are due to ex-colleagues there and Mrs J. Wells who assisted in the updating of the statistics.

2 See ILO (1926) Methods of Compiling Statistics of Industrial Disputes, Studies and Reports Series no. 10, Geneva: ILO.

3 The British Evidence is summarized in S.W. Creigh and G. Poland (1983) 'Differences in strike activity between industrial countries in the post-war period', Adelaide: National Institute of Labour Studies, Working Paper no. 59, November.

4 Japanese dispute statistics distinguish between strikes lasting half a day or more, which are included in the nation's official stoppage statistics and so form the basis for international comparisons, and strikes coming to the attention of the statistical agency lasting less than one half day. New Zealand statistics differentiate 'complete strikes' from 'partial stoppages' leading to a reduction in output.

5 See ILO (1926), op. cit., especially pp. 115-18 and D. Jackson and T.G. Sweet (1978) 'The classification and interpretation of strike statistics: an international comparative analysis', Birmingham: University of Aston Management Centre, Working Paper no. 97. The British Government made attempts to collect statistical information on strikes and lock-outs in 1887 and records are available on a broadly comparable basis from 1893 onwards. In the USA the statistics date back to 1881. Japan began to collect statistics in 1897. For a discussion of these early experiments, see

S.W. Creigh (1982) 'The origins of British strike statistics', Business History, vol. 24, no. 1: 96-106.

6 The 14th International Conference of Labour Statisticians, held from 28 October to 6 November 1987 in Geneva, proposed an amended set of guidelines relating to industrial disputes.

7 The current industrial groups are the major divisions of the International Standard Industrial Classification of Economic Activities (ISIC - 1968):

1 Agriculture, hunting, forestry, and fishing
2 Mining and quarrying
3 Manufacturing
4 Electricity, gas, and water
5 Construction
6 Wholesale and retail trade, and restaurants and hotels
7 Transport, storage, and communication
8 Financing, insurance, real estate, and business services
9 Community, social, and personal services
10 Activities not adequately defined

8 Key segments of the Forchheimer and Ross and Hartman studies are conveniently reprinted in E.W. Evans and S.W. Creigh (eds.) (1977) Industrial Conflict in Britain, London: Cass.

9 Royal Commission on Trade Unions and Employers' Associations (1968) (chairman: Lord Donovan), Final Report, Cmnd 3623, London: HMSO.

10 See H.A. Turner (1969) Is Britain Really Strike-Prone? A Review of the Incidence, Character and Costs of Industrial Conflict, Department of Applied Economics Occasional paper no. 20, Cambridge: Cambridge University Press (especially pp. 10-11) and W.E.J. McCarthy (1970) 'The nature of Britain's strike problem', British Journal of Industrial Relations, vol. 8, no. 1: 224-36.

11 See M. Fisher (1973) Measurement of Labour Disputes and their Economic Effects, Paris: OECD; Jackson and Sweet (1978) op. cit; S.W. Creigh, N. Donaldson, and E. Hawthorn (1980) 'Differences in strike activity in OECD countries', Employment Gazette, vol. 88, no. 11: 1174-81; and M. Shalev 'Lies damned lies and strike statistics: the measurement of trends in industrial conflict' and Appendix II in C. Crouch and A. Pizzorno (eds.) (1978) The Resurgence of Class Conflict in Western Europe since 1968, vol. 1, London: Macmillan.

12 The full set of data for all the various classifications is, of course, usually available only on an annual basis. However, the major countries usually produce relatively brief monthly or quarterly analyses of stoppage data shortly after the end of the period concerned.

13 In most cases lock-outs are dealt with in a brief note, although Canada and West Germany provide rather more information.

14 See, for instance, E. Batstone, I. Boraston, and S. Frenkel (1978) The Social Organization of Strikes, Oxford: Basil Blackwell.

15 The situation with regard to the available classifications of recorded stoppages by duration, size (workers involved), and working days lost across the OECD countries is set out in Creigh and Poland (1983) op. cit., tables 2, 3, and 4 respectively.

16 See W. Brown (ed.) (1981) The Changing Contours of British Industrial Relations: A Survey of Manufacturing Industry, Oxford: Basil Blackwell.

17 The merits of the various measures of strike action and their usefulness in measuring the economic impact of disputes are discussed in

S.W. Creigh (1978) 'The economic costs of strikes', Industrial Relations Journal, vol. 9, no. 1: 19-26.

18 Statistics ought to relate solely to stoppages in mining, manufacturing, construction, and transport. Unfortunately, the data for several countries do not always meet this requirement:

> Australian data includes electricity and gas but exclude communication.
> Denmark included manufacturing only up to 1974.
> Italy includes gas, water, and electricity.
> Sweden included all industries until 1971.
> Switzerland includes gas, electricity, and water.
> USA includes gas, water, and sanitary services.

19 The contrary approach is to focus attention more narrowly. The manufacturing sector may have special significance in terms of strike activity. Mining operations are, of course, tied to natural resource endowments, while much construction and transport activity is likewise closely linked to particular population and production centres. In contrast, manufacturing industry operations are relatively 'footloose' in locational terms both within and between countries. Furthermore, manufactured goods are a major item in international trade and have played a vital role in the growth of trade during the post-war period, especially in the massive growth in trade between the industrialized countries themselves. The manufacturing sector is thus relatively 'open' and exposed to foreign competition in a way unknown in the more sheltered sectors of the economy. (Creigh and Poland (1983) provide one of the few recent examples of this approach.)

20 See H.A. Clegg (1976) Trade Unionism under Collective Bargaining, Oxford: Blackwell: table 2, p.69.

21 C.T.B. Smith, R. Clifton, P. Makeham, S.T. Creigh, and R.V. Burn (1978) Strikes in Britain: A Research Study of Industrial Stoppages in the United Kingdom, London: HMSO: 94-7.

22 For example, Statistical Office of the European Communities (Eurostat) (1980) Employment and Unemployment 1972-1978, Brussels: Eurostat.

23 A recent example is 'International comparisons of industrial stoppages in 1984' (1986) Employment Gazette, vol. 94, no. 6: 266-9.

24 The ILO appears to have been well aware of the problem posed by Sweden's strike pattern. In fact, prior to 1972 it adopted the simple expedient of providing stoppage incidence rates relating to all industries for Sweden, while maintaining its industrial sector coverage elsewhere.

25 See, for instance, Organization for Economic Co-operation and Development (1982) Labour Force Statistics 1969-1980, Paris: OECD. Prior to the appearance of these OECD data analysts had no choice but to utilize the less satisfactory civilian labour force base which includes employers, the self-employed, and family workers - e.g. Smith et al. (1978), op. cit.

26 S.W. Creigh, G. Poland, and M. Wooden (1984) 'The reasons for international differences in strike activity', Adelaide: National Institute of Labour Studies, Working Paper no. 61, February.

Part 2: Labour statistics for individual countries

10 LABOUR STATISTICS FOR TWENTY-FOUR OECD COUNTRIES

DEFINITIONS

Employment	Wage and salaried employees with a job during a specified period, together with employers, own-account workers and unpaid family workers
Civilian employment	Persons in employment (including employers and self-employed) but excluding the armed forces
Labour force	Employed and unemployed

Unemployment is expressed as a percentage of the total labour force and is based on either sample surveys or employment-office statistics. It refers to those in the reference period of working age who are without work, currently available for work, and seeking work.

Hours of work = average hours actually worked per worker (except, where specified, hours paid for).

GNP (Gross National Product) per head is in US dollars.

Earnings (excluding agriculture) are expressed in the currency of the country concerned.

AUSTRALIA

Size 7,687,000 km^2
Population (1986) 15,974,000. Annual change 1981-6: +1.4 per cent
Per capita GNP (1985) $10,830

Labour force (000s)	1985	1986	1987
Total	7,345	7,606	7,775
Males	4,526	4,605	4,681
Females	2,819	3,001	3,094

Activity rates	1984	1985	1986
Labour force as percentage of population of all ages			
Total	45.9	46.3	47.3
Male	57.5	57.3	57.6
Female	34.4	35.3	37.0

Activity rates	1984	1985	1986
Labour force as percentage of population aged 15-64			
Total	69.6	69.9	71.1
Male	85.8	85.3	85.4
Female	52.9	54.1	56.5

Civilian employment (000s)	1985	1986	1987
Total	6,676	6,946	7,079
Males	4,108	4,198	4,256
Females	2,568	2,748	2,823

Civilian employment by sector (%)	1986
Agriculture	6.1
Industry	26.8
Services	67.1

Employment by industry (000s)	1985
Agriculture	414.3
Extractive industries	102.4
Manufacturing	1,109.4
Electricity, gas, water	137.9
Construction	468.8
Wholesale and retail trade (and hotels)	1,318.8
Transport and communications	523.4
Finance, insurance, and business services	663.7
Community, social, and personal services	1,907.3

Unemployment	1985		1986		1987	
	000s	%	000s	%	000s	%
Total	598	8.1	590	7.8	626	8.1
Males	353	7.8	343	7.4	360	7.7
Females	246	8.7	247	8.2	266	8.6
Aged 15-24 (as percentage of total)	% 47.0		% 45.1		% 45.5	

Average hours of work per week in manufacturing	1983	1984	1985	1986
	36.9	37.7	37.2	37.7

Industrial disputes	1983	1984	1985	1986
Number of disputes	1,787	1,965	1,845	1,687
Workers involved (000s)	470.2	560.3	570.5	691.7
Working days lost (000s)	1,614.4	1,307.4	1,256.2	1,390.7

Average weekly earnings ($)	1984	1985	1986
	398.10	423.10	455.20

Consumer prices (percentage increase)	1985	1986	1987
	6.7	9.1	8.4

Trade unions

Total membership (1986)	3,186,200 in 326 unions
As percentage of total employees	55.0
Central organization	Australian Council of Trade Unions (ACTU) 2,699,120 members in 161 unions

Membership of major ACTU unions (1985)

Australian Teachers' Federation	170,104
Shop, Distributive and Allied Employees Association	169,000
Australian Public Service Federation	143,990
Amalgamated Metal Workers Union	131,029
The Federated Miscellaneous Workers Union of Australia	123,665
The Australian Workers' Union	118,656

Trade union membership by size, 1986

Number of members	Number of unions	Percentage of total unions	Percentage of total members
Under 100	40	12.3	0.1
100 and under 250	40	12.3	0.2
250 and under 500	32	9.8	0.4
500 and under 1,000	43	13.2	1.0
1,000 and under 2,000	45	13.8	2.0
2,000 and under 5,000	39	12.0	4.1
5,000 and under 10,000	23	7.1	5.0
10,000 and under 20,000	19	5.8	8.6
20,000 and under 30,000	12	3.7	9.2
30,000 and under 40,000	7	2.1	7.9
40,000 and under 50,000	10	3.1	14.3
50,000 and under 80,000	8	2.5	16.6
80,000 and over	8	2.5	30.7
Total	**326**	**100.0**	**100.0**

Source Australian Bureau of Statistics

AUSTRIA

Size	84,000 km²
Population (1986)	7,565,000
Per capita GNP (1985)	$9,120

Labour force (000s)	1984	1985	1986
Total	3,363	3,355	3,385
Males	2,029	2,031	2,042
Females	1,334	1,324	1,343

Activity rates Labour force as percentage of population of all ages	1984	1985	1986
Total	44.5	44.4	44.8
Male	56.7	56.7	57.0
Female	33.6	33.3	33.8

Activity rates Labour force as percentage of population aged 15-64	1984	1985	1986
Total	66.3	65.8	66.3
Male	81.7	81.2	81.3
Female	51.5	51.0	51.1

Civilian employment (000s)	1984	1985	1986
Total	3,235	3,235	3,279
Males	1,949	1,957	1,978
Females	1,286	1,277	1,301

Civilian employment by sector (%)	1986
Agriculture	8.7
Industry	37.8
Services	53.6

Employment by industry (000s)	1985
Agriculture	36.6
Extractive industries	23.3
Manufacturing	843.3
Electricity, gas, water	34.8
Construction	239.3
Wholesale and retail trade (and hotels)	516.3
Transport and communications	211.4
Finance, insurance, and business services	175.1
Community, social, and personal services	752.7

Unemployment	1985		1986		1987	
	000s	%	000s	%	000s	%
Total	139.5	4.8	152.0	5.2	164.5	5.6
Males	84.2	4.9	88.9	5.1	95.0	5.5
Females	55.3	4.7	63.1	5.2	69.5	5.7
Aged under 30 (as percentage of total)	% 28.6		% 31.0		% 30.3	

Average hours of work per month in manufacturing	1984	1985	1986	1987
	145.2	144.9	142.1	139.9

Industrial disputes	1984	1985	1986
Number of disputes	2	4	11
Workers involved (000s)	0.268	35.531	3.222
Working days lost (000s)	0.543	22.752	3.253

Average hourly earnings in manufacturing (Schillings)

1985

Range from 125.90 in Oil to 50.60 in Clothing

Consumer prices (percentage increase)	1985	1986	1987
	3.3	1.7	1.5

Trade unions

Total membership (1986)	1,671,217 in 15 OGB affiliated unions
As percentage of total employees	59.0
Central organization	OGB (Austrian Federation of Trade Unions)

Membership of major unions (1986)

Gewerkschaft der privatangestellten (Private Salaried Employees' Union)	348,117
Gewerkschaft Metall-Bergbau-Energie (Union of Metal Workers, Miners, and Power-Supply Workers)	251,112
Gewerkschaft Offentlicher Dienst (Union of Public Employees)	226,328
Gewerkschaft der Bau- und Holzarbeiter (Building, Construction, and Woodworkers Union)	184,361
Gewerkschaft der Gemeindebediensteten (Union of Municipal Employees)	169,128
Gewerkschaft der Eisenbahner (Railway Workers Union)	117,021

BELGIUM

Size	31,000 km²
Population (1986)	9,910,000
Per capita GNP (1985)	$8,280

Labour force (000s)	1984	1985	1986
Total	4,214	4,202	4,212
Males	2,561	2,531	2,514
Females	1,653	1,671	1,698

Activity rates Labour force as percentage of population of all ages	1984	1985	1986
Total	42.8	42.6	42.8
Male	53.2	52.6	52.3
Female	32.8	33.1	33.1

Activity rates Labour force as percentage of population aged 15-64	1984	1985	1986
Total	63.6	63.3	63.4
Male	77.1	75.9	75.4
Female	50.1	51.3	51.3

Civilian employment (000s)	1984	1985	1986
Total	3,579	3,607	3,644
Males	2,225	2,227	2,231
Females	1,354	1,380	1,414

Civilian employment by sector (%)	1985
Agriculture	2.9
Industry	29.7
Services	67.4

Employment by industry (000s)	1985
Agriculture	105
Extractive industries	24
Manufacturing	811
Electricity, gas, water	32
Construction	203
Wholesale and retail trade (and hotels)	703
Transport and communications	262
Finance, insurance, and business services	290
Community, social, and personal services	1,144

Unemployment	1984		1985		1986		1987	
	000s	%	000s	%	000s	%	000s	%
Total	595.8	14.4	558.3	13.5	516.8	12.3	500.8	11.9
Males	273.7	11.1	246.0	9.9	217.6	8.7	208.9	8.3
Females	322.1	19.5	312.3	18.9	299.1	17.6	292.0	17.2

Average hours of work per week in manufacturing	1983	1984	1985	1986
	33.5	33.7	33.1	33.0
Average hourly earnings (Francs)	1984	1985	1986	
	283.35	295.17	296.37	
Average hourly labour cost per employee in manufacturing (Francs)	593	* *	* *	
Consumer prices (percentage increase)	1985	1986	1987	
	4.9	1.3	1.6	

Trade unions

Total membership (1985)	2,600,000
As percentage of labour force	75.0
Central organizations	Confédération des Syndicats Chrétiens (1.3 million members in 17 unions) Fédération Générale du Travail de Belgique (1 million members in 14 unions)

CANADA

Size 9,976,000km²
Population (1986) 25,675,000. Annual change 1981-6: +1.1 per cent
Per capita GNP (1985) $13,680

Labour force (000s)	1985	1986	1987
Total	12,716	12,947	13,200
Males	7,327	7,416	7,498
Females	5,389	5,531	5,702

Activity rates Labour force as percentage of population of all ages	1984	1985	1986
Total	49.6	50.1	50.6
Male	58.2	58.4	58.6
Female	41.3	42.0	42.7

Activity rates Labour force as percentage of population aged 15-64	1984	1985	1986
Total	72.9	73.6	74.3
Male	84.6	84.9	85.1
Female	61.2	62.4	63.5

Civilian employment (000s)	1985	1986	1987
Total	11,311	11,634	11,954
Males	6,508	6,657	6,793
Females	4,804	4,977	5,161

Civilian employment by sector (%)	1986
Agriculture	5.1
Industry	25.3
Services	69.6

Employment by industry (000s)	1985
Agriculture	590
Extractive industries	191
Manufacturing	1,981
Electricity, gas, water	124
Construction	587
Wholesale and retail trade (and hotels)	2,634
Transport and communications	760
Finance, insurance, and business services	1,126
Community, social, and personal services	3,319

Unemployment	1985		1986		1987	
	000s	%	000s	%	000s	%
Total	1,328	10.4	1,236	9.5	1,167	8.9
Males	750	10.2	690	9.3	634	8.5
Females	578	10.7	546	9.9	533	9.4
Aged 15-24 (as percentage of total)	% 35.6		% 35.1		% 33.0	

Average hours of work (paid) per week in manufacturing	1984	1985	1986	1987
	38.5	38.8	38.7	38.8

Industrial disputes	1984	1985	1986
Number of disputes	717	824	741
Workers involved (000s)	186.75	159.71	483.87
Working days lost (000s)	3,871.8	3,188.7	7,133.8

Average weekly earnings ($)	1985	1986	1987
	419.20	435.35	442.76

Consumer prices (percentage increase)	1985	1986	1987
	4.0	4.1	4.4

Trade unions

Total membership (1986)	3,730,000 (in 219 national unions and 67 international unions)
As percentage of non-agricultural paid workers	37.7
Central organization	Canadian Labour Congress 2,164,000 members in 80 unions

Membership of major unions (1986)

Canadian Union of Public Employees	304,300
National Union of Provincial Government Employees	254,300
Public Service Alliance of Canada	182,000
United Steelworkers of America	160,000
United Food and Commercial Workers International Union	156,000
International Union, United Automobile, Aerospace and Agricultural Implement Workers of America	140,000

Size of international and national unions, 1986

	International		National	
Membership groups	Number of unions	Number of members	Number of unions	Number of members
		000s		000s
50 - 999	14	5	77	32
1,000 - 9,999	21	88	101	364
10,000 - 29,999	17	291	26	434
30,000 or more	15	1,075	15	1,302
Total	**67**	**1,459**	**219**	**2,132**

DENMARK

Size 43,000 km²
Population (1986) 5,116,000. Annual change 1981-6: 0.0 per cent
Per capita GNP (1985) $11,200

Labour force (000s)	1984	1985	1986
Total	2,720	2,753	2,816
Males	1,481	1,499	1,526
Females	1,239	1,254	1,290

Activity rates	1984	1985	1986
Labour force as percentage of population of all ages			
Total	53.2	53.8	55.0
Male	58.6	59.5	60.5
Female	47.8	48.3	49.7

Activity rates	1984	1985	1986
Labour force as percentage of population aged 15-64			
Total	80.3	81.0	82.5
Male	86.7	87.4	88.4
Female	73.8	74.5	76.5

Civilian employment (000s)	1984	1985	1986
Total	2,457	2,522	2,630
Males	1,338	1,383	1,438
Females	1,118	1,139	1,192

Civilian employment by sector (%)	1985
Agriculture	6.7
Industry	28.1
Services	65.2

Employment by industry (000s)	1985
Agriculture	168.8
Extractive industries	4.3
Manufacturing	515.3
Electricity, gas, water	18.7
Construction	170.9
Wholesale and retail trade (and hotels)	391.9
Transport and communications	179.7
Finance, insurance, and business services	192.6
Community, social, and personal services	905.9

Unemployment	1984		1985		1986		1987	
	000s	%	000s	%	000s	%	000s	%
Total	276.3	10.2	251.8	9.3	217.3	8.0	219.5	8.0
Males	129.9	8.9	110.9	7.6	89.5	6.1	95.1	6.5
Females	146.4	11.9	140.9	11.5	127.8	10.2	124.3	9.9

Average hours of work per week in manufacturing	1984	1985	1986
	33.0	32.1	33.0

Industrial disputes	1984	1985	1986
Number of disputes	157	820	215
Workers involved (000s)	50.764	581.3	56.735
Working days lost (000s)	131.7	2,332.7	93.200

	1985	1986
Average hourly earnings (Kroner)	84.78	89.43
Average hourly labour cost per wage earner (Kroner)	88.45	92.60

Consumer prices (percentage increase)	1985	1986	1987
	4.8	3.5	4.0

Trade unions

Total membership (1985)	2,000,000
As percentage of labour force	78
Central organizations	LO (Danish Federation of Trade Unions) 1,397,346 members in 31 unions FTF (Public Servants and Salaried Workers) 270,000 members in 50 unions AC (Academics) 95,000 members

Membership of major unions (affiliated to LO), 1985

National Union of General Workers	311,597
National Union of Commercial and Clerical Employees	309,549
National Union of Metalworkers	138,626
National Union of Municipal Workers	118,833
National Union of Female Workers	101,213

FINLAND

Size 337,000 km²
Population (1986) 4,919,000. Annual change 1981-6: +0.5 per cent
Per capita GNP (1985) $10,890

Labour force (000s)	1985	1986	1987
Total	2,597	2,596	2,583
Males	1,370	1,372	1,367
Females	1,227	1,224	1,216

Activity rates	1984	1985	1986
Labour force as percentage of population of all ages			
Total	52.6	52.9	52.8
Male	57.5	57.6	57.6
Female	48.0	48.5	48.3

Activity rates	1984	1985	1986
Labour force as percentage of population aged 15-64			
Total	77.2	77.6	77.7
Male	81.7	81.7	81.9
Female	72.7	73.5	73.5

Civilian employment (000s)	1985	1986	1987
Total	2,427	2,421	2,414
Males	1,255	1,253	1,250
Females	1,172	1,168	1,164

Civilian employment by sector (%)	1986
Agriculture	11.0
Industry	32.0
Services	57.0

Employment by industry (000s)	1985
Agriculture	280
Extractive industries	**
Manufacturing	598
Electricity, gas, water	**
Construction	178
Wholesale and retail trade (and hotels)	355
Transport and communications	186
Finance, insurance, and business services	156
Community, social, and personal services	681

Unemployment	1985		1986		1987	
	000s	%	000s	%	000s	%
Total	130	5.0	138	5.3	130	5.1
Males	76	5.5	82	6.0	78	5.8
Females	57	4.6	56	4.6	53	4.3
Aged 15-24 (as percentage of total)	% 30.0		% 29.0		% 28.5	

Average hours of work per week in manufacturing	1984	1985	1986
	32.3	32.3	31.9

Industrial disputes	1984	1985	1986
Number of disputes	1,679	833	1,236
Workers involved (000s)	558.70	170.02	589.04
Working days lost (000s)	1,526.9	174.27	2,787.5

Average hourly earnings in manufacturing (Markkaa)	1985	1986
	32.10	34.00
Average hourly labour cost per employee in manufacturing (Markkaa)	53.39	57.00

Consumer prices (percentage increase)	1985	1986	1987
	6.3	3.6	3.3

Trade unions

Total membership (1985)	1,764,882
As percentage of labour force	80
Central organizations	SAK (Central Organization of Finnish Trade Unions) 1,052,762 members in 27 unions TVK (Confederation of Salaried Employees in Finland) 370,000 members in 14 unions AKAVA (Central Organization of Professional Associations in Finland) 207,000 members in 44 unions STTK (Confederation of Technical Employee Organizations in Finland) 120,396 members in 15 unions

FRANCE

Size 547,000 km^2
Population (1986) 55,379,000. Annual change 1981-6: +0.4 per cent
Per capita GNP (1985) $9,540

Labour force (000s)	1984	1985	1986
Total	23,865	23,902	24,038
Males	13,988	13,901	13,976
Females	9,877	10,001	10,062

Activity rates Labour force as percentage of population of all ages	1984	1985	1986
Total	43.4	43.3	43.3
Male	52.1	51.6	51.5
Female	35.2	35.3	36.6

Activity rates Labour force as percentage of population aged 15-64	1984	1985	1986
Total	66.1	65.7	65.8
Male	77.4	76.5	76.3
Female	54.8	55.0	55.3

Civilian employment (000s)	1984	1985	1986
Total	20,981	20,900	20,965
Males	12,358	12,203	12,245
Females	8,625	8,697	8,720

Civilian employment by sector (%)	1986
Agriculture	7.3
Industry	31.3
Services	61.3

Employment by industry (000s)	1985
Agriculture	1,583
Extractive industries	115
Manufacturing	4,838
Electricity, gas, water	211
Construction	1,517
Wholesale and retail trade (and hotels)	3,484
Transport and communications	1,369
Finance, insurance, and business services	1,689
Community, social, and personal services	6,084

Unemployment	1984		1985		1986	
	000s	%	000s	%	000s	%
Total	2,312	9.7	2,442	10.1	2,513	10.3
Males	1,071	7.7	1,155	8.3	1,188	8.5
Females	1,241	12.6	1,288	12.9	1,324	13.2

Average hours of work per week in manufacturing	1984	1985	1986	1987
	38.7	38.6	38.6	38.7

Industrial disputes	1984	1985	1986
Number of disputes	2,537	1,901	1,391
Workers involved (000s)	42.1	22.8	21.8
Working days lost (000s)	1,316.8	726.7	567.6

Average hourly earnings (Francs)	1984	1985	1986
	22.88	37.51	38.74
Average hourly labour cost per employee in manufacturing (Francs)	84.35	* *	* *

Consumer prices (percentage increase)	1985	1986	1987
	5.8	2.7	3.3

Trade unions

Total membership (1985)	3,900,000
As percentage of labour force	19
Central organizations	Confédération Générale du Travail (CGT) 1,200,000 members in 46 unions CGT-FO (Force Ouvrière) 1,100,000 members in 36 unions Confédération Française Démocratique du Travail (CFDT) 850,000 members in 26 unions Confédération Française des Travailleurs Chrétiens (CFTC) 180,000 members in 45 unions Confédération Générale des Cadres (CGC) 220,000 members

GERMANY (FR)

Size	249,000 km²
Population (1986)	61,048,000. Annual change 1981-6: -0.2 per cent
Per capita GNP (1984)	$11,130

Labour force (000s)	1984	1985	1986
Total	27,624	27,838	28,014
Males	16,982	17,078	17,115
Females	10,647	10,766	10,909

Activity rates	1984	1985	1986
Labour force as percentage of population of all ages			
Total	45.2	45.6	45.9
Male	58.1	58.5	58.5
Female	33.3	33.8	34.3

Activity rates	1983	1984	1985
Labour force as percentage of population aged 15-64			
Total	65.1	64.8	65.2
Male	80.6	79.9	79.9
Female	49.7	49.7	50.4

Civilian employment (000s)	1984	1985	1986
Total	24,835	25,004	25,257
Males	15,178	15,256	15,381
Females	9,657	9,748	9,876

Civilian employment by sector (%)	1986
Agriculture	5.3
Industry	40.9
Services	53.8

Employment by industry (000s)	1985
Agriculture	1,390
Extractive industries	316
Manufacturing	8,009
Electricity, gas, water	236
Construction	1,691
Wholesale and retail trade (and hotels)	3,805
Transport and communications	1,513
Finance, insurance, and business services	1,652
Community, social, and personal services	6,388

Unemployment	1984		1985		1986	
	000s	%	000s	%	000s	%
Total	2,143	8.2	2,151	8.3	2,046	8.0
Males	1,155	7.5	1,132	7.5	1,040	7.0
Females	988	9.3	1,091	9.4	1,006	9.4
	%		%		%	
Aged under 25 (as percentage of total)	27.2		26.2		24.6	

Average hours of work (paid) per week in manufacturing	1984	1985	1986	1987
	41.0	40.7	40.4	40.1

Industrial disputes	1983	1984	1985
Number of disputes	* *	* *	* *
Workers involved (000s)	94.07	537.26	78.19
Working days lost (000s)	40.84	5,617.6	34.40

Average hourly earnings (Marks)	1985	1986	1987
	16.39	16.99	17.68

Average hourly labour cost per employee in manufacturing (Marks)	1984	
	31.72	* *

Consumer prices (percentage increase)	1985	1986	1987
	2.2	-0.2	0.3

Trade unions

Total membership (1986)	9,350,526
As percentage of total employees	39
Central organization	Deutscher Gewerkschaftsbund (DGB) 7.76 million members in 17 unions

Membership of major DGB unions (1986)

I G Metall (Metalworkers)	2,598,323
OTV (Public Sector and Transport Employees)	1,198,567
I G Chemie (Chemical and Paper Workers)	653,776

Non-DGB Salaried Employees Organizations

Deutscher Angestellten Gewerkschaft (DAG)	496,299
Deutscher Beamtenbund (DBB)	782,059

GREECE

Size	132,000 km²
Population (1986)	9,970,000
Per capita GNP (1985)	$3,550

Labour force (000s)	1984	1985	1986
Total	3,868	3,892	3,888
Males	2,529	2,513	2,505
Females	1,339	1,379	1,383

Activity rates Labour force as percentage of population of all ages	1984	1985	1986
Total	39.1	39.2	39.0
Male	52.0	51.4	51.1
Female	26.6	27.3	27.3

Activity rates Labour force as percentage of population aged 15-64	1983	1984	1985
Total	59.9	59.8	59.6
Male	80.0	79.0	77.7
Female	40.4	40.9	41.8

Civilian employment (000s)	1984	1985	1986
Total	3,553	3,588	3,601
Males	2,376	2,371	2,378
Females	1,177	1,217	1,223

Civilian employment by sector (%)	1985
Agriculture	28.9
Industry	27.3
Services	43.8

Employment by industry (000s)	1985
Agriculture	1,037
Extractive industries	29
Manufacturing	679
Electricity, gas, water	32
Construction	243
Wholesale and retail trade (and hotels)	571
Transport and communications	250
Finance, insurance, and business services	133
Community, social, and personal services	616

Unemployment	1983		1984		1985		1986	
	000s	%	000s	%	000s	%	000s	%
Total	61.647	3.8	72.216	4.2	88.972	5.1	110.5	6.1
Males	37.148	**	42.020	**	51.167	**	61.0	**
Females	24.498	**	29.196	**	37.805	**	49.4	**

Average hours of work (paid) per week in manufacturing	1985	1986
	39.3	39.1

Industrial disputes	1986
Number of disputes	213
Workers involved (000s)	1,106.3
Working days lost (000s)	1,262.8

Average weekly earnings in manufacturing (Drachmas)	1987
	14,933 (ranging from 12,169 in Clothing and Shoes to 22,376 in Metals)

Average hourly labour cost per employee in manufacturing Drachmas)	441.0

Consumer prices (percentage increase)	1985	1986	1987
	19.3	23.0	16.4

Trade unions

Total membership (1983)	675,000
As percentage of labour force	35
Central organization	GSEE (Greek General Confederation of Labour) with 350,000 members in 1985

ICELAND

Size	103,000 km²
Population (1986)	241,000
Per capita GNP (1985)	$10,480

Labour force (000s)	1983	1984	1985
Total	114.5	115.8	116

Activity rates	1983	1984	1985
Labour force as percentage of population of all ages			
Total	48.3	48.4	48.3

Activity rates	1983	1984	1985
Labour force as percentage of population aged 15-64			
Total	76.2	76.1	* *

Civilian employment (000s)	1983	1984	1985
Total	113.3	114.3	116

Civilian employment by sector (%)	1985
Agriculture	10.5
Industry	36.8
Services	52.7

Employment by industry (000s)	1983
Agriculture	14.9
Extractive industries	-
Manufacturing	29.2
Electricity, gas, water	1.3
Construction	11.7
Wholesale and retail trade (and hotels)	16.0
Transport and communications	8.0
Finance, insurance, and business services	4.3
Community, social, and personal services	29.7

Unemployment	1983		1984		1985		1986	
	000s	%	000s	%	000s	%	000s	%
Total	1.187	1.0	1.481	1.2	1.108	0.9	0.823	0.7

Average hours of work (paid) per week per wage earner	1984	1985	1986
	48.9	48.6	48.5

Industrial disputes	1984	1985	1986
Number of disputes	7	13	4
Workers involved (000s)	12.000	6.000	1.000
Working days lost (000s)	301	91.000	1.000

Average hourly earnings (Kronur)	1986
All manufacturing industries	282.62 (ranging from metal working 373.37, to paper products 207.85)

Consumer prices (percentage increase)	1985	1986	1987
	31.9	21.3	17.8

Trade unions

Total membership (1985)	100,000
As percentage of labour force	94
Central organization	Icelandic Federation of Labour (ASI) 61,874 members in 238 unions. (Also 4 smaller bodies)

Membership of major unions (1985)

Reykjavik Shop and Office Workers Union	8,140
State Institutions Employees Union	4,872
Union of Unskilled Male Workers in Reykjavik	3,924

IRELAND

Size	70,000 km²
Population (1986)	3,540,000
Per capita GNP (1985)	$4,850

Labour force (000s)	1984	1985	1986
Total	1,308	1,302	1,308
Males	922	917	915
Females	386	385	393

Activity rates	1984	1985	1986
Labour force as percentage of population of all ages			
Total	37.1	36.7	36.9
Male	52.1	51.7	51.7
Female	21.9	21.7	22.2

Activity rates	1984	1985	1986
Labour force as percentage of population aged 15-64			
Total	62.1	61.4	61.4
Male	86.6	85.7	85.1
Female	37.0	36.6	37.2

Civilian employment (000s)	1984	1985	1986
Total	1,090	1,059	1,068
Males	752	727	729
Females	338	332	339

Civilian employment by sector (%)	1985
Agriculture	16.0
Industry	28.9
Services	55.1

Employment by industry (000s)	1985
Agriculture	169
Extractive industries	10
Manufacturing	202
Electricity, gas, water	15
Construction	78
Wholesale and retail trade (and hotels)	190
Transport and communications	68
Finance, insurance, and business services	77
Community, social, and personal services	244

Unemployment	1984		1985		1986		1987	
	000s	%	000s	%	000s	%	000s	%
Total	214.2	16.3	230.6	17.4	236.4	18.2	247.3	19.0
Males	159.1	17.1	170.2	18.6	172.0	18.8	176.2	* *
Females	55.1	14.3	60.4	15.7	64.4	16.6	71.1	* *

Average hours of work per week in manufacturing	1983	1984	1985	1986
	40.8	41.1	41.1	41.4

Industrial disputes	1983	1984	1985
Number of disputes	154	192	116
Workers involved (000s)	30.48	30.99	168.67
Working days lost (000s)	319.01	386.42	417.73

Average hourly earnings in manufacturing (£)	1984	1985	1986
	3.90	4.17	4.43*

(*ranging from 6.26 in Drink and Tobacco, to 2.73 in Clothing)

Average hourly labour cost per employee in manufacturing (£)	6.17	* *	* *

Consumer prices (percentage increase)	1985	1986	1987
	5.4	3.9	3.2

Trade unions

Total membership (1986)	518,000 in 77 unions (Dept. of Labour statistics)
As percentage of labour force	55 (excluding unemployed)
Central organization	Irish Congress of Trade Unions (ICTU) 446,066 members in 61 unions

Membership of major unions (1986)

Irish Transport and General Workers Union	177,672
Federated Workers Union of Ireland	44,272
Amalgamated Transport and General Workers Union	23,667
Irish National Teachers Organization	18,580
Irish Distributive and Administrative Trade Union	16,092
Local Government and Public Services Union	15,350

Ireland: trade union membership by size, 1986

Size band	No. of unions	Aggregate membership
- 500	19	4,828
501 - 1000	8	6,018
1001 - 1500	6	7,292
1501 - 2000	5	9,146
2001 - 3000	12	28,232
3001 - 5000	7	26,913
5001 - 7500	4	25,199
7501 - 10000	5	48,281
10001 - 15000	5	66,833
15001 - 20000	3	50,022
20001 -	3	245,611
Total	**77**	**518,375**

Source Department of Labour

ITALY

Size	301,000 km²
Population (1986)	57,221,000. Annual change 1981-6: +0.3 per cent
Per capita GNP (1985)	$6,520

Labour force (000s)	1985	1986	1987
Total	23,459	23,851	24,103
Males	15,306	15,379	15,453
Females	8,189	8,473	8,650

Activity rates	1984	1985	1986
Labour force as percentage of population of all ages			
Total	41.3	41.5	42.2
Male	55.5	55.6	55.8
Female	27.8	28.1	29.2

Activity rates	1984	1985	1986
Labour force as percentage of population aged 15-64			
Total	59.7	59.7	60.5
Male	79.4	79.2	79.3
Female	40.6	40.8	42.3

Civilian employment (000s)	1985	1986	1987
Total	20,508	20,614	20,646
Males	13,677	13,638	13,601
Females	6,831	6,977	7,046

Civilian employment by sector (%)	1986
Agriculture	10.9
Industry	33.1
Services	56.0

Employment by industry (000s)	1985
Agriculture	2,296
Extractive industries	209
Manufacturing	4,766
Electricity, gas, water	**
Construction	1,921
Wholesale and retail trade (and hotels)	4,365
Transport and communications	1,091
Finance, insurance, and business services	716
Community, social, and personal services	5,143

Unemployment	1984		1985		1986	
	000s	%	000s	%	000s	%
Total	2,304	9.9	2,382	10.1	2,610	10.9
Males	987	6.5	1,024	6.7	1,115	7.3
Females	1,317	16.3	1,358	16.6	1,496	17.7
Aged 14-24 (as percentage of total)	% 60.3		% 59.8		% 56.5	

Average hours of work per day in manufacturing	1983	1984	
	7.7	7.8	

Industrial disputes	1984	1985	1986
Number of disputes	1,816	1,341	1,469
Workers involved (000s)	7,356.5	4,842.8	3,606.7
Working days lost (000s)	8,703.3	3,830.8	5,643.7

Average hourly earnings (Lire)	1983	1984	
	7,804	8,674	

Consumer prices (percentage increase)	1985	1986	1987
	9.2	5.8	4.8

Trade unions

Total membership (1985)	6,800,000
As percentage of labour force	40
Central organizations	Confederazione Generale Italiana del Lavoro (CGIL) 4,150,000 members Confederazione Italiana del Sindicati Lavoratori (CISL) 2,900,000 members Unione Italiana del Lavoro (UIL) 900,000 members

JAPAN

Size	372,000 km²
Population (1986)	121,440,000. Annual change 1981-6:+0.7 per cent
Per capita GNP (1985)	$11,300

Labour force (000s)	1985	1986	1987
Total	59,634	60,202	60,836
Males	35,960	36,260	36,550
Females	23,670	23,950	24,290

Activity rates Labour force as percentage of population of all ages	1984	1985	1986
Total	49.4	49.4	49.6
Male	60.6	60.5	60.7
Female	38.5	38.6	38.8

Activity rates Labour force as percentage of population aged 15-64	1984	1985	1986
Total	72.7	72.4	72.4
Male	88.4	87.8	87.6
Female	57.2	57.2	57.4

Civilian employment (000s)	1985	1986	1987
Total	58,070	58,530	59,110
Males	35,030	35,260	35,510
Females	23,040	23,270	23,600

Civilian employment by sector (%)	1986
Agriculture	8.5
Industry	34.5
Services	57.1

Employment by industry (000s)	1985
Agriculture	5,090
Extractive industries	90
Manufacturing	14,530
Electricity, gas, water	330
Construction	5,300
Wholesale and retail trade (and hotels)	13,180
Transport and communications	3,430
Finance, insurance, and business services	3,920
Community, social, and personal services	11,970

Unemployment	1985		1986		1987	
	000s	%	000s	%	000s	%
Total	1,560	2.6	1,670	2.8	1,730	2.9
Males	930	2.6	990	2.7	1,040	2.8
Females	630	2.7	670	2.8	690	2.8
Aged 15-24 (as percentage of total)	% 22.4		% 23.4		% 23.1	

Average hours of work per week in manufacturing	1984	1985	1986	1987
	41.7	41.5	41.1	42.3

Industrial disputes	1984	1985	1986
Number of disputes	596	627	620
Workers involved (000s)	155.06	123.39	118.03
Working days lost (000s)	354.05	264.05	253.42

Average monthly earnings (Yen)	1986	1987
	327,041	335,860

Average monthly labour cost per employee in manufacturing (Yen)	1984	1985
	355,780	365,918

Consumer prices (percentage increase)	1985	1986	1987
	2.0	0.6	0.1

Trade unions

Total membership (1985)	12,418,000
As percentage of all employees	28.9
Central organizations	Sohyo (General Council of Trade Unions of Japan) 4,365,000 members in 50 federations Domei (Japanese Confederation of Labour) 2,161,000 members in 29 federations Churitsuroren (Federation of Independent Unions of Japan) 1,557,000 members in 10 federations Shinsanbetsu (National Federation of Industrial Organizations) 61,000 members in 5 federations

Number of unions

34,539 individual unions
74,499 unit - unions

Japan: private-sector union membership by size of firm, 1985

Size	Membership (000)	%
1,000 or more employees	5,334	57.9
300 - 999	1,417	15.4
100 - 299	1,029	11.2
30 - 99	451	4.9
29 or less	67	0.7
Others	919	10.0
Total	**9,217**	**100**

Source Ministry of Labour

LUXEMBURG

Size	2,586 km²
Population (1986)	369,500

Labour force (000s)	1984	1985	1986
Total	161.4	164.0	167.4
Males	107.2	108.2	110.4
Females	54.2	55.4	57.0

Activity rates	1984	1985	1986
Labour force as percentage of population of all ages			
Total	44.1	44.6	45.3
Male	60.2	60.5	61.4
Female	28.8	29.4	30.0

Activity rates	1984	1985	1986
Labour force as percentage of population aged 15-64			
Total	63.4	63.9	64.9
Male	84.5	84.7	85.6
Female	42.5	43.2	44.3

Civilian employment (000s)	1984	1985	1986
Total	158.0	160.3	164.4
Males	105.1	106.1	108.5
Females	52.9	54.2	55.9

Civilian employment by sector (%)	1985
Agriculture	4.2
Industry	33.4
Services	62.3

Employment by industry (000s)	1985
Agriculture	6.8
Extractive industries	0.2
Manufacturing	38.0
Electricity, gas, water	1.4
Construction	13.7
Wholesale and retail trade (and hotels)	35.1
Transport and communications	10.6
Finance, insurance, and business services	17.5
Community, social, and personal services	36.2

Unemployment	1985		1986		1987	
	000s	%	000s	%	000s	%
Total	2.588	1.7	2.290	1.5	2.660	1.7
Males	1.343	1.4	1.220	1.2	1.511	1.5
Females	1.245	2.3	1.070	1.9	1.148	2.0

Average hours of work (paid) per week in manufacturing	1984	1985	1986
	39.7	40.3	40.5
Average hourly earnings (Francs)	1984	1985	1986
	297.30	306.20	316.70

Average monthly industrial wage (1986) 90,587 (minimum monthly gross wage 26,689)

Average hourly labour cost per employee in manufacturing (Francs)	525	**	**
Consumer prices (percentage increase)	1985	1986	1987
	4.1	0.3	0.8

Trade unions

Total membership as percentage of labour force (1984)	60
Central organizations	Confédération Générale du Travail 30,000 members Confédération des Syndicats Chrétiens 18,000 members Also a number of smaller federations

NETHERLANDS

Size	41,000 km²
Population (1986)	14,563,000. Annual change 1981-6: +0.5 per cent
Per capita GNP (1985)	$9,290

Labour force (000s)	1984	1985	1986
Total	5,773	5,812	5,843
Males	3,800	3,806	3,812
Females	1,973	2,005	2,031

Activity rates Labour force as percentage of population of all ages	1984	1985	1986
Total	40.0	40.1	40.1
Male	53.2	53.1	52.9
Female	27.1	27.4	27.6

Activity rates Labour force as percentage of population aged 15-64	1984	1985	1986
Total	58.8	58.6	58.3
Male	76.5	75.8	75.1
Female	40.7	40.9	41.1

Civilian employment (000s)	1984	1985	1986
Total	4,980	5,076	5,135
Males	3,283	3,334	3,365
Females	1,696	1,742	1,770

Civilian employment by sector (%)	1985
Agriculture	4.9
Industry	26.5
Services	68.6

Employment by industry (000s)	1985
Agriculture	268.1
Extractive industries	11.3
Manufacturing	993.4
Electricity, gas, water	44.2
Construction	385.7
Wholesale and retail trade (and hotels)	906.5
Transport and communications	322.6
Finance, insurance, and business services	457.3
Community, social, and personal services	1,716.1

Unemployment	1984		1985		1986		1987	
	000s	%	000s	%	000s	%	000s	%
Total	822.4	14.1	761.0	12.9	710.7	12.0	685.5	11.5
Males	555.2	14.6	498.0	13.0	453.5	11.8	428.7	11.1
Females	267.2	13.3	263.0	12.8	257.2	12.3	256.8	12.1

Average hours of work (paid) per week in manufacturing	1984	1985	1986
	40.3	40.4	40.1

Industrial disputes	1984	1985	1986
Number of disputes	11	45	35
Workers involved (000s)	16.158	22.570	17.029
Working days lost (000s)	29.181	89.390	38.858

Average hourly earnings (Guilders)	1984	1985
	18.46	18.55

Average hourly labour cost per employee in manufacturing (Guilders)	34.41	36.25

Consumer prices (percentage increase)	1985	1986	1987
	2.3	0.2	-0.5

Trade unions

Total membership (1985)	1,541,000
As percentage of employed labour force	29
Central organizations	Federation of Dutch Trade Unions (FNV) 898,000 members in 24 unions Christian National Trade Union (CNV) 300,000 members in 13 unions Trade Unions of Middle and Higher Personnel (MHP) 108,000 members

NEW ZEALAND

Size	269,000 km²
Population (1986)	3,279,000
Per capita GNP (1985)	$7,010

Labour force (000s)	1983	1984	1985
Total	1,355	1,371	1,399
Males	884	889	894
Females	471	482	505

Activity rates Labour force as percentage of population of all ages	1983	1984	1985
Total	42.0	42.1	42.7
Male	55.1	54.9	54.9
Female	29.0	29.4	30.6

Activity rates Labour force as percentage of population aged 15-64	1983	1984	1985
Total	65.3	65.0	65.5
Male	84.7	83.7	83.2
Female	45.7	46.0	47.6

Civilian employment (000s)	1984	1985
Total	1,281	1,329

Civilian employment by sector (%)	1985
Agriculture	11.1
Industry	32.4
Services	56.5

Employment by industry (000s)	1985
Agriculture	148
Extractive industries	5
Manufacturing	318
Electricity, gas, water	16
Construction	91
Wholesale and retail trade (and hotels)	231
Transport and communications	104
Finance, insurance, and business services	104
Community, social, and personal services	324

Unemployment	1983		1984		1985		1986	
	000s	%	000s	%	000s	%	000s	%
Total	76.475	5.7	66.534	5.0	53.179	4.0	67.200	5.0
Males	48.304	5.5	41.367	4.7	33.459	3.8	45.040	* *
Females	28.171	6.2	25.167	5.5	19.720	4.3	22.161	* *

Average hours of work (paid) per week in manufacturing	1983	1984	1985	1986
	39.5	40.4	40.2	39.5

Industrial disputes	1983	1984	1985	1986
Number of disputes	333	364	383	213
Workers involved (000s)	140.73	160.28	182.15	91.1
Working days lost (000s)	371.77	424.92	756.43	1,323.4

Average hourly earnings ($)	1984	1985
	7.92	8.56

	1986	1987
Average weekly earnings	373.89	427.46*

(*ranging from 543.04 in Mining & Quarrying, to 277.31 in Restaurants & Hotels)

Consumer prices (percentage increase)	1985	1986	1987
	15.4	13.2	15.7

Trade unions

Total membership (1986)	489,763 in 227 unions
As percentage of labour force	40
Central organization	New Zealand Federation of Labour

Membership of major unions (1986)

New Zealand Amalgamated Engineering and Related Trades COT	45,000
New Zealand Meat Processors, Packers, Preservers, Freezing Works, and Related Trades	24,023
New Zealand Labourers, General Workers, and Related Trades	20,206
Northern Hotel, Hospital, Restaurant, and Related Trades Employees	18,643
New Zealand Bank Officers	18,500
Northern Clerical, Administrative, and Related Workers	15,264

NORWAY

Size 324,000 km²
Population (1986) 4,167,000. Annual change 1981-6: +0.3 per cent
Per capita GNP (1985) $14,370

Labour force (000s)	1985	1986	1987
Total	2,064	2,128	2,171
Males	1,174	1,190	1,209
Females	893	938	962

Activity rates	1984	1985	1986
Labour force as percentage of population of all ages			
Total	49.1	49.7	51.0
Male	56.6	56.7	57.8
Female	41.7	42.8	44.5

Activity rates	1984	1985	1986
Labour force as percentage of population aged 15-64			
Total	76.6	77.3	79.3
Male	86.2	86.0	87.3
Female	66.7	68.3	71.0

Civilian employment (000s)	1985	1986	1987
Total	2,012	2,071	2,126
Males	1,141	1,154	1,188
Females	871	916	938

Civilian employment by sector (%)	1986
Agriculture	6.9
Industry	27.6
Services	65.3

Employment by industry (000s)	1985
Agriculture	144
Extractive industries	23
Manufacturing	365
Electricity, gas, water	21
Construction	151
Wholesale and retail trade (and hotels)	343
Transport and communications	171
Finance, insurance, and business services	132
Community, social, and personal services	658

Unemployment	1985		1986		1987	
	000s	%	000s	%	000s	%
Total	54	2.6	42	2.0	45	2.1
Males	25	2.1	18	1.5	21	1.7
Females	28	3.1	24	2.6	25	2.6
Aged 16-24 (as percentage of total)	% 42.6		% 45.2		% 46.7	

Average hours of work per week in manufacturing	1984	1985	1986
	38.0	38.4	38.4

Industrial disputes	1983	1984	1985
Number of disputes	9	21	11
Workers involved (000s)	1.018	30.635	6.557
Working days lost (000s)	5.897	104.35	66.473

Average hourly earnings in manufacturing (Kroner)	1984	1985	1986
	57.06	61.56	71.05*

(*ranging from 50.53 in footwear manufacture, to 109.63 in newspaper printing)

Average yearly labour cost per employee in manufacturing (Kroner)		
	127,869	140,197

Consumer prices (percentage increase)	1985	1986	1987
	5.5	7.3	8.5

Trade unions

Total membership (1986)	1,231,602
As percentage of labour force	66
Central organizations	LO (Norwegian Federation of Trade Unions) 785,573 members in 34 unions
	YS (Confederation of Vocational Unions) 131,739 members
	AF (Federation of Norwegian Professional Associations) 144,108 members
	Other associations of wage earners 170,182

Membership of major LO unions (1986)

Municipal Employees	172,789
Federation of State Employees' Union	114,350
Iron and Metalworkers	101,163
Building Workers	61,089
Norwegian Union of Employees in Commerce and Offices	60,815
Government Employees	41,487

PORTUGAL

Size	92,000 km²
Population (1986)	10,290,000
Per capita GNP (1985)	$1,970

Labour force (000s)	1984	1985	1986
Total	4,544	4,505	4,481
Males	2,687	2,661	2,655
Females	1,857	1,844	1,825

Activity rates Labour force as percentage of population of all ages	1984	1985	1986
Total	47.3	46.6	46.2
Male	57.9	57.0	56.6
Female	37.3	36.9	36.4

Activity rates Labour force as percentage of population aged 15-64	1984	1985	1986
Total	73.2	71.8	70.8
Male	89.0	87.2	86.1
Female	58.2	57.2	56.2

Civilian employment (000s)	1984	1985	1986
Total	4,063	4,030	4,045
Males	2,434	2,412	2,412
Females	1,630	1,618	1,634

Civilian employment by sector (%)	1982
Agriculture	25.2
Industry	37.5
Services	37.3

Employment by industry (000s)	1985
Agriculture	1,018
Extractive industries	24
Manufacturing	1,037
Electricity, gas, water	30
Construction	354
Wholesale and retail trade (and hotels)	592
Transport and communications	187
Finance, insurance, and business services	120
Community, social, and personal services	917

Unemployment	1985		1986		1987	
	000s	%	000s	%	000s	%
Total	384.7	8.5	381.6	8.4	319.6	7.1
Males	165.5	6.3	170.4	6.5	139.3	5.4
Females	219.2	11.3	211.2	11.1	180.3	9.3

Average hours of work per week in manufacturing	1984	1985	
	38.6	38.1	

Industrial disputes	1983	1984	1985
Number of disputes	500	525	476
Workers involved (000s)	237.6	230.5	199.0
Working days lost (000s)	650.7	269.7	275.4

Average hourly earnings (Escudos)	1984	1985
	173.7	204.3
Average yearly labour cost per employee in manufacturing (Escudos)	478,500	* *

Consumer prices (percentage increase)	1984	1985	1986
	29.3	19.3	11.6

Trade unions

Total membership (1986)	2,790,000 in 361 unions
As percentage of total employees	81
Central organizations	Confederacao Geral dos Trabalhadores Portugueses, Intersindical Nacional (CGTP-IN) - with 193 affiliated unions
	Uniao Geral dos Trabalhadores (UGT) - with 52 affiliated unions

SPAIN

Size	505,000 km²
Population (1986)	38,688,000. Annual change 1981-6: +0.5 per cent
Per capita GNP (1985)	$4,290

Labour force (000s)	1985	1986	1987
Total	13,938	14,147	14,668
Males	9,791	9,840	9,896
Females	4,147	4,307	4,772

Activity rates Labour force as percentage of population of all ages	1984	1985	1986
Total	36.3	36.4	36.6
Male	52.1	51.9	51.8
Female	21.0	21.5	21.9

Activity rates Labour force as percentage of population aged 15-64	1984	1985	1986
Total	56.2	56.1	56.1
Male	79.6	78.7	78.2
Female	33.0	33.6	34.1

Civilian employment (000s)	1985	1986	1987
Total	10,567	10,815	11,370
Males	7,462	7,599	7,901
Females	3,105	3,215	3,470

Civilian employment by sector (%)	1986
Agriculture	15.6
Industry	32.4
Services	52.1

Employment by industry (000s)	1985
Agriculture	1,763.4
Extractive industries	81.6
Manufacturing	2,399.4
Electricity, gas, water	85.6
Construction	769.9
Wholesale and retail trade (and hotels)	2,130.8
Transport and communications	617.9
Finance, insurance, and business services	450.1
Community, social, and personal services	2,018.0

Unemployment	1985		1986		1987	
	000s	%	000s	%	000s	%
Total	2,983	21.4	2,972	21.0	2,954	20.1
Males	1,941	19.7	1,881	19.1	1,653	16.7
Females	1,042	25.1	1,091	25.3	1,302	27.3
Aged 16-24 (as percentage of total)	% 48.1		% 47.8		% 47.5	

Average hours of work per week in manufacturing	1984	1985	1986
	36.7	36.5	36.9

Industrial disputes	1983	1984	1985
Number of disputes	1,451	1,498	1,092
Workers involved (000s)	1,483.6	2,242.2	1,511.2
Working days lost (000s)	4,416.7	6,357.8	3,223.5

Average hourly earnings (Pesetas)	1984	1985	1986
	508	558	611

Consumer prices (percentage increase)	1985	1986	1987
	8.8	8.8	5.2

Trade unions

Membership as percentage of labour force (1985)	16
Central organizations	Union General de Trabajadores (UGT) 663,000 members Comisiones Obreras (CCOO) 500,000 members

SWEDEN

Size	450,000 km²
Population (1986)	8,369,000. Annual change 1981-6: +0.1 per cent
Per capita GNP (1985)	$11,890

Labour force (000s)	1985	1986	1987
Total	4,424	4,384	4,421
Males	2,341	2,298	2,300
Females	2,082	2,087	2,121

Activity rates Labour force as percentage of population of all ages	1984	1985	1986
Total	52.0	52.3	52.4
Male	55.5	55.5	55.6
Female	48.5	48.9	49.2

Activity rates Labour force as percentage of population aged 15-64	1984	1985	1986
Total	80.3	81.0	81.3
Male	83.9	84.2	84.1
Female	76.7	77.6	78.3

Civilian employment (000s)	1985	1986	1987
Total	4,299	4,269	4,337
Males	2,277	2,238	2,256
Females	2,022	2,031	2,081

Civilian employment by sector (%)	1986
Agriculture	4.2
Industry	30.2
Services	65.6

Employment by industry (000s)	1985
Agriculture	208
Extractive industries	15
Manufacturing	968
Electricity, gas, water	40
Construction	260
Wholesale and retail trade (and hotels)	591
Transport and communications	300
Finance, insurance, and business services	321
Community, social, and personal services	1,594

Unemployment	1985		1986		1987	
	000s	%	000s	%	000s	%
Total	125	2.8	117	2.7	84	1.9
Males	65	2.8	61	2.6	44	1.9
Females	60	2.9	56	2.7	40	1.9
Aged 16-24 (as percentage of total)	% 32.2		% 33.0		% 35.2	

Average hours of work per week in manufacturing	1984	1985	1986
	38.1	38.3	38.3

Industrial disputes	1984	1985	1986
Number of disputes	206	160	75
Workers involved (000s)	23.676	124.51	66.304
Working days lost (000s)	31.29	504.21	682.65

Average hourly earnings in manufacturing (Kronor)	1985	1986
	58.58	62.65

Average hourly labour cost per employee in manufacturing (Kronor)		
	84.20	91.34

Consumer prices (percentage increase)	1985	1986	1987
	7.4	4.2	4.2

Trade unions

Total membership (1986)	3,750,000
As percentage of total employees	90
Central organizations	LO (Swedish Trade Union Confederation) 2,250,000 members in 24 unions TCO (Central Organization of Salaried Employees) 1,200,000 members in 21 unions SACO/SR (Swedish Confederaton of Professional Associations/National Federation of Civil Servants) 300,000 members in 25 unions

Membership of major unions (1986)

Municipal Workers (LO)	640,000
Metal Workers (LO)	460,000
Union of Salaried Employees in Industry (TCO)	280,000
State Employees (LO)	210,000
Local Government Salaried Employees Union (TO)	170,000
Commercial Employees (LO)	160,000

SWITZERLAND

Size	41,000 km²
Population (1985)	6,533,000
Per capita GNP (1985)	$16,370

Labour force (000s)	1984	1985	1986
Total	3,177	3,201	3,244
Males	2,002	2,016	2,039
Females	1,175	1,185	1,206

Activity rates Labour force as percentage of population of all ages	1984	1985	1986
Total	48.8	49.0	49.4
Male	62.8	62.9	63.2
Female	35.4	35.6	36.0

Activity rates Labour force as percentage of population aged 15-64	1984	1985	1986
Total	71.4	71.4	71.8
Male	89.5	89.4	89.5
Female	53.1	53.2	53.9

Civilian employment (000s)	1984	1985	1986
Total	3,142	3,171	3,219
Males	1,982	1,999	2,025
Females	1,160	1,172	1,193

Civilian employment by sector (%)	1986
Agriculture	6.5
Industry	37.7
Services	55.8

Employment by industry (000s)	1985
Agriculture	210
Extractive industries	5
Manufacturing	946
Electricity, gas, water	21
Construction	224
Wholesale and retail trade (and hotels)	596
Transport and communications	196
Finance, insurance, and business services	293
Community, social, and personal services	681

Unemployment	1985		1986		1987	
	000s	%	000s	%	000s	%
Total	30.3	1.0	25.7	0.8	24.7	0.8
Males	16.4	0.8	13.4	0.7	12.5	0.6
Females	13.9	1.2	12.3	1.1	12.1	1.1
Aged under 30 (as percentage of total)	% 41.2		% 40.5		% * *	

Average hours of work (paid) per week in manufacturing	1983	1984	1985	1986
	43.2	43.0	42.9	42.6

Industrial disputes	1984	1985	1986
Number of disputes	2	3	1
Workers involved (000s)	0.050	0.366	0.036
Working days lost (000s)	0.662	0.662	0.072

Average hourly earnings (Francs)	1984	1985
	17.82	18.36*

(*ranging from 24.68 in printing, to 16.49 in cleansing and chimney sweeping)

Consumer prices (percentage increase)	1985	1986	1987
	3.4	0.7	1.5

Trade unions

Total membership (1985)	850,000
As percentage of labour force	32
Central organizations	4 major confederations. Largest is Schweizerischer Gewerkschaftsbund (SGB) with 443,584 members in 12 affiliated unions (largest are Metalworkers and Watchmakers union with 118,314 members, and Construction and Timber Union with 115,190 members)

TURKEY

Size	781,000 km^2
Population (1986)	50,300,000
Per capita GNP (1985)	$1,080

Labour force (000s)	1984	1985	1986
Total	18,516	18,769	19,012

Activity rates Labour force as percentage of population of all ages	1984	1985	1986
Total	37.5	37.7	37.3

Activity rates Labour force as percentage of population aged 15-64	1984	1985	1986
Total	64.5	63.5	62.6

Civilian employment (000s)	1984	1985	1986
Total	15,111	15,290	15,632

Civilian employment by sector (%)	1985
Agriculture	57.1
Industry	17.5
Services	25.4

Employment by industry (000s)	1985
Agriculture	8,725
Extractive industries	119
Manufacturing	1,802
Electricity, gas, water	132
Construction	623
Wholesale and retail trade (and hotels)	763
Transport and communications	541
Finance, insurance, and business services	229
Community, social, and personal services	2,083

Unemployment	1985		1986		1987	
	000s	%	000s	%	000s	%
Total	934.6	**	1,053.4	**	1,124	**
Males	781.7	**	876.9	**	929	**
Females	152.8	**	176.5	**	195	**

Industrial disputes	1985	1986
Number of disputes	21	28
Workers involved (000s)	2.410	7.926
Working days lost (000s)	194.30	234.94

Average daily earnings (Liras)	1983	1984
	944.37	1,307.6

Average daily wage level (1986) 3,601 (legal minimum wage 1,112)

Consumer prices (percentage increase)	1984	1985	1986
	48.4	45.0	34.6

Trade unions

Total membership (1986)	1,977,066
As percentage of total employees	63
Central organizations	Türkiye Isci Sendikalari Konfederasyonu (Türk-Is) 1,457,604 members in 32 unions Türkiye Milliyetci Isci Sendikalari Konfederasyonu (MISK) 139,746 members in 9 unions Türkiye Hak Isci Sendikalari 155,810 members in 6 unions

Membership of major unions (1986)

Tek Gida Is (Food)	183,365
Teksif (Textiles)	178,157
Yol-Is (Construction)	123,130
Türk Metal (Metal)	120,530
Belediye Is (General Workers)	108,608
Tes-Is (Energy)	99,467

UK

Size	245,000 km²
Population (1986)	56,760,000
Per capita GNP (1985)	$8,460

Labour force (000s)	1985	1986	1987
Total	27,594	27,772	27,814
Males	16,449	16,414	16,344
Females	11,175	11,359	11,470

Activity rates Labour force as percentage of population of all ages	1984	1985	1986
Total	48.0	48.7	48.9
Male	59.1	59.6	59.4
Female	37.5	38.4	39.0

Activity rates Labour force as percentage of population aged 15-64	1984	1985	1986
Total	73.1	74.3	74.5
Male	87.5	88.3	87.9
Female	58.6	60.1	61.0

Civilian employment (000s)	1985	1986	1987
Total	24,090	24,239	24,590
Males	13,937	13,908	14,019
Females	10,152	10,331	10,572

Civilian employment by sector (%)	1986
Agriculture	2.6
Industry	31.1
Services	66.4

Employment by industry (000s)	1985
Agriculture	620
Extractive industries	291
Manufacturing	5,728
Electricity, gas, water	321
Construction	1,447
Wholesale and retail trade (and hotels)	5,096
Transport and communications	1,407
Finance, insurance, and business services	2,201
Community, social, and personal services	6,960

Unemployment	1985		1986		1987	
	000s	%	000s	%	000s	%
Total	3,271	11.9	3,289	11.8	2,953	10.6
Males	2,252	13.7	2,252	13.5	2,046	12.4
Females	1,019	9.1	1,036	9.0	907	7.8
Aged under 25 (as percentage of total)	% 38.1		% 35.9		% 33.6	

	1983	1984	1985	1986
Average hours of work per week in manufacturing	41.5	41.7	41.8	41.6

Industrial disputes	1984	1985	1986
Number of disputes	1,206	903	1,074
Workers involved (000s)	1,464.3	791.3	720.2
Working days lost (000s)	27,135	6,402	1,920

	1985	1986
Average hourly earnings (£)	3.747	4.006
Average hourly labour cost per employee in manufacturing (£)	**	**

	1985	1986	1987
Consumer prices (percentage increase)	6.1	3.4	4.2

Trade unions

Total membership (1985)	10,716,000 in 373 unions
As percentage of labour force	43
Central organization	Trades Union Congress (TUC) 9,585,729 members in 88 unions

Membership of major unions (1985)

Transport and General Workers' Union	1,434,005
Amalgamated Engineering Union	974,904
General, Municipal, Boilermakers, and Allied Trades Union	826,920
National and Local Government Officers Association	752,131
National Union of Public Employees	663,776

Trade unions: numbers and membership, 1985

Number of members	Number of unions	All membership (000s)	Percentage of: Number of unions	Percentage of: Membership of all unions
Under 100	74	3	19.8	0.0
100 - 499	94	23	25.2	0.2
500 - 999	37	28	9.9	0.3
1,000 - 2,499	57	95	15.3	0.9
2,500 - 4,999	26	102	7.0	1.0
5,000 - 9,999	14	87	3.8	0.8
10,000 - 14,999	4	48	1.1	0.4
15,000 - 24,999	11	202	2.9	1.9
25,000 - 49,999	23	805	6.2	7.5
50,000 - 99,999	9	655	2.4	6.1
100,000 - 249,999	14	2,351	3.8	21.9
250,000 and more	10	6,317	2.7	58.9
Total	**373**	**10,716**	**100.0**	**100.0**

Source Employment Gazette (Department of Employment)

USA

Size 9,363,000 km²
Population (1986) 241,600,000. Annual change 1981-6: +1.0 per cent
Per capita GNP (1985) $16,690

Labour force (000s)	1985	1986	1987
Total	117,167	119,540	121,602
Males	65,967	66,973	67,784
Females	51,200	52,568	53,818

Activity rates Labour force as percentage of population of all ages	1984	1985	1986
Total	48.8	49.2	49.7
Male	57.0	57.0	57.3
Female	41.4	41.8	42.5

Activity rates Labour force as percentage of population aged 15-64	1984	1985	1986
Total	73.6	74.1	74.8
Male	84.8	84.6	85.0
Female	62.8	63.9	64.9

Civilian employment (000s)	1985	1986	1987
Total	107,150	109,597	112,440
Males	59,891	60,892	62,107
Females	47,259	48,706	50,334

Civilian employment by sector (%)	1986
Agriculture	3.1
Industry	27.7
Services	69.3

Employment by industry (000s)	1985
Agriculture	3,338
Extractive industries	938
Manufacturing	20,879
Electricity, gas, water	1,486
Construction	6,987
Wholesale and retail trade (and hotels)	22,296
Transport and communications	6,062
Finance, insurance, and business services	11,005
Community, social, and personal services	34,158

Unemployment	1985		1986		1987	
	000s	%	000s	%	000s	%
Total	8,312	7.1	8,237	6.9	7,425	6.1
Males	4,521	6.9	4,530	6.8	4,101	6.2
Females	3,791	7.4	3,707	7.1	3,324	6.2
Aged 15-24 (as percentage of total)	% 38.6		% 37.7		% 37.7	

Average hours of work per week in manufacturing	1984	1985	1986	1987
	40.7	40.5	40.7	41.0

Industrial disputes	1984	1985	1986
Number of disputes	62	54	69
Workers involved (000s)	376.0	323.9	533.2
Working days lost (000s)	8,498.8	7,079.1	11,861

Average hourly earnings ($)	1984	1985
	8.32	8.58*

(*ranging from 15.36 in malt beverage industry, to 4.36 in eating and drinking places)

Average hourly labour cost per employee in manufacturing ($)	12.47	12.97

Consumer prices (percentage increase)	1985	1986	1987
	3.5	1.8	3.7

Trade unions

Total membership (1985)	17,000,000
As percentage of labour force	16
Central organization	AFL-CIO 14,000,000 members in 100 unions

Membership of major unions (1985)

United Food and Commercial Workers International Union	1,203,000
United Auto Workers	1,026,000
American Federation of State, County and Municipal Employees	955,000
International Brotherhood of Electrical Workers	869,000
United Steelworkers of America	694,000
Carpenters and Joiners of America	678,000
(Non AFL-CIO) Teamsters Union	1,800,000

11 LABOUR STATISTICS* FOR TWENTY NON-OECD COUNTRIES

* Definitions as on p. 205

ARGENTINA

Size	2,767,000 km²
Population (1986)	31,030,000
Per capita GNP (1985)	$2,130

Labour force (000s)	1985
Total	11,452
Males	8,400
Females	3,000

Activity rates	1985
Labour force as percentage of population of all ages	
Total	37.5
Male	55.3
Female	19.9

Employment (000s) (Gran Buenos Aires)	1984
Total	4,039.9
Males	2,678.7
Females	1,361.2

Labour force by sector (%)	1980
Agriculture	13
Industry	34
Services	53

Estimated average annual growth of labour force (%)	
1980-85	1.1
1985-2000	1.5

Employment by industry (000s)	1984
Agriculture	10.19
Extractive industries	2.17
Manufacturing	962.15
Electricity, gas, water	21.19
Construction	219.31
Wholesale and retail trade (and hotels)	635.01
Transport and communications	218.45
Finance, insurance, and business services	252.49
Community, social, and personal services	1,101.08

Unemployment (Gran Buenos Aires)	1983		1984		1985	
	000s	%	000s	%	000s	%
Total	159.4	4.2	152.1	3.8	216.2	5.3
Males	98.9	**	92.8	**	142.9	**
Females	60.5	**	59.3	**	73.3	**

Average hours worked per month in manufacturing	1984	1985	1986
	178.4	179.7	188.4
Consumer prices (percentage increase)	1985	1986	1987
	672.2	90.1	131.3

Trade unions

Central organization	Confederacion General del Trabajo (CGT) with 2,500,000 members

BRAZIL

Size	8,512,000 km^2
Population (1986)	138,490,000
Per capita GNP (1985)	$1,640

Labour force (000s)	1985
Total	55,098
Males	36,625
Females	18,473

Employment (000s)	1983	1984	1985
Total	48,467	50,209	53,237
Males	32,460	33,648	35,463
Females	16,006	16,561	17,774

Employment by industry (000s)	1982
Agriculture	14,139
Manufacturing	7,790
Construction	3,423
Wholesale and retail trade (and hotels)	4,954
Transport and communications	1,831
Finance, insurance, and business services	2,555
Community, social, and personal services	13,234

Labour force by sector (%)	1980
Agriculture	31
Industry	27
Services	42

Estimated average annual growth of labour force (%)	
1980-85	2.3
1980-2000	2.1

Unemployment	1982		1985	
	000s	%	000s	%
Total	2,533	**	1,862	**
Males	1,678	**	1,162	**
Females	855	**	699	**

Consumer prices (percentage increase)	1984	1985	1986
	172.3	201.6	67.2

Trade unions

Total membership (1986)	43,000,000 in 4,646 unions
Central confederations	CNTI (Confederacao Nacional dos Trabalhadores na Industria) 65 Federations and 1,296 unions affiliated, covering 11 million workers
	CNTC (Confederacao Nacional dos Trabalhadores no Comércio) 32 Federations and 550 unions affiliated, covering 9 million workers
	CONTAG (Confederacao Nacional dos Trabalhadores na Agricultura) 22 Federations and 2,800 unions affiliated, covering 9 million workers

Major central unions (1986)

CGT (Confederacao Geral dos Trabalhadores)
1,500 unions affiliated with 30 million workers

CUT (Central Unica dos Trabalhadores)
1,014 unions affiliated with 13 million workers

CHILE

Size	757,000 km²
Population (1986)	12,330,000
Per capita GNP (1985)	$1,430

Labour force (000s)	1986
Total	4,269
Males	2,989
Females	1,280

Activity rates	1986
Labour force as percentage of population of all ages	
Total	35.1
Male	50.2
Female	20.6

Employment (000s)	1985	1986
Total	3,720.6	3,895.7
Males	2,620.9	2,739.0
Females	1,099.7	1,156.7

Labour force by sector (%)	1980
Agriculture	31
Industry	27
Services	42

Estimated average annual growth of labour force (%)	
1980-85	2.6
1985-2000	1.7

Employment by industry (000s)	1985
Agriculture	751.1
Extractive industries	86.1
Manufacturing	494.7
Electricity, gas, water	26.1
Construction	145.5
Wholesale and retail trade (and hotels)	644.6
Transport and communications	214.4
Finance, insurance, and business services	150.8
Community, social, and personal services	1,206.9

Unemployment	1983		1984		1985		1986	
	000s	%	000s	%	000s	%	000s	%
Total	551.9	14.6	541.3	13.9	516.7	12.2	374.1	8.7
Males	381.7	14.6	351.1	13.0	355.4	11.9	250.0	8.4
Females	170.2	14.7	190.1	15.9	161.3	12.8	124.0	9.7

Industrial disputes	1984	1985	1986
Number of disputes	38	42	41
Workers involved (000s)	3.600	8.500	3.900
Working days lost (000s)	41.980	131.63	60.700

Average monthly earnings (Pesos)	1985	1986
	59,574	73,101

Consumer prices (percentage increase)	1985	1986	1987
	30.7	19.5	19.9

Trade unions

Major national centre — Coordinadora Nacional Sindical (CNS) 700,000 members in some 30 confederations and unions

EGYPT

Size	1,001,000 km^2
Population (1986)	49,610,000
Per capita GNP (1985)	$610

Labour force (000s)	1983
Total	13,842
Males	11,128
Females	2,714

Activity rates	1983
Labour force as percentage of population of all ages	
Total	31.4
Male	49.8
Female	12.5

Employment (000s)	1982	1983
Total	10,115	11,526
Males	9,319	9,581
Females	796	1,945

Labour force by sector (%)	1980
Agriculture	46
Industry	20
Services	34

Estimated average annual growth of labour force (%)	
1980-85	2.6
1985-2000	2.7

Employment by industry (000s)	1983
Agriculture	4,722
Extractive industries	32.8
Manufacturing	1,697
Electricity, gas, water	100.1
Construction	619.1
Wholesale and retail trade (and hotels)	1,019.1
Transport and communications	570.7
Finance, insurance, and business services	149.2
Community, social, and personal services	2,428.2

Unemployment	1982		1983	
	000s	%	000s	%
Total	606.2	5.7	812.7	6.6
Males	400.7	4.1	582.4	5.7
Females	205.5	20.5	230.3	**

Industrial disputes	1981	1982	1983
Number of disputes	6	4	1
Workers involved (000s)	2.886	0.771	0.050
Working days lost (000s)	2.886	0.771	0.100

Consumer prices (percentage increase)	1984	1985	1986
	17.0	14.0	21.8

Trade unions

Central organization	Egyptian Trade Union Federation with 3,000,000 members in 23 unions

GHANA

Size	239,000 km^2
Population (1986)	14,040,000
Per capita GNP (1985)	$380

Labour force by sector (%)	1980
Agriculture	56
Industry	18
Services	26

Estimated average annual growth of labour force (%)	
1980-85	2.7
1985-2000	2.9

Unemployment	1983	1984	1985	1986
	000s	000s	000s	000s
Total	23.700	21.154	24.229	25.790
Males	**	15.397	19.160	22.455
Females	**	5.757	5.069	3.335

Industrial disputes	1982
Number of disputes	6
Workers involved (000s)	3.554
Working days lost (000s)	2.747

Consumer prices	1984	1985
(percentage increase)	39.6	10.4

Trade unions
Total membership (1987) 608,438

Central organization — Trade Union Congress of Ghana with 608,438 members in 17 national unions

Membership of major unions (1987)

Industrial and Commercial Workers' Union	120,000
Central Agricultural Workers' Union	120,000
Public Service Workers' Union	65,000
Teachers and Educational Workers' Union	50,000
Construction and Building Trades Workers' Union	40,000
Maritime and Dockworkers' Union	35,000

HONG KONG

Size	1,000 km²
Population (1986)	5,530,000
Per capita GNP (1985)	$6,230

Labour force (000s)	1986
Total	2,754
Males	1,716
Females	1,037

Activity rates	1986
Labour force as percentage of population of all ages	
Total	51.0
Male	61.9
Female	39.5

Employment (000s)	1984	1985	1986
Total	2,505.2	2,543.3	2,625.4
Males	1,577.6	1,613.0	1,663.7
Females	927.5	930.4	961.7

Labour force by sector (%)	1985
Agriculture	1.7
Industry	43.6
Services	53.9

Estimated average annual growth of labour force (%)	
1980-85	2.5
1985-2000	1.4

Employment by industry (000s)	1985
Agriculture	41.5
Extractive industries	0.7
Manufacturing	918.8
Electricity, gas, water	17.0
Construction	191.8
Wholesale and retail trade (and hotels)	573.8
Transport and communications	206.5
Finance, insurance, and business services	147.4
Community, social, and personal services	445.7

Unemployment	1984		1985		1986	
	000s	%	000s	%	000s	%
Total	101.0	3.9	83.6	3.2	76.1	2.8
Males	68.8	4.2	58.6	3.5	51.1	3.0
Females	32.2	3.4	25.1	2.6	24.9	2.5

International labour statistics

Average hours of work per week in manufacturing	1984	1985	1986
	44.8	44.8	45.2

Industrial disputes	1984	1985	1986
Number of disputes	11	3	9
Workers involved (000s)	2.325	0.440	2.136
Working days lost (000s)	3.083	1.160	4.907

Average daily wage rate ($)	1985	1986
	100.80	109.20

Average annual labour cost per employee in manufacturing ($)	1984	1985
	35,614	38,974

Consumer prices (percentage increase)	1984	1985	1986
	8.2	3.1	5.5

Trade unions

Total membership (1985)	367,560 in 391 unions
As percentage of labour force	16.1

Membership of major unions (1985)

Hong Kong Professional Teachers' Union	31,750
Motor Transport Workers' Union	27,345
Hong Kong Seamen's Union	18,864
Hong Kong Union of Chinese Workers in Western Style Employment [Real estate and business services, etc.]	15,815
Hong Kong and Kowloon Restaurant and Cafe Workers' General Union	12,508
Hong Kong and Kowloon Spinning, Weaving, and Dyeing Trades Workers' General Union	10,045

Hong Kong: Trade unions by size of membership, 1985

Declared membership	Number of unions	Declared membership
Under 51	63	2,140
51 - 250	155	18,123
251 - 1,000	102	49,953
1,001 - 5,000	57	112,291
5,001 and over	14	185,053
Total	**391**	**367,560**

Source Registrar of Trade Unions in Hong Kong

INDIA

Size	3,288,000 km²
Population (1986)	766,140,000
Per capita GNP (1985)	$270

Labour force (000s)	1981
Total	244,605
Males	181,100
Females	63,500

Activity rates	1981
Labour force as percentage of population of all ages	
Total	36.8
Male	52.7
Female	19.8

Employment (000s)	1984	1985
Total	24,214	24,578
Males	21,156	21,416
Females	3,058	3,162

Labour force by sector (%)	1980
Agriculture	70
Industry	13
Services	17

Estimated average annual growth of labour force (%)	
1980-85	2.0
1985-2000	1.8

Employment by industry (000s)	1984
Agriculture	1,308
Extractive industries	1,040
Manufacturing	6,191
Electricity, gas, water	772
Construction	1,186
Wholesale and retail trade (and hotels)	399
Transport and communications	2,921
Finance, insurance, and business services	1,128
Community, social, and personal services	9,269

Unemployment	1983	1984	1985	1986
	000s	000s	000s	000s
Total	20,802	23,034	24,861	28,261
Males	17,454	19,186	20,628	23,476
Females	3,348	3,848	4,233	4,785

Industrial disputes	1984	1985	1986
Number of disputes	2,094	1,755	1,581
Workers involved (000s)	1,949.0	1,078.8	1,263.9
Working days lost (000s)	56,025	29,239	22,119

Average monthly earnings in manufacturing (Rupees)	1982	1983
	622.5	786.3

Consumer prices (percentage increase)	1984	1985	1986
	9.2	6.4	9.0

Trade unions

Central organizations

All-India Centre of Trade Unions (A-ICTU) with 1,400,000 members in 300 unions

All-India Trade Union Congress (AITUC) with 3,470,000 members in 3,622 unions

Centre of Indian Trade Unions (CITU) with 1,800,000 members in 3,000 unions

Indian Labour Association with 2,500,000 members

Indian National Trade Union Congress with 4,200,000 members

INDONESIA

Size	1,919,000 km²
Population (1986)	166,940,000
Per capita GNP (1985)	$530

Labour force (000s)	1985
Total	63,826
Males	40,849
Females	22,977

Activity rates	1985
Labour force as percentage of population of all ages	
Total	38.9
Male	50.0
Female	27.9

Labour force by sector (%)	1980
Agriculture	57
Industry	13
Services	30

Estimated average annual growth of labour force (%)	
1980-85	2.4
1985-2000	2.2

Employment by industry (000s)	1982
Agriculture	31,593
Extractive industries	391
Manufacturing	6,022
Electricity, gas, water	62
Construction	2,146
Wholesale and retail trade (and hotels)	8,554
Transport and communications	1,796
Finance, insurance, and business services	113
Community, social, and personal services	7,125

Unemployment	1983		1984		1985	
	000s	%	000s	%	000s	%
Total	353.51	**	577.01	**	785.24	**
Males	279.81	**	430.72	**	552.27	**
Females	73.62	**	146.29	**	232.97	**

International labour statistics

Industrial disputes	1984	1985	1986
Number of disputes	29	78	73
Workers involved (000s)	2.773	21.148	15.778
Working days lost (000s)	1.708	557	109.36

Consumer prices (percentage increase)	1984	1985	1986
	10.4	4.7	6.0

Trade unions

Central organization	All-Indonesia Union of Workers (SPSI) with 2,500,000 members

KENYA

Size	583,000 km^2
Population (1986)	21,160,000
Per capita GNP (1985)	$290

Employment (000s)	1984	1985	1986
Total	1,119.7	1,174.4	1,220.5
Males	910.6	943.5	972.0
Females	209.1	230.9	248.5

Labour force by sector (%)	1980
Agriculture	81
Industry	7
Services	12

Estimated average annual growth of labour force (%)	
1980-85	3.5
1985-2000	3.7

Employment by industry (000s)	1985
Agriculture	240.9
Extractive industries	4.8
Manufacturing	158.8
Electricity, gas, water	17.7
Construction	49.9
Wholesale and retail trade (and hotels)	89.7
Transport and communications	55.7
Finance, insurance, and business services	53.4
Community, social, and personal services	503.5

Industrial disputes	1983	1984	1985
Number of disputes	75	69	87
Workers involved (000s)	12.851	7.663	17.207
Working days lost (000s)	18.518	39.395	28.961

Average monthly earnings (Shillings)	1984	1985	1986
	1,870.4	2,015.6	2,204.1

Consumer prices (percentage increase)	1984	1985	1986
	8.8	11.2	7.7

Trade unions

Membership as percentage of labour force	10-20
Central organization	Central Organization of Trade Unions of Kenya (COTU)

REPUBLIC OF KOREA

Size	98,000 km^2
Population (1986)	41,570,536
Per capita GNP (1985)	$2,150

Labour force (000s)	1986
Total	16,116
Males	9,819
Females	6,296

Activity rates	1986
Labour force as percentage of population of all ages	
Total	38.8
Male	46.8
Female	30.6

Employment (000s)	1984	1985	1986
Total	14,417	14,935	15,505
Males	8,874	9,107	9,339
Females	5,544	5,828	6,165

Labour force by sector (%)	1980
Agriculture	36
Industry	27
Services	37

Estimated average annual growth of labour force (%)	
1980-85	2.7
1985-2000	1.9

Employment by industry (000s)	1985
Agriculture	3,722
Extractive industries	154
Manufacturing	3,500
Electricity, gas, water	41
Construction	908
Wholesale and retail trade (and hotels)	3,370
Transport and communications	698
Finance, insurance, and business services	561
Community, social, and personal services	1,980

Unemployment	1983		1984		1985		1986	
	000s	%	000s	%	000s	%	000s	%
Total	614	4.1	567	3.8	619	4.0	611	3.8
Males	486	5.2	443	4.8	478	5.0	480	4.9
Females	128	2.2	124	2.2	141	2.4	131	2.1

Average hours worked per week in manufacturing	1984	1985	1986
	54.3	53.8	54.7

Industrial disputes	1984	1985	1986
Number of disputes	114	265	276
Workers involved (000s)	16.400	28.700	46.900
Working days lost (000s)	19.900	64.300	72.000

Average monthly earnings (Won)	1984	1985	1986
	296,907	324,283	350,966

Average monthly labour cost per employee in manufacturing (Won)	348,070	384,160	**

Consumer prices (percentage increase)	1984	1985	1986
	2.3	2.5	2.0

Trade unions

Total membership (1982) 839,000 in 2,418 unions

MALAYSIA

Size	330,000 km^2
Population (1986)	16,110,000
Per capita GNP (1985)	$2,000

Labour force (000s) **Peninsular Malaysia**	1980
Total	4,924
Males	3,300
Females	1,600

Activity rates	1980
Labour force as percentage of population of all ages	
Total	37.5
Male	49.6
Female	25.3

Employment (1983) (000s)	Sabah	Sarawak
Total	111.74	117.4
Males	**	88.6
Females	**	28.8

Labour force by sector (%)	1980
Agriculture	42
Industry	19
Services	39

Estimated average annual growth of labour force (%)	
1980-85	2.9
1985-2000	2.6

Unemployment

	Peninsular Malaysia	Sabah	Sarawak
	1985	1983	1982
	000s	000s	000s
Total	76.71	1.606	9.217
Males	46.35	1.237	6.738
Females	30.36	0.369	2.479

Employment by industry (1982) (000s)	Sabah	Sarawak
Agriculture	59.557	21.013
Extractive industries	1.591	3.153
Manufacturing	7.154	25.440
Electricity, gas, water	1.075	0.894
Construction	6.916	29.959
Wholesale and retail trade (and hotels)	2.426	21.453
Transport and communications	3.530	13.374
Finance, insurance, and business services	**	1.941
Community, social, and personal services	15.655	8.874

Average hours worked per week in manufacturing (1979)	Peninsular Malaysia	Sabah	Sarawak
	47.5	52.0	46.2

Industrial disputes (Peninsular Malaysia)

	1983
Number of disputes	**
Workers involved (000s)	2.458
Working days lost (000s)	7.880

Consumer prices (percentage increase)	1984	1985	1986
Peninsular Malaysia	3.9	0.3	0.7
Sabah	1.2	0.9	**
Sarawak	3.5	-0.1	**

Trade unions

Central organization	Malaysian Trades Union Congress (MTUC) with 396,000 members in 152 unions

MEXICO

Size	1,973,000 km^2
Population (1986)	79,560,000
Per capita GNP (1985)	$2,080

Labour force (000s)	1980
Total	22,066
Males	15,900
Females	6,100

Activity rates	1980
Labour force as percentage of population of all ages	
Total	33.0
Male	48.2
Female	18.2

Employment (000s)	1984	1985	1986
Total	6,429	6,700	6,884
Males	4,546	4,730	4,807
Females	1,882	1,970	2,077

Labour force by sector (%)	1980
Agriculture	37
Industry	29
Services	34

Estimated average annual growth of labour force (%)	
1980-85	3.2
1985-2000	3.0

Unemployment	1984		1985		1986	
	000s	%	000s	%	000s	%
Total	**	6.0	**	4.8	**	4.9
Males	**	5.3	**	4.0	**	4.2
Females	**	7.6	**	6.3	**	6.1

	1983	1984
Average hours worked per week in manufacturing	45.8	46.4

Industrial disputes	1986
Number of disputes	312
Workers involved (000s)	82.833
Working days lost (000s)	121.1

	1984	1985	1986
Consumer prices (percentage increase)	65.5	57.7	86.2

NIGERIA

Size	924,000 km²
Population (1986)	98,500,000
Per capita GNP (1985)	$800

Labour force (000s)	1983
Total	29,453
Males	20,000
Females	9,400

Activity rates	1983
Labour force as percentage of population of all ages	
Total	32.0
Male	43.1
Female	20.6

Labour force by sector (%)	1980
Agriculture	68
Industry	12
Services	20

Estimated average annual growth of labour force (%)	
1980-85	2.6
1985-2000	2.9

Unemployment	1985		1986	
	000s	%	000s	%
Total	32.827	**	33.039	**

Industrial disputes	1985	1986
Number of disputes	56	101
Workers involved (000s)	18.55	28.8
Working days lost (000s)	317.93	224.55

Consumer prices (percentage increase)	1984	1985	1986
	39.5	5.5	5.4

Trade unions (1985)

Central organization	Nigerian Labour Congress 2,100,000 members in 42 unions

PAKISTAN

Size	804,000 km²
Population (1986)	99,160,000
Per capita GNP (1985)	$380

Labour force (000s)	1985
Total	28,596
Males	25,300
Females	3,300

Activity rates	1985
Labour force as percentage of population of all ages	
Total	30.2
Male	51.5
Female	7.2

Employment (000s)	1984	1985
Total	27,481	27,798
Males	**	**
Females	**	**

Labour force by sector (%)	1980
Agriculture	52
Industry	19
Services	28

Estimated average annual growth of labour force (%)	
1980-85	3.2
1985-2000	2.8

Employment by industry (000s)	1984
Agriculture	14,053
Extractive industries	29
Manufacturing	3,582
Electricity, gas, water	301
Construction	1,279
Wholesale and retail trade (and hotels)	3,183
Transport and communications	1,224
Finance, insurance, and business services	219
Community, social, and personal services	2,715

Unemployment	1984		1985		1986	
	000s	%	000s	%	000s	%
Total	183.6	**	212.3	**	224.6	**

Industrial disputes	1984	1985
Number of disputes	81	58
Workers involved (000s)	30.702	35.858
Working days lost (000s)	157.75	159.43

Consumer prices	1984	1985	1986
(percentage increase)	6.7	5.8	3.8

Trade unions

Central organizations	All Pakistan Federation of Trade Unions (APFTU) with 589,000 members All Pakistan Federation of Labour (APFOL) with 380,000 members, and six other federations

PHILIPPINES

Size	300,000 km²
Population (1986)	55,000,000
Per capita GNP (1985)	$580

Labour force (000s)	1985
Total	21,643
Males	13,400
Females	8,200

Employment (000s)	1983	1984	1985	1986
Total	19,366	19,368	20,327	19,366
Males	11,958	12,289	12,758	**
Females	7,408	7,079	7,569	**

Labour force by sector (%)	1980
Agriculture	51
Industry	16
Services	33

Estimated average annual growth of labour force (%)	
1980-85	2.5
1985-2000	2.4

Employment by industry (000s)	1985
Agriculture	10,085
Extractive industries	129
Manufacturing	1,926
Electricity, gas, water	79
Construction	678
Wholesale and retail trade (and hotels)	2,650
Transport and communications	913
Finance, insurance, and business services	351
Community, social, and personal services	3,515

Unemployment	1983		1984		1985	
	000s	%	000s	%	000s	%
Total	1,003	4.9	1,465	7.0	1,316	6.1
Males	458	3.7	675	5.2	644	4.8
Females	545	6.7	790	10.0	672	8.2

Industrial disputes	1983	1984	1985
Number of disputes	155	282	366
Workers involved (000s)	33.638	65.306	111.26
Working days lost (000s)	581.29	1,907.8	2,457.7

Average daily wage rates (Pesos)	1984	1985
Skilled	58.20	64.24
Unskilled	50.48	56.48

Consumer prices (percentage increase)	1985	1986	1987
	23.1	1.0	3.8

Trade unions

Total membership (1986) 4,840,000

As percentage of wage and salary workers 55

Central organizations

National Congress of Farmers' Organizations
2,800,000 members
Trade Union Congress of the Philippines
814,000 members in 34 affiliated organizations
May First Movement
217,000 members in 9 affiliated organizations

Membership of major unions (1986)

Federation of Free Farmers (FFF)	200,000
Associated Labour Union (ALU)	187,000
Philippine Social Security Labour Union (PSSLU)	98,000
National Federation of Sugar Workers (NFSW)	82,000
National Labour Union (NLU)	80,000

SINGAPORE

Size	1,000 km²
Population (1986)	2,590,000
Per capita GNP (1985)	$7,420

Labour force (000s)	1985
Total	1,204
Males	800
Females	400

Activity rates	1985
Labour force as percentage of population of all ages	
Total	47.1
Male	59.8
Female	34.3

Employment (000s)	1984	1985	1986
Total	1,174.8	1,154.3	1,149.0
Males	748.0	734.3	719.0
Females	426.8	420.0	430.1

Labour force by sector (%)	1985
Agriculture	0.9
Industry	37.7
Services	61.3

Estimated average annual growth of labour force (%)	
1980-85	1.9
1985-2000	0.8

Employment by industry (000s)	1985
Agriculture	8.1
Extractive industries	2.4
Manufacturing	293.8
Electricity, gas, water	7.7
Construction	102.8
Wholesale and retail trade (and hotels)	271.1
Transport and communications	117.0
Finance, insurance, and business services	100.7
Community, social, and personal services	248.3

Unemployment	1984		1985		1986	
	000s	%	000s	%	000s	%
Total	32.54	2.7	49.78	4.1	79.55	6.5
Males	20.19	2.6	31.88	4.2	54.40	7.0
Females	12.35	2.8	17.90	4.1	25.15	5.5

Average hours of work per week in manufacturing	1983	1984	1985
	48.9	48.6	47.0

Industrial disputes	1984	1985	1986
Number of disputes	0	0	1
Workers involved (000s)	0	0	0.061
Working days lost (000s)	0	0	0.122

Average hourly earnings ($)	1984	1985
	3.45	3.62
Average annual labour cost per employee in manufacturing ($)	13,519	14,972

Consumer prices (percentage increase)	1985	1986	1987
	0.5	-1.4	0.5

Trade unions

Total membership (1985)	201,132 in 84 unions
As percentage of labour force	17
Central organization	National Trades Union Congress 195,858 members in 69 unions

Membership of major unions (1985)

United Workers of Electronics and Electrical Industries	21,777
Amalgamated Union of Public Employees	20,312
Singapore Manual and Mercantile Workers Union	13,106

SOUTH AFRICA

Size	1,221,000 km²
Population (1986)	33,220,000
Per capita GNP (1985)	$2,050

Labour force (000s)	1980
Total	8,690
Males	5,900
Females	2,800

Activity rates	1980
Labour force as percentage of population of all ages	
Total	34.7
Male	46.2
Female	22.8

Labour force by sector (%)	1980
Agriculture	17
Industry	35
Services	49

Estimated average annual growth of labour force (%)

1980-85	2.8
1985-2000	2.8

Unemployment	1983		1984		1985		1986	
	000s	%	000s	%	000s	%	000s	%
Total	35.775	**	31.969	**	62.106	**	77.80	**
Males	22.886	**	18.890	**	37.428	**	48.00	**
Females	12.88	**	13.079	**	24.677	**	29.00	**

Paid employment in non-agricultural activities (000s)	1984	1985	1986
Total	4,900.6	4,824.1	4,857.9

Average hours of work per week in manufacturing	1984	1985	1986
	46.5	46.2	46.7

Average monthly earnings in manufacturing (Rand)	1984	1985	1986
	688	749	860

Consumer prices (percentage increase)	1984	1985	1986
	11.7	16.2	18.6

Trade unions (1985)

Four central federations with 1,020,000 members in 86 unions (largest is Confederation of South African Trade Unions with 450,000 members)

TANZANIA

Size	945,000 km²
Population (1986)	22,460,000
Per capita GNP (1985)	$290

Labour force (000s)	1978
Total	7,845
Males	3,800
Females	4,000

Activity rates	1978
Labour force as percentage of population of of all ages	
Total	44.8
Male	44.4
Female	45.2

Employment (000s)	1981	1982
Total	631.83	601.26
Males	419.47	503.36
Females	79.90	93.98

Labour force by sector (%)	1980
Agriculture	86
Industry	5
Services	10

Estimated average annual growth of labour force (%)	
1980-85	2.8
1985-2000	3.0

Employment by industry (Tanganyika) (000s)	1981
Agriculture	119.48
Extractive industries	6.57
Manufacturing	104.31
Electricity, gas, water	23.98
Construction	45.63
Wholesale and retail trade (and hotels)	39.64
Transport and communications	55.23
Finance, insurance, and business services	17.54
Community, social, and personal services	209.45

Consumer prices	1984	1985	1986
(percentage increase)	42.9	28.2	44.0

Trade unions

Degree of unionization (as percentage of labour force, including peasants)	40-50

Union of Tanzania Workers (JUWATA) is the single trade union centre

ZAMBIA

Size	753,000 km²
Population (1986)	6,900,000
Per capita GNP (1985)	$390

Labour force (000s)	1984
Total	2,032
Males	1,400
Females	600

Activity rates	1984
Labour force as percentage of population of all ages	
Total	31.6
Male	46.0
Female	17.4

Employment (000s)	1985	1986
Total	361.50	360.50

Labour force by sector (%)	1980
Agriculture	73
Industry	10
Services	17

Estimated average annual growth of labour force (%)	
1980-85	3.2
1985-2000	3.5

Employment by industry (000s)	1984
Agriculture	35.40
Extractive industries	58.47
Manufacturing	48.20
Electricity, gas, water	7.85
Construction	33.61
Wholesale and retail trade (and hotels)	30.25
Transport and communications	24.00
Finance, insurance, and business services	22.41
Community, social, and personal services	105.00

Industrial disputes	1985	1986
Number of disputes	50	35
Workers involved (000s)	23.749	5.344
Working days lost (000s)	66.176	8.932

Average monthly earnings (Kwacha)	1984
	237

Average annual earnings (1983) 2,392 (ranging from 3.256 in mining, to 1,037 in agriculture)

Consumer prices (percentage increase)	1984	1985	1986
	20.0	8.0	14.0

Trade unions

Central organization — Zambia Congress of Trade Unions (ZCTU) with 400,000 members in 18 unions

ZIMBABWE

Size	391,000 km²
Population (1986)	8,400,000
Per capita GNP (1985)	$680

Labour force (000s)	1982
Total	2,484
Males	1,500
Females	1,000

Activity rates	1982
Labour force as percentage of population of all ages	
Total	33.1
Male	41.1
Female	25.4

Employment (000s)	1984	1985
Total	1,036.4	1,058.7
Males	864.5	**
Females	172.0	**

Labour force by sector (%)	1980
Agriculture	73
Industry	11
Services	17

Estimated average annual growth of labour force (%)	
1980-85	2.7
1985-2000	3.0

Employment by industry (000s)	1983
Agriculture	263.5
Extractive industries	60.3
Manufacturing	173.4
Electricity, gas, water	6.9
Construction	49.3
Wholesale and retail trade (and hotels)	80.6
Transport and communications	49.6
Finance, insurance, and business services	15.8
Community, social, and personal services	334.0

Industrial disputes	1982	1983
Number of disputes	94	32
Workers involved (000s)	14.404	0.744
Working days lost (000s)	21.286	0.379

Average monthly earnings ($)	1986
Electricity	661
Transport	599
Manufacturing	462
Mining	353
Construction	316

Consumer prices (percentage increase)	1984	1985	1986
	20.2	8.5	15.0

Trade unions

Total membership (1986)	173,000 in 30 unions
As percentage of employees	16
Central organization	Zimbabwe Congress of Trade Unions (to which all unions are affiliated)

Membership of major unions (1986)

Associated Mine Workers' Union	26,000 members
Zimbabwe Construction Workers' Union	15,000 members
Commercial Workers Union of Zimbabwe	11,000 members
General Agriculture and Plant Workers' Union	10,000 members
Zimbabwe Catering and Hotel Workers' Union	9,500 members
Zimbabwe National Union of Clothing	9,165 members

APPENDIX:

MEMBERSHIP OF THE INTERNATIONAL TRADE SECRETARIATS

Table A1.1 Membership of the trade secretariats affiliated to the International Confederation of Free Trade Unions

Name	Year	Number of member unions	Total affiliated membership
International Federation of Building and Woodworkers (IFBWW)	1987	126	3,100,000
International Federation of Chemical, Energy and General Workers' Unions (ICEF)	1984	209	6,300,000
International Federation of Commercial, Clerical, Professional, and Technical Employees (FIET)	1987	248	8,369,568
International Secretariat for Arts, Mass Media, and Entertainment Trade Unions (ISETU/FIET since 1985)	1987		100,000
International Federation of Free Teachers' Unions (IFFTU)	1986	70	6,500,000
International Graphical Federation (IGF)	1984	39	764,802
International Federation of Journalists (IFJ)	1986	38	122,891
International Metalworkers' Federation (IMF)	1984	145	13,549,000

Number of countries	Regional distribution		
	Number of unions		Membership
58	Europe	47	**
	Asia & Pacific	30	**
	Americas	29	**
	Africa	20	**
72	Europe	48	1,684,000
	Asia & Pacific	58	1,750,000
	Americas	66	2,156,000
	Africa	36	710,000
93	Europe	79	4,573,000
	Asia & Pacific	56	1,341,000
	Americas	75	2,045,000
	Africa	38	410,000
51	Europe	19	**
	Asia & Pacific	21	**
	Americas	17	**
	Africa	13	**
37	Europe	25	523,100
	Asia & Pacific	7	13,400
	Americas	3	170,000
	Africa	4	58,300
32	Europe	22	98,500
	Asia & Pacific	9	9,300
	Americas	2	13,300
	Africa	5	1,700
68	Europe	28	6,108,000
	Asia & Pacific	47	2,721,000
	Americas	46	4,435,000
	Africa	24	285,000

Table A1.1 (Cont.)

Name	Year	Number of member unions	Total affiliated membership
Miners' International Federation (MIF)	1986	**	1,200,000
International Federation of Plantation, Agricultural, and Allied Workers (IFPAAW)	1987	100	4,000,000
Postal, Telegraph, and Telephone International (PTTI)	1984	198	3,924,419
Public Services International (PSI)	1986	242	10,208,586
International Textile, Garment, and Leather Workers' Federation (ITGLWF)	1986	158	4,965,832
International Transport Workers' Federation (ITF)	1985	398	4,372,194
International Union of Food and Allied Workers' Associations (IUF)	1986	211	2,147,244
Universal Alliance of Diamond Workers	1986	**	10,000

Number of countries	Regional distribution		
	Number of unions		Membership
31	**		**
73	Europe	**	1,400,000
	Asia & Pacific	**	1,560,000
	Americas	**	400,000
	Africa	**	640,000
93	Europe	71	1,459,000
	Asia & Pacific	40	1,119,000
	Americas	69	1,189,000
	Africa	18	157,000
77	Europe	74	6,046,000
	Asia & Pacific	72	1,547,000
	Americas	56	2,286,000
	Africa	40	328,000
73	Europe	41	1,145,000
	Asia & Pacific	30	2,072,000
	Americas	59	1,063,000
	Africa	28	685,000
88	Europe	123	2,346,800
	Asia & Pacific	102	943,800
	Americas	128	896,600
	Africa	45	183,500
68	Europe	62	1,161,507
	Asia & Pacific	57	332,785
	Americas	69	627,071
	Africa	23	25,878
3	Europe	3	10,000

INDEX

Note: the figure and tables from Part I, together with all the information from Part II, are entered in **bold.**

For Product Safety Concerns and Information please contact our EU representative GPSR@taylorandfrancis.com Taylor & Francis Verlag GmbH, Kaufingerstraße 24, 80331 München, Germany

Batch number: 10731596

Printed by Printforce, the Netherlands